The Enlightened Investor

Eugene Wolfe

CONTENTS

ACKNOWLEDGMENTS

I am indebted to the work and teachings of the late Joseph Campbell. When I first encountered his work in 1989, it provided a template around which I could organize my thoughts regarding the spiritual quest. I also thank those in the field of behavioral economics who have informed much of my thinking

1 FOREWORD

It was May 25, 1984, a beautiful spring evening on Lake Minnetonka, Minnesota. It was also the evening before my wedding day. As is often the custom, our wedding rehearsal dinner involved a fair amount of food and drink. Late in the evening, in response to a question I cannot now remember, I declared, "Life is a crap shoot, get on with it." It was, and continues to be a succinct summary of my philosophy towards life. And nothing in the last thirty years has dissuaded me of its truth. It has been my unofficial credo. And if I should ever forget it, I have thirty or so friends who are more than happy to remind me of it.

Mark Twain once remarked, "The only certainties in life are death and taxes." He almost had it right. In the hundred years since his death we have come to understand a world in which, as the philosopher Wittgenstein put it, "The only certainty is uncertainty."

Think back to 1999. How far away it all now seems. The economy was roaring along and the stock market, driven ever upwards by the dot.com phenomenon, was reaching new highs almost every day. As we approached the millennium, it seemed as if Professor Pangloss was right, that we truly "lived in the best of all possible times in the best of all possible worlds." It was not a question of if we all were going to be rich, just how soon it would happen.

Fast forward. What a difference several years makes. It was a beautiful Tuesday morning in Oklahoma City. I was preparing for another day of appointments with investment advisors. As was my custom, I ordered room service for breakfast, did some stretching exercises, showered, and read USA Today. As I was getting ready to leave for the day's work suddenly it was on the television screen, a live shot of the World Trade Center as smoke poured out of the top of the north tower. On the Today Show, Katie Couric spoke about an apparent airplane crash into the tower. "How could any small plane pilot be so stupid?" I asked myself. It was only several minutes later when I and millions of other Americans watched in amazement and horror as the second plane crashed into the south tower. How ironic it was, to be in Oklahoma City, which, up until that moment, had been the site of the worst terrorism event in United States history.

I decided to continue on my appointments. It was a surreal day, empty streets and freeways. Every office I visited had the television tuned to the news stations, instead of the investment and market news channels such as CNBC. The reaction of those I met was one of horror and anger. However, another response I found to be most interesting can be summarized as, "How could this happen?" And to think that this response came from the good people of Oklahoma City. The 1995 bombing of the Alfred P. Murrah Federal Building killed 168 and injured more than 600 people. People who had stared terrorism straight in the face were asking, "How could such a thing happen?" Human memory is short. As Nassim Taleb has said, "Rare events are always unexpected, otherwise they would not occur."[i] Terrorism is not a new phenomenon. The FBI, in a 1999 report, cited 327 incidents or suspected incidents of terrorism in the United States between 1980 and 1999. Over 200 people were killed and over 2000 injured in these attacks. Perhaps more than any other time in history, the only certainty is uncertainty.

During the three year period from 2000-2002, the markets were hammered by a succession of three events, 1) the bursting of the speculative internet bubble, 2) 9/11, and 3) corporate executive and accounting scandals. Billions of dollars were lost by investors. Just as Americans asked, "How could this happen?' in regards to terrorism; so also they were asking, "How could this happen?" in regards to their investments. All the sure bets of the late 1990's and all the sophisticated strategies were for naught. Nobody saw it coming. And then, seemingly out of thin air, the bull market roared back. Twenty-seven months after 9/11, the stock markets staged a remarkable, and in the end, unsustainable recovery from the crushing bear market of 2000-2002. Investors were again poised to make the same mistakes they made in the late 1990's.

And so they did. We do not need to recite the litany of financial horrors that began in the autumn of 2008. Suffice it to say that if the internet bubble was the financial sinking of the Titanic, the Housing bubble and Great Recession is a financial Pearl Harbor. However, unlike Pearl Harbor, America appears to be unwilling or unable to mobilize the energy and will to vanquish its financial enemies.

The last eleven years have destroyed many Americans' faith in the American Dream. The headlong pursuit of financial riches has subverted the pursuit of happiness. This book is a response to these events and the new reality. Perhaps this time it really is different.

Why "The Enlightened Investor?" The Enlightenment was a philosophical movement of the 18th century which was characterized by skepticism about established dogmas and a rationalistic approach to solving problems. It was the Enlightenment that informed many of the core principles of our Founding Fathers and provided the philosophical underpinning of our Declaration of Independence. Enlightenment also entails the revealing and broadening of knowledge. In thirty years in the investment and insurance business I have become a skeptic. During these years I have come to question the dogma of the investment industry. I have come to believe that the conventional wisdom is almost always wrong. I have seen investors make mistake after mistake because of irrational behavior. Unfortunately, the investment industry almost always exacerbates the problem.

This book proposes an alternative to the conventional investment wisdom. It proposes a path to financial independence based upon the spiritual wisdom of the ages, psychological research into the roots of investor behavior, exposing the investment fallacies that prevent most families from achieving financial independence, and finally, explaining the simple, straightforward investment strategies that have stood the test of time.

Fundamentally, it seeks to answer the question: How can I find financial independence and security in an uncertain world?

2 THE WAY WE ARE

Money doesn't buy happiness. People with ten million are no happier than people with nine million dollars." Hobart Rowen

You may find yourself living in a shotgun shack.
You may find yourself in another part of the world.
You may find yourself behind the wheel of a large automobile.
You may find yourself in a beautiful house with a beautiful wife.
You may ask yourself, "How did I get here?"

You may ask yourself, "How do I work this?"

You may ask yourself, "Where is that large automobile?"
You may tell yourself, "This is not my beautiful house!"
You may tell yourself, "This is not my beautiful wife!"
<u>Once in a Lifetime</u>, The Talking Heads

We shall begin by taking a look at America in terms of income and wealth. The idea of being rich is usually expressed in terms of either net worth or in terms of income. If you have a high net worth you are considered "wealthy," and if you have high income you are considered "affluent." The terms "wealthy" and "affluent" have come to be used synonymously and interchangeably as if they meant the same thing, namely being rich. However, we must draw a distinction between wealth and affluence. They are not the same when it comes to a discussion of financial independence.

The word "wealth" comes to us from the old English "to weal", which means to have in abundance. Thus wealth signifies net worth. Net worth is the sum of all your assets less your indebtedness. "Affluence" comes to us from the Latin "afflue", which means "to flow". Income, or cash flow, is the amount of money you can earn either by your labors or by investing assets which pay interest or dividends.

By either measure, most Americans are not doing very well. A recent survey by Allianz Life Insurance Company of North America revealed that, in the event of serious financial setback such as unemployment or illness, 58% of the respondents said they would need financial assistance after less than six months. The Pew Research Center conducted a poll in March of 2007, several months before the economic collapse of the Great Recession. Even then, many Americans were pessimistic about their future economic prospects and doubted whether their children would be as prosperous. Seventy-three percent of respondents agreed with the statement, "Today it's really true that the rich just get richer while the poor get poorer."

Unfortunately, for many Americans the American dream is turning into an American nightmare. The promise of America has always been that it is the "land of opportunity." Put in more blunt terms, "You can get rich here!" One of the core values of the American Dream has always been the idea of upward economic mobility. However, a growing body of evidence indicates that economic mobility is not as real as many would think. The Economic Mobility Project, conducted by the Pew Charitable Trusts, The American Enterprise Institute, The Brookings Institution, The Heritage Foundation, and the Urban Institute, has found that of all developed countries; currently the United States has the lowest economic mobility and highest income inequality. The study also indicated that there is a strong correlation between lack of economic mobility and income inequality.

A large part of the American Dream is the belief that happiness is synonymous with monetary wealth. As a result we look upon the rich with a combination of admiration and envy. As Mark Twain put it, "I am opposed to millionaires; however it would be dangerous to offer me the position."

Let us first consider income. According to information from the U.S. Census Bureau, from 1947 to 1979, the rate of real (inflation-adjusted) income growth was about the same at all income levels. Real incomes grew at an annual rate of 2.5% for the lowest 20% of American income earners and at a rate of 2.2% for the highest 20%. However, from 1979 to 2010 annual incomes fell by 0.4% in the lowest 20% and rose by 1.2% in the highest 20%. When you factor in the effect of the Bush administration tax cuts, which overwhelmingly benefited high income and net worth Americans, the discrepancy in income growth is startling. According to the Congressional Budget Office, from 1979 to 2004, real after-tax income rose by 9% for the lowest 20%, 69% for the top 20%, and an astounding 176% for the top 1%!

Income inequality is a fact of economic life in America. We have witnessed the rise of a nationwide movement, Occupy Wall Street, which has drawn attention to this disparity. Their rallying cry has been "We are the 99 percent." They wish to draw attention between the top 1% of income earners versus the other 99%. Income disparity is a fact of economic life, it has always been so. However the disparity between the lower 80% of income and the top 20% has increased dramatically. According to a study of income and tax trends by the Congressional Budget Office (CBO), the top 20% of income earners received approximately half of the country's after-tax income in 2007, and the share of after-tax income received by each of the bottom four-fifths of income earners fell from 1979 to 2007[ii]

The CBO study contains data over the period from 1979-2007. It is considered superior to other income studies because it combines Census data with Internal Revenue Service data from income tax returns. The study is also important in that it contains information on after-tax income adjusted for inflation and expressed in 1997 dollars.

The results are startling. From 1979 to 2007 the average real after-tax income of the poorest 20 percent of U.S. households rose 19 percent. The three-fifths of American households in the middle of the income scale, the proverbial "middle-class", saw their average real after-tax income rise 40 percent over the 28 year period. On the other hand, the average real after-tax income of the top 20 percent of households increased by 65%. And most shocking of all, the top 1 percent of income earners saw their average real after-tax income increase by an amazing 275%.

The report succinctly summarizes the state of income inequality in America. Consider that:

- The share of after-tax income of the top 1 percent of the American working population more than doubled from 1979-2007. In 2007, the top 1 percent takes home 17% of all after-tax income compared to 8 percent in 1979.

- The share of after-tax income of the top 20% take home 53% of all after-tax income in 2007 compared to 43% in 1979. Consider this: the top 20% of the most affluent Americans exceeded the amount of the remaining 80% of working Americans.

- The share of after-tax income of the middle 60% declined by 3% from 1979 to 2007.

- The share of after-tax income of the bottom 20% declined by 2% from 1979 to 2007, from 7% in 1979 to only 5% in 2007.

Furthermore, the following statistics illustrate just how great the income disparity is between those in the top 1% and the rest of American incomes:

- The approximately 14,000 American families who comprise the top 1/100th % of income earned an average of $31,000,000/yr.

- The 135,000 families who occupy the top 99.90% - 99.99%, received an average of $3,900,000/yr.

- The 1,350,000 families in the top 99% - 99.90% received an average of $386,000/yr.

- The 13,200,000 families in the top 90% - 99% received an average of $108,000/yr.

- The 132,000,000 families that comprise the bottom 90% received an average of $36,000/yr.

As a result, the United States has the highest income inequality of any country in the western world (U.S, Canada, Europe, and Australia/New Zealand)

Market Income Plus Transfers, 1979 -2007 Category Minimums (2007 dollars)

Income Category	1979	1994	2007	% Change 1979-2007	$ Change 1979-2007
Lowest quintile	$ 0	$ 0	$ 0	0%	$ 0
Second quintile	17,394	17,077	20,488	18%	$ 3,094
Middle quintile	27,563	28,896	34,261	24%	$ 6,698
Fourth quintile	37,861	42,051	49,960	32%	$ 12,099
81-90 percentile	52,803	60,718	74,732	42%	$ 21,929
91-95 percentile	67,496	80,455	102,918	52%	$ 35,422
96-99 percentile	85,634	105,247	141,914	66%	$ 56,280
Top 1 percentile	167,365	221,474	352,875	111%	$185,510

Source: Congressional Budget Office, Trends in the Distribution of Household Income Between 1979-2007

The gap between lower and upper income households in the United States continues to widen. There is a wide-spread belief that the gap between the highest and lowest household incomes grew dramatically during the decade of the 1980's, but stopped altogether during the economic prosperity of the 1990's. The Congressional Budget Office study demonstrates that this is not the case. The supply-side economists' maxim of "a rising tide lifts all boats" is nothing more than a hollow promise for most Americans. The income disparities did indeed widen during the 1980's, but also continued to grow dramatically during the 1990's and 2000's as well. The study reports that from 1979-2007, the minimum income of the top one percent increased 111%, or $185,510 per household. This was 4.6 times the percentage increase, and an astounding 27.7 times the dollar increase that the middle-fifth received![iii]

The fact of the matter is that the average American's prospects for economic security have become more uncertain over the last forty years. A University of

Michigan Panel Study of Income Dynamics reports that the instability of American family incomes was roughly five times greater in the 2000's than in the 1970's.

This disparity is causing serious distress among increasing numbers of Americans. Evidence of such distress is provided by the Institute for Innovation in Social Policy at the Fordham University Graduate Center. The institute analyzes government statistics in areas such as infant mortality, children in poverty, teenage suicide, health insurance coverage, and homicide rates as a method of taking the pulse of the "social well-being of the nation." In their most recent Index of Social Health, it revealed a dramatic decrease in the social health of the United States. In fact, it was the biggest decline in the index in twenty years. The categories that saw severe declines in the latest index were child abuse, average weekly earnings, children in poverty, health insurance coverage, the gap between rich and poor, and out-of-pocket health costs for those over age 65. Of these, income inequality reached its worst level on record.

The reasons for the increasing income gap are many. One can look at economic and tax policy and it is clear that the field is tilted to the advantage of high-income earners. The Congressional Budget Office study notes that the percentage of income that Americans paid in federal income taxes declined between 1979 and 2001 among all income groups; however the top one percent of households again had the advantage. They had the largest percentage decrease in income tax rates, from an average of 37.3 percent of income in 1979 to 33.3 percent in 1997. Furthermore, the tax cuts that President Bush proposed and Congress passed in 2001 and 2003 continue to widen the chasm between after-tax incomes of the top, middle, and bottom households.

When fully phased in, the top one percent of households realized an average increase in after-tax income of 6 to 7 percent. Contrast this with the increase for the middle fifth of households of 2.2 percent, and an increase of 0.8% for the bottom fifth of households.[iv] The economic stimulus plan that President Bush introduced in January of 2003 continued the recent trend in tax cuts which favor the top 10% of American income earners. According to the Citizens for Tax Justice, half of the proposed $350 billion package would go to the top 1% of American income earners. In contrast, the typical American in the middle-fifth of income received a few hundred dollars in tax relief while those in the bottom fifth received almost nothing.

These tax cuts and the corresponding increase in income of the top one percent also has a profound effect on the overall economy. From 1979 to 2007, the top one percent of income earners saw their share of national wealth increase by 13.5%, equal to approximately $1.10 trillion. We know that the wealthy save about fifty percent of their income increases as opposed to only ten percent for the population as a whole. As a result, the redirected income from the lower ninety-nine percent to the top one percent reduced annual consumption by approximately $440 billion. This translates into reduced demand for goods and services which then results in lower economic growth.

Critics of the income gap argue that the numbers may be true, but that they do not tell the whole story. They contend that households move up the income ladder as they progress in their financial lives. When they are young, they may be in the lower income groups, but as their careers progress they earn higher incomes. If only this were true. Although some families may see their income rise over time, studies of income mobility demonstrate that the majority of low-income households continue to have low incomes for many years.

The Economic Mobility Project referenced earlier found that 42% of children born to parents in the bottom twenty percent of income earners remain in the bottom, while 39% born to parents in the top twenty percent remain at the top. Only about one-third of Americans were ranked as "upwardly mobile," which required earning more than their parents as well as moving into a higher quintile on the income scale.

Many Americans are laboring under a false notion that they can count on an ever-increasing income to lead them to financial independence. The evidence clearly demonstrates that for most Americans, climbing the income ladder is no longer a fait accompli. The gap between rich and middle to lower income earners is a fact. Between 1973 and 1998, the real hourly wages of the average American worker fell by 9% such that by 1998 the average inflation-adjusted hourly wage was about the same as it was in 1967. This is in stark contrast to the previous twenty-five year period (1947-1973) when wages grew by 75%.[v]

The wealthy have the means to contribute large amounts of money to political candidates and as a result, economic and tax policy is severely skewed to their benefit. The middle- and lower-income classes do not have the financial means to contribute large sums of money, nor do they have the time to become politically involved as they are working longer and longer hours just to get by. In terms of political and economic policy, there is no one to speak for the great majority of Americans. Unfortunately, I do not see this state of affairs changing in the foreseeable future. Thus, the Enlightened Investor understands that if she is to succeed in the search for financial independence, she will have to take matters into her own hands. She will realize that the key to financial independence lies not with government policies and programs, but rather with her own financial decisions.

Even if one is fortunate enough to enjoy high income, in and of itself it provides no guarantee of achieving financial independence. Consider the example of doctors. In their book, <u>The Millionaire Next Door</u>, Stanley and Danko stated that, "Physicians do not tend to be wealth accumulators. Among all major high-income producing occupations, physicians have a significantly low propensity to accumulate wealth."[vi] If one doctor buys a Porsche, it won't be long until all the doctors in the clinic or hospital have one. Such spending is not confined merely to physicians.

Many Americans lead lifestyles that put them in a precarious financial situation should they encounter an unexpected financial event such as the loss of a job. Professor Edward Wolff of the Jerome Levy Economics Institute has determined that the financial reserves of the average middle-class family would only sustain their lifestyle between 0-2 months.[vii] In an economy where jobs are eliminated at the drop of a hat, such financial vulnerability is certainly not a path to financial independence.

Even those Americans lucky enough to hit the jackpot of the lottery are not immune. Consider the fact that one-third of all lottery winners end up in bankruptcy.[viii] Most Americans have obviously embraced the words of William Thackeray when he said, "To be thought rich is as good as being rich", or, in the words of the late eighteenth century humorist Artemus Ward, "Let us be happy and live within our means, even if we have to borrow to do so!"

This malady, which some have termed "affluenza," was revealed in its comic splendor to me some twenty years ago. I was dating a young woman who was divorced with two young children, ages three and five. Her former husband was a successful physician in Miami. For his daughter's fifth birthday he bought her a gold Rolex watch. Five years old with a Rolex! Some months later the watch stopped working. My lady friend brought the watch into one of the finest jewelers in Minneapolis and was forthwith humiliated when the jeweler told her that the gold Rolex was a fake! Buying your five year old daughter a fake Rolex, who or what in the world was her father trying to impress? As Friedrich von Schiller put it, "Against stupidity, the very gods themselves contend in vain."

The other measure of financial well-being is net worth. Net worth is comprised of the value of all your assets, house, cars, furnishings, business interests, mutual funds, checking and savings accounts, etc. less the amount you owe. In America we tend to define financial well-being in terms of net worth more so than in terms of income. I suspect that if you asked the average American how much money it would take to be financially independent, the nearly universal response would be, "A million dollars!" As we shall see, a million dollars isn't what it used to be. Sad to say, most Americans aren't even close to having a net worth of a million dollars.

The total net worth of average Americans hasn't increased since 1989. Losses in the stock market over the last decade, combined with the housing value collapse have left many Americans with less net worth than they had twenty years ago.

One way to measure the growing gap between the wealthy and the middle class is to compare mean net worth to median net worth of American households. Mean household wealth is the average of all American households, in other words, the total wealth of all households divided by the total number of households. However, median household wealth is the point at which there are an equal number of households above and below the line.   As such it is much more accurate representation of the wealth of the typical American household. To the extent that the mean household wealth exceeds the median household wealth is one measure of wealth inequality.

For example, if there were five households with net worth's of $100,000 each, and one household with a net worth of $1,000,000; the mean net worth would be $250,000; ($1,000,000) + ($100,000 x 5) = $1,500,000 divided by 6 equals $250,000. The median net worth of this sample would be $100,000.

The Bill Gates' and Warren Buffett's of the world dramatically skew the mean. The Survey of Consumer Finances which is conducted periodically by the Federal Reserve Board has revealed a dramatic increase in the gap between mean and median household wealth from 1983 to 1998. In 1983, the median net worth of American households was $54,600 and the mean net worth was $212,600. In 1998, the median net worth of American households was $91,300 and the mean net worth was $359,700. In 2007, the median was $120,300 and the mean $556,300. As noted earlier, the greater the gap between median and mean net worth, the greater the difference between the rich and the middle-class.[ix]

In 1998, the richest one percent of American households held half of all outstanding stock, financial securities, and trust equity, two-thirds of all business equity, and thirty-six percent of investment real estate.[x]

For most Americans, if it were not for the equity in their home and value of their cars, they would have a minimal or negative net worth. In fact, a recent study found that 25% of American families had no net worth beyond consumer goods. If you ignore real estate, the number jumps to 55%.[xi] The following chart illustrates the mean net worth and the mean net worth minus home equity for U.S. families classified by quintiles of net worth.

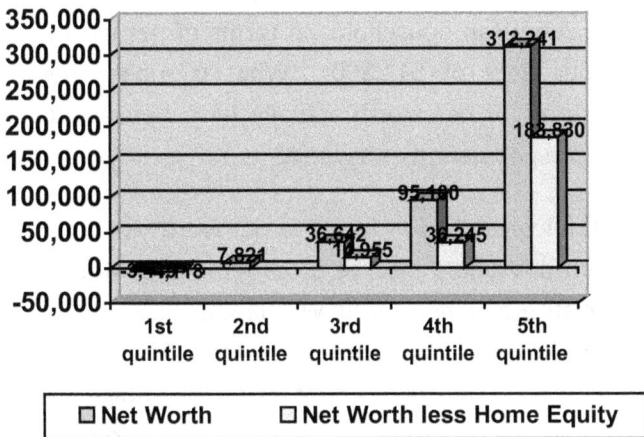

Source: Capital Research Associates

For all their hard work, most Americans have no assets other than the house they live in, and all the stuff that goes into it. For all the talk radio, magazines, television stations, financial self-help gurus, financial planners, and stockbrokers talking about how to achieve financial success; for most Americans, it just isn't working. It seems that every passing year a new record in the number of personal and business bankruptcies filed in the United States is achieved. Consider that the number of Americans filing for non-business bankruptcy in 2011 was 1,536,799 up 9.0% over filings in 2009 according to the Administrative Office of the U.S. Courts.

Perhaps these Americans have taken the words of Lionel Stander to heart when he quipped, "Anyone who lives within their means suffers from a lack of imagination!" If these current trends continue, nearly one in seven families with children will declare bankruptcy by the end of the decade, according to Dr. Elizabeth Warren, a Harvard Law School professor and the co-author of *The Two-Income Trap: Why Middle Class Mothers and Fathers Are Going Broke.*

According to Dr. Warren, "This year, more people will end up bankrupt than will suffer a heart attack. More adults will file for bankruptcy than will be diagnosed with cancer. More people will file for bankruptcy than will graduate from college. And, in an era when traditionalists decry the demise of the institution of marriage, Americans will file more petitions for bankruptcy than for divorce."

As mentioned earlier, more and larger income is not a guarantee of financial independence. Americans, by-and-large, make decent incomes especially compared to the rest of the world. However, we know that this does not translate into significant net worth. One of the most important reasons for the low levels of household net worth is that most American households have extremely high levels of debt, primarily consumer debt. What is most striking and revealing is that the lowest 20% of American households in terms of net worth have the highest median consumer debt of $11,500. What is more, the households in the lowest 20% in terms of net worth actually have household incomes that are about the same as the population as a whole!

The median household income of the lowest 20% in terms of net worth is about $31,700 as compared to the median household income of all families of about $29,000.[xii] The Economic Policy Institute, a non-profit Washington, D.C. think tank, reported that the ratio of household debt to income grew from 72% at the end of 1992 to 83% by March of 2001. Household debt as a percentage of disposable income is at its highest level ever in the United States. The reason for this explosion in debt isn't hard to explain: The Federal Reserve estimates that 43% of American families spend more than they earn, on average spending $1.22 for every dollar they earn.

According to the 2010 Census Bureau report, the average American household has more than $5,000 of credit card debt, up from $3,000 in 1990. According to CardWeb.com, the average American has 2.7 bank credit cards, 3.8 retail credit cards, and 1.1 debit cards. During the second quarter of 2010, as astounding $21,827,510,600 of credit card payments were more than 180 days overdue.

Unfortunately, many Americans turned to the equity in their homes to bail themselves out of debt or to finance consumer consumption. From 2003-2007, U.S. households took out $2.2 trillion in home equity loans and cash-out financing. Low interest rates on mortgages and a tax code that encourages consolidating debt into mortgages had accelerated the trend toward using home equity to support spending to maintain lifestyle. It is estimated that 20% of the $2.2 trillion went to fund consumption. This strategy has had catastrophic consequences as generations of Americans will now reach retirement age with no hope of ever paying off their mortgage. According to the U.S. Census Bureau's American Housing Survey 2009, more than eight hundred thousand homeowners have three or more mortgages on their property. According to a CNBC report in November of 2011, 55% of all homeowners have outstanding loans that equal 100% or more of the value of their homes.

All of this spending has resulted in the personal savings rate in the United States to fall to unprecedented levels. The Commerce Department reported that the personal savings rate fell to a record low level in October, 2004 when American households saved only two-tenths of 1 percent of disposable income. In other words, an individual with take-home pay of $40,000 would only save $1.50 per week. As of November 2011, the personal savings rate has risen to 3.5%. However, this statistic is misleading. Most of the increase in the personal savings rate is a function of consumers shedding debt through housing foreclosures and bankruptcies. Two-thirds of household debt reduction is due to defaults on home loans and consumer debt. And it is estimated that as of January 2012, there are still $254 billion dollars of mortgage foreclosures in the pipeline.

And yet we strive for higher paying jobs or play the lottery in the false hope that, "if we can only make just a little more money, then we'll be able to achieve financial security." Unfortunately, for most Americans, there is little light, if any, at the end of this tunnel.

The Roper Center at the University of Connecticut conducted a study over a number of years starting in 1978. They surveyed Americans who had incomes at or near the median income of Americans as a whole, which at that time was $17,640. They surveyed Americans who had income at or near $17,640. They were asked, "How much more income would it take for you to feel financially comfortable?" In other words, how much more income would it take to be able to pay for your wants and needs? The response to the question was $19,600.

What the respondents were saying is, "If I only had $1,960 more, then I would be happy and content and well on my way to financial independence. In 1985, the median income was $27,734, the response to the question, $30,600. Now they only needed $2,866 more. In 1994, the median income was $38,782, the response to the question, $40,000. If they only had $1,218 more![xiii] Year after year, the result is consistent. If we only had just a little bit more. It is like trying to chase a rainbow to find the pot of gold at the end.

In my college years, we coined the phrase, "The Theory of the Unsatisfied Man" to describe our desires as humans for more, ever more. The psychologists call it the "hedonic treadmill". Our materialist, consuming-oriented culture is caught in an upward-spiraling arms race of "gimme I want" and "gimme I need". And I will admit that I am as guilty as anyone when it comes to wanting the newest thing. I am amazed at how each succeeding generation comes to expect more and more as its birthright. Teen-age children with their own cell phones and automobiles! And to think that the parents of my generation thought we were spoiled when we were able to drive the family automobile a couple of times a week! In surveys of children age 10 to 13, Juliet Schor, an economist and professor of sociology at Boston College, found that the children's' overriding goal was to get rich. In response to the statement, "I want to make a lot of money when I grow up," 63 percent agreed and only 7 percent disagreed. I'm sure the parents of today's generation would like to cry out like King Lear when he responded to his daughters,

O, reason not the need! Our basest beggars are in the poorest thing superfluous. Allow not nature more than nature needs. King Lear Act II, Sc. IV

I think Shakespeare distilled the essence of the problem to several concise lines. What do we want? Most of us want as much as we can get! But how much do we truly need? Ah, there's the rub. Lear's insight is that we call our wants needs, in hopes of rationalizing to others and to ourselves that they are truly necessary. We are caught in a whirlpool of our own making. We work hard to earn an income in order to buy what we want. What we want eventually becomes what we think we need. At some point, what we need is no longer what we now want.

Not unlike Sisyphus, we are caught in an endless act of rolling the stone of want and need up the hill of higher expectations. The gods punished Sisyphus by letting him get the stone almost up to the summit of the hill, then tripping him up and having the stone roll down to the bottom. Sisyphus' dilemma was that he was destined to keep rolling the stone up the hill; our dilemma is that no matter how high we roll the stone; the summit of the hill keeps rising higher and higher into the sky.

Make your desire for wealth your god and it will plague you like the devil! In fact, most American families have attained a level of affluence where additional purchases and consumption no longer have an appreciable effect on their general welfare. Study after study demonstrates that a materialistic attitude, in other words wanting more and never satisfied, increases the probability that a person will suffer from depression, anxiety, and low self-esteem.

The root cause of this dilemma is our compulsion to compare ourselves to our neighbors, relatives, and co-workers. As H.L. Mencken put it, "A wealthy man is the one who makes more money than his brother-in-law!" This phenomenon of human nature has been confirmed by science. The psychologists Kahneman and Tversky, who have done ground-breaking work in the field of investor behavior, demonstrated that people prefer to make $70,000 per year when others around them are making $60,000, rather than to make $80,000 when their familiars are making $90,000. Perhaps the economic historian, Charles Kindleberger put it best when he said, "There is nothing as disturbing to one's well-being and judgment as to see a friend get rich."

The truth of the matter is that it is much easier in America to earn a large income, than it is to accumulate wealth. Put another way, being affluent is no guarantee of becoming financially independent. As long as you focus only on the income side of the equation, and not on the expense side, you are doomed to failure. If you spend more than you make, financial independence is not in your future. All the good advice in the world will not help as much as an interest-free loan! You'll end up like the comedian Henny Youngman when he quipped, "I've got all the money I'll ever need, as long as I die by four o'clock! Perhaps we would do well to keep in mind the timeless wisdom of Edward Gibbon,

"I am indeed rich, since my income is superior to my expense, and my expense equal to my desires."

In the following chapters I will put forth a new vision of financial independence, a new philosophy of money and how we relate to it. We have discussed the hard facts of our current financial environment in terms of income and wealth. We will dispel the illusions under which most investors' labor. We will construct a framework for pursuing financial independence, regardless of income, by integrating time-tested investment strategies with the perennial wisdom of the ages.

3 THE CIRCLES OF LIFE

"I see no special heroism is accumulating money, particularly if the person is foolish enough to not even try to derive any tangible benefit from such wealth."
Nassim Taleb

Our lives are not cut out of whole cloth. We all are comprised of many different dimensions, or circles which are interwoven to create the quilt that we call life. At any given minute, day, month, or perhaps year, one circle may be predominant, yet all are in play.

Before we begin to explore the path to financial independence, let's step back and take a larger view of what I call the "Circles of Life." The symbol I use to illustrate the Circles of Life is not unlike that of the Olympics. Five circles, intertwined, each representing a different dimension of life. Just as the Olympic circles represent continents, separate and distinct geographically, yet also intertwined culturally, economically, and politically; so it is with the Circles of Life. Each circle represents a distinct aspect of our life, yet each has a profound effect on the other.

The five Circles of Life are:

Spiritual-   The relationship between, and/or identification with, ourselves and a transcendent presence. The search for meaning and/or wisdom.

Emotional- The whole range of human response. Love, anger, envy, joy, jealousy, melancholy, lust, compassion, etc.

Physical-   The interplay of the body and all of its organic systems. The elements of hunger, the senses, movement, sickness, and health.

Social- The relationship between ourselves and others, as well as society as a whole. Our relationship and response to societal mores and ethics.

Financial- The striving for the means to provide shelter, food, material goods, status, etc. Quite simply, money!

The Circles of Life

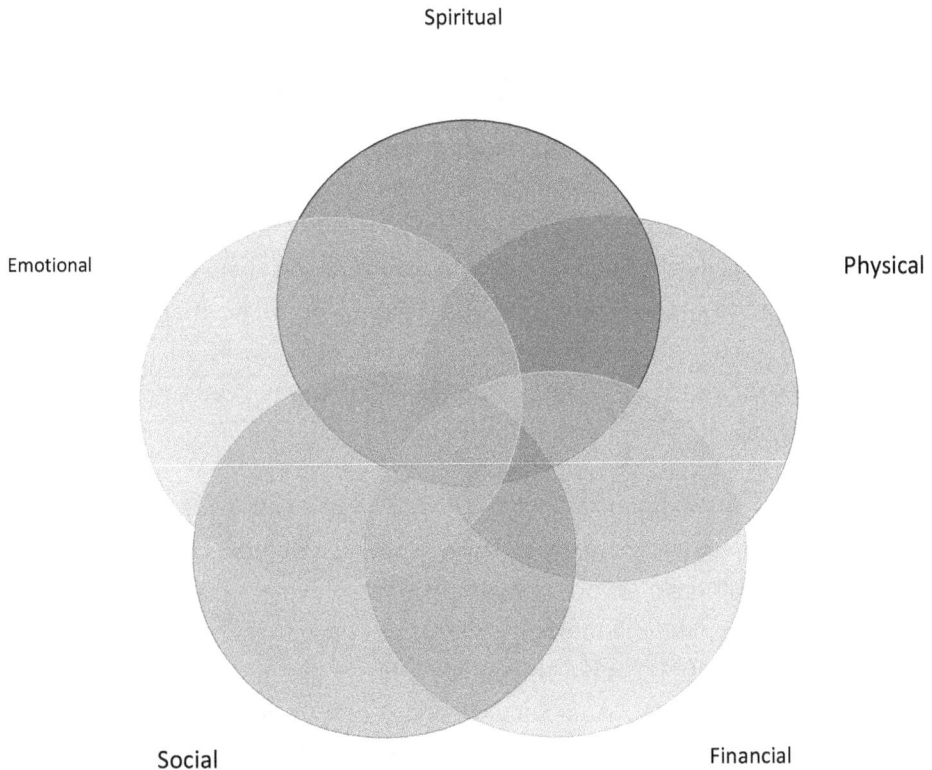

Spiritual

Emotional

Physical

Social

Financial

Each dimension of life overlaps and interplays with the others. And whether for good or for ill, in our capitalist society the financial circle is important indeed. We may agree with the playwright Clifford Odets when he wrote, "Life shouldn't be printed on dollar bills", however our actions belie the notion. We find ourselves at a point in history where the financial circle has come to dominate the other Circles of Life. We can debate whether this is the best of all possible worlds, but the fact remains that money, and how we deal with it has a profound and pervasive influence on our ability to enjoy and derive meaning from the other Circles of Life. We ignore it at our own peril.

At this point we need to explore the idea of a financial lifetime. We may speculate on the possibility of a spiritual life after death, but we do know for certain that our financial lifetime survives beyond our mortal life. Very few of us will ever die dead even, so to speak. We will either have more assets than we needed, or we will be in debt. Our financial lifetime survives by way of our estate. One of the responsibilities of financial independence is to ensure that when our living time here on earth is finished, that the consequences of our financial life are not a burden on our surviving family and society as a whole.

The reality of a financial lifetime has changed dramatically over the last twenty years. The Old Paradigm of a financial lifetime was one where you had one career with one company. You had one mortgage and lived in the same house for most of your life. You had a defined benefit pension plan that you knew would pay you in your retirement no matter how long you lived. You knew that you could depend on Social Security and Medicare. And you would spend 10-15 years in retirement until your death. The financial lifetime of the typical American was much less complicated!

The New Paradigm of the financial lifetime is one where you will have multiple careers working for multiple companies. You will spend a number of years in self-employment. You will have several periods of unemployment. You will live in many houses and have multiple mortgages. You will have a defined contribution pension plan such as a 401(k) in which you will bear all the investment risk. You will be more heavily in debt. Social Security and Medicare may not provide the level of benefits that they did in the past. You will probably work, either full- or part-time during your retirement years. And you will live from 20-40 years in retirement. The financial lifetime has become infinitely more complicated. As a result, the new reality of a financial lifetime is much more uncertain and hazardous than that of the post-World War II generation. The path to financial independence is not as well-defined as it used to be.

In thinking about our financial lifetime, it is helpful to use the analogy of a river. As a river makes its way to the ocean, it is not an entirely straight or calm course. The river is comprised of many twists and bends, stretches of turbulent whitewater rapids, calm stretches of languid flows, perhaps even a waterfall or two. We are, each of us, on a financial raft trip on our own river. It will be our first and only trip. We do not have the benefit of a map or GPS satellites. How long the trip will last, none of us knows.

We can approach our journey in one of three ways: The first is to lie back, let the current take us where it will. We will not try to anticipate what might be around the next bend. The second approach is to focus obsessively on the goal of reaching the ocean. We will try to get down the river as fast as we can, we will paddle furiously, and we will lie awake at night worrying about what might be around the next bend. We will focus intently on the tasks at hand every day. We will realize at the end of the trip that we have missed the entire journey. The final approach is that of the enlightened rafter. We will have the courage to face the river. Although we have no map, we will embrace the challenge and enjoy the trip. We will employ the knowledge and wisdom of other rafters who have left a record of their own journey. We will anticipate what may be around the next bend, but will not lose sight of the beauty of the moment. We will be open to, and enjoy, the mystery of the river.

The other symbol that I use in discussing the pursuit of financial independence is the Circles of Financial Concern.

Circles of Financial Concern

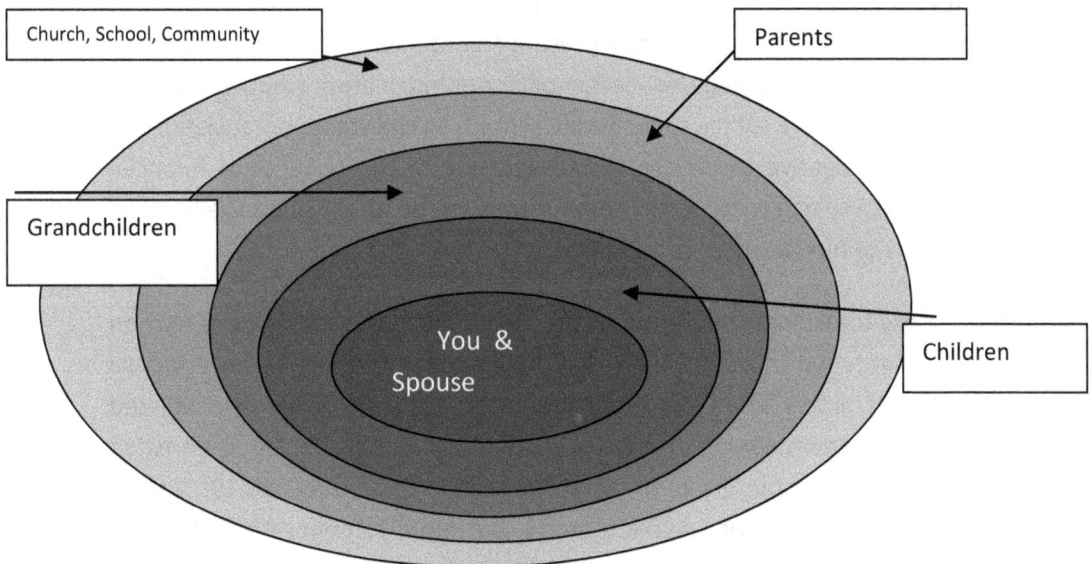

These circles encompass the great financial opportunities/challenges that we may encounter as we move through our financial lifetime. They can be summarized as follows:

1) Personal financial independence

2) Raising and educating children

3) Providing for the education of grandchildren

4) Providing support for parent's in their later years

5) Leaving a legacy to a school, church, or other charitable organization

At any given moment during our financial lifetime, we may be confronted with one or more of these opportunities/challenges. I refer to them as opportunities/challenges because they represent the opposite sides of the same coin. If we have been successful in our pursuit of financial independence, they present marvelous opportunities to lend a helping hand to those we care about the most. However, they may present difficult, if not impossible, challenges to those who haven't taken the steps to achieve financial independence.

This is not to suggest that we should feel obligated to meet each and every one of these opportunities/challenges as they present themselves. We may choose not to pay for our children's college education or our grandchildren's education. We may not want to leave a legacy to a church, school, or charitable organization. It is clearly our prerogative to choose. However, one of the rewards of financial independence is the ability, at some point in time, to be able to financially assist other members of our family or community.

This book seeks to explore the notion of the Enlightened Investor. I have chosen the term "Enlightened Investor" because I believe that the key to an effective relationship with money lies in a spiritual approach. We are profoundly conflicted when it comes to the meaning of money, particularly within the Judeo-Christian tradition. In the Old Testament of the Bible we read in Ecclesiastes 10:19 "A feast is made for laughter, and wine maketh merry, but money answereth all things." And then we turn to the New Testament where St. Paul writes in 1 Timothy 6:10 "The love of money is the root of all evil." The same quote has also been attributed to the Greek philosopher Phocyclides. Whoever said it first is immaterial, what is important is that the sentiment has obviously been around quite a while. More recently, Bob Dylan epitomized the 1960's era of rebellion and protest in his lyric, "Money doesn't talk, it swears," which was in counterpoint to the writer O. Henry's infamous line that, "Money talks." To which I would add that not only does money talk and swear, sometimes it curses.

So which is it, the end, the means to the end, or the bitter end? The philosopher Arthur Schopenhauer describes the conundrum of money thus, "Money is human happiness in the abstract. He, who is no longer capable of enjoying human happiness in the concrete, devotes his heart entirely to money." For many Americans the pursuit of wealth or income is a poor substitute for the joy and meaning that is lacking in everyday life. However, as a society we have made materialism the highest expression of our dreams. The god of commerce is predominant in every expression of American life. It has come to the point where, in many American religious traditions, the unfettered pursuit of wealth is equated with God's will.

It is imperative to draw the distinction between material well-being and an insatiable quest for wealth or income. The distinction is simply, "How much is enough?" "How much is necessary for a good life?" When a society believes that buying and selling is the sine qua non of life, when the citizens are called consumers, what does this say about our values? Henry David Thoreau is known for his statement that, "Most people lead lives of quiet desperation." In our modern age I would modify Thoreau's maxim thus: "Most people lead lives of quiet economic desperation."

In my thirty years in the investment and insurance business, I have come to believe that there is indeed a path to financial independence. However it is also my firm conviction that there are thousands of things better to do in life than worry about money and investments. We have become a culture obsessed with affluence and wealth. We are all now like the Gilded Age entrepreneur, Collis Huntington when he boasted, "Whatever is not nailed down is mine. And whatever I can pry loose is not nailed down!" And we pay a heavy price in terms of life satisfaction and fulfillment. Modern American life is characterized by families where both spouses are working, and working longer and longer hours. They despair over the lack of time to spend with each other and with their children. They are sleep-deprived and debt-ridden. They worry about if their job will be eliminated or if they'll have a chance to be promoted. They worry about how they're going to pay for college for their children, to say nothing of the anxiety over funding their retirement. Need I go on?

Is there a way to pursue and achieve financial independence without giving yourself over to an obsession with money? I believe there certainly is. The path is not easy and it is fraught with hazards. Just as the knights of King Arthur's court sought the Holy Grail in times past, we too are on a quest for the holy grail of financial independence. And just as Parsifal found the Grail by seeking the middle path between the pairs of opposites, so we shall also seek the grail of financial independence by seeking the middle path. The path is not a pursuit of money for money's sake, nor is it a condemnation of money as evil. It is a path that recognizes that money is a critical aspect of modern life that forswears the accumulation of wealth for its own sake that seeks to minimize the amount of time we need to devote investments; such that we can better use that time to pursue the passions of life.

Antoine St. Exupery, the author of <u>The Little Prince</u> put it eloquently when he said, "Perfection is attained, not when there is nothing left to add, rather it is when there is nothing left to take away." O Sancta Simplicitas. The path to financial independence rejects the notion of love of money as a possession; rather it is to use money as a means to the enjoyments and realities of life: family, friends, philosophical or religious pursuits, athletic activities, music and the arts, the beauty of the natural world, education, politics, and community activities.

It is not my purpose to be a financial guru. I do not propose that you walk in my shoes and follow in my footsteps. I do not have all the answers. It is my intention to explore the path to financial independence, to expose the fallacies that are predominant in our financial and investment culture, and to reveal the simple strategies for achieving financial independence.

4 FINANCIAL INDEPENDENCE

"A man is rich in proportion to the number of things he can afford to let alone."
Henry David Thoreau

"It is better to live rich, than to die rich." *Samuel Johnson*

The Enlightened Investor has one over-arching mission in her financial life: to achieve and maintain financial independence. Believe it or not, financial independence encompasses much more than income and wealth. The concept of financial independence is not to make as much income as possible or to accumulate as much wealth as possible. Income and wealth are means to an end. We work and invest for one of two possible goals. Either we strive, 1) to maximize our possibility of getting rich, or 2) to minimize the probability of failing to meet our income needs. In other words, the objective is to make the likelihood of retiring poor as low as possible. Most Americans believe that these two goals are inseparable, one from the other. The prevailing belief seems to be, "If I'm rich, I've got it made!" Our culture certainly promotes this idea. The first step towards financial maturity is the realization that it's not just about more and more money. The revelation of the Enlightened Investor is that the desire to get as rich as possible, and the goal of an adequate and secure lifetime income, more often than not are mutually exclusive. You can have one or the other, not both.

This seems like heresy. How can this be? Consider the words of the renowned behavioralist, Ernest Maslow,

Man is a wanting animal and rarely reaches a state of complete satisfaction, except for a short time. As one desire is satisfied, another one pops up to take its place. When this is satisfied, still another comes into the foreground. It is a characteristic of the human being throughout his whole life that he is practically always desiring something.

If the purpose of our financial life is to accumulate as much money as we possibly can, we set ourselves up for failure. The mindless pursuit to invest for ever-greater wealth creates an ever-greater possibility that the unexpected risk will wipe you out. Peter L. Bernstein, the author of *Against the Gods: The Amazing Story of Risk*, summarized the issue when he wrote, "At the extremes, the market is not a random walk. At the extremes the market is more likely to destroy fortunes than to create them." In an uncertain world, that which can come by luck can be taken away by luck."

The problem of pursuing the means with no thought to the end can be illustrated by recent history. Since the beginning of the market meltdown in March of 2000 and continuing through the Great Recession, I have been asked by financial advisors to accompany them on appointments with their clients. The situation is the same almost every time. The client's are in their mid to late-fifties. At the height of the bull market of the late '90's, they were flush with newly created wealth due to investment success. As such they were convinced, as was their financial advisor that they could quit work and retire. Their 401(k) and IRA's were worth hundreds of thousands of dollars. They thought they had it made. Because most of their assets were in retirement accounts, they were subject to the 10% penalty tax for withdrawals prior to age 59½. However, by taking distributions under the IRS code Sec. 72(t), they could avoid the 10% penalty. Under a 72(t) distribution, they had to choose a distribution amount based on their age and one of three calculations: 1) Amortization, 2) Annuitization, or 3) Life Expectancy.

They were full of confidence and unbridled optimism. Their financial advisor had for years encouraged them to invest in stocks because the historical performance charts told them that stocks returned an average of 12.00% a year. And now their investments were returning 25-50% a year in the market! Who wouldn't be tempted to leave the work-a-day world behind and retire early? Being full of optimism they chose the distribution method that gave them the largest income. The disadvantage of the 72(t) distribution was that they were locked into taking that distribution every year for the later of five years, or until they reached age 59½. No matter what happened, they could not change the amount they took out each year.

As the old saying goes, "Whatever goes around comes around." Unfortunately, the bear market that started in March of 2000 decimated the value of their investments. It was not uncommon to see portfolios with 50-80% losses. Their investments were dropping off of the proverbial cliff, and yet they still had to withdraw the same large amount from their qualified retirement accounts. In almost every case, they were facing the distinct probability that their accounts would be depleted in several years. I was brought in to these sad situations to see if there was anything that could be done. Optimism had turned to despair. Unfortunately, they had two options, none of which they found appealing. I told them they could go back to work and/or cut their living expenses.

What happened? How did this sad state of affairs come to pass? Unfortunately, they, along with thousands of other Americans, made the all-too-human mistake of thinking their good fortune would continue indefinitely. They invested to get rich, and they paid the price. Perhaps they would have had some consolation had I told them that theirs was not the first time nor would it be the last, that fate would deal a tragic blow to the best laid plans. We can go back in history to find the same fateful story played out time after time.

The story of Croesus, the King of Lydia, and Solon, the law-giver of Athens is perhaps the most eloquent example. Croesus was the richest man in the world because Lydia had the richest gold mines in history. Croesus was an earlier day Bill Gates. And so it came, that one day, Solon the wise man of Athens came to visit the court of King Croesus. Croesus, took great delight in showing Solon the wealth and grandeur of his kingdom. At one point, Croesus solicited Solon's reaction. Expecting praise and admiration, Croesus instead heard:

"The observation of the numerous misfortunes that attend all conditions forbids us to grow insolent upon our present enjoyments, or to admire a man's happiness that may yet, in the course of time, suffer change. For the uncertain future has yet to come."

Not exactly what Croesus was expecting. Croesus made the mistake of identifying his good fortune with his imagined invulnerability. John Kenneth Galbraith put it best when he wrote:

"Men possessed of money, like men earlier favored by noble birth and great title, have infallibly imagined that the awe and admiration that money inspires were really owing to their own wisdom or personality."

We have an unfortunate propensity to translate our good fortune into thinking that we are infallible, that God or luck has smiled upon us, now and forevermore. The Enlightened Investor turns the equation around; because we are fallible we fail to see good fortune for what it is, a random event in an uncertain world.

The quest for financial independence will never depend on investment performance. Market performance comes and goes, is here today and gone tomorrow. The quest for financial independence will depend on what you do to manage risk and uncertainty today, and more importantly, tomorrow. The Enlightened Investor knows that investing is a gamble that the future will be better than the past, but that there is no guarantee that this will be true. The risk is that our investments may not provide us with the income we need now or in the future.

Whatever happened to Croesus, king of Lydia? He established the first imperial currency in the history of the world. He also decided to make war on the Persian king Cyrus. In consulting the Oracle at Delphi he was told that he would, "destroy a great empire." Unfortunately, it was his own.

As he was being prepared to be burned at the stake by the victorious Persians, Croesus cried out for Solon. Curious, the Persians inquired as to who this Solon was. To which Croesus replied, "A man I would give a great fortune to see talking with all the tyrants on earth." Impressed, the Persians released him. From this point on we know no more of the great king of Lydia, Croesus.

Being rich is not necessarily a permanent condition. There are countless ways to lose your wealth: bad luck, bad decisions, political revolution, war, death, disability, or disease to name only a few. Life is uncertain. Nothing can predict risk; there are only considerations of risk.

I recall an appointment I attended with a financial advisor and his client, a successful attorney who had retired and was now providing full-time home care for his wife who was suffering from Alzheimer's disease. He had invested aggressively during the bull market of the 1990's and now was suffering the full force of the bear market of the early 2000's. It was evident after reviewing his financial situation that he had enough money to last around three more years. At the end of our appointment, in a voice full of anger, grief, and despair, he declared that if his wife did not die by the time the money ran out, he intended to kill her and then himself, and be done with it. "Fool that I am," he said, "I always thought I was rich. It's only now that I realize that there is no such thing."

In light of this man's experience and the experience of the early retirees discussed earlier, one may be compelled to ask: Is there such a thing as financial independence, and if so, what is it? If we are to walk the path to financial independence, we should start by defining our terms. First and foremost, financial independence is a personal goal. Each person or family has the right, and I would daresay the obligation to define financial independence in their own terms. Just as we all walk differently and at different speeds, so it is with the walk along the path to financial independence. We must temper our human tendencies to compare ourselves to others and to compete with them.

With this in mind, I have come to a working definition of financial independence which encompasses these considerations.

Financial independence is when you have enough capital and assets to produce the income you want, for as long as you will need it, such that work is optional and retirement is affordable.

This definition encompasses two critical requirements, 1) attention to the objective levels of economic resources (what you have and what you will need), and, 2) attention to the subjective perceptions of financial satisfaction (what you want).

I have embraced this definition of financial independence because it allows everyone to determine for themselves what it means to be financially independent. It is not my job, nor is it your financial advisor's job, nor anyone else's job to tell you how much money you should have. Nor is it to make you as rich as possible. Instead, it is to help you determine how much income you will require to fulfill your financial needs, test that goal against reality, and then help you assemble investments and investment strategies that will help you achieve financial independence in the most efficient and prudent manner possible consistent with your capacity to deal with financial risk.

What is it that we truly want and need our money to buy for us? It has been my experience in working with clients and financial advisors that very few people ever take the time to really sit down and think about this question. We tend to let the days, months, and the years go rolling by. Our minds may turn to thoughts of "If only". If only I had a better job. If only I didn't have to work fifty hours a week to try to get ahead. If only I could get out of debt. If only I could stop putting my money in stupid "get rich quick" schemes. If only I had more time to spend with my family. And yet very few people ever take the steps necessary to turn "If only" into reality.

The path to financial independence begins with the personal decision to take control of our financial life. If you were to ask average Americans how much money it would take to be financially independent I'm sure the common response would be "a million dollars". Let's get one thing straight, financial independence is not a million dollars or ten million dollars. I have known clients who have achieved financial independence on $30,000 income per year. I have also known others where $500,000 income per year wasn't enough! There is no right or wrong when it comes to financial independence.

In fact, financial independence may be more of an attitude towards money as opposed to an actual amount of money or income. Because of the uncertainties of life, and especially modern economic life, actual financial independence may come and go several times during a financial lifetime. The ultimate problem in an uncertain world is that you never know when fate will turn against you. The loss of a job, accident, sickness, bad investments, etc. can destroy any semblance of financial independence in short order. Bad things happen and they may happen to you. The path to financial independence is comprised of accumulating adequate wealth and also of protecting that wealth.

At some point during your financial lifetime, you must move beyond "How much" and come to grips with "how much is enough?" You must have the courage to turn the quest for more into the quest for enough.

Research tells us that our perceptions of financial satisfaction are largely dependent on a comparison of our achievements to our aspirations. The smaller the difference between achievement and aspiration, the higher the level of satisfaction. Absolute levels of achievement are not important in terms of financial satisfaction. Or, as your grandmother might have said, "Money can't buy happiness." If there are large differences between achievement and aspiration, the research indicates that people use two strategies to bring them closer together. You can try to increase achievement, or you can reduce your aspirations.[xiv]

Could it be that lowering our aspirations is the path to true financial independence, rather than a mark of failure? Could it be that "enough" money is often much less than we think? The Enlightened Investor knows that "enough" will never be "enough" until she realizes that "enough" will never be "enough" until she decides how much is truly "enough"!

Beyond the first step of determining how much income will satisfy our needs, there are three additional steps that must be taken to achieve financial independence.

The second step is to determine what kind of return we can expect on our capital and assets. In other words, how much income can I expect to generate from my capital and assets. This step is fraught with danger. Many people find themselves within reach of financial independence only to be tripped up by faulty assumptions and decisions.

The third step is to determine the variability of the returns on capital and assets. What sorts of risks will my capital and assets be subjected to, such as market- or interest-rate risk? What other catastrophic risks may befall my income and assets? What is my best-case and worst-case scenario? Doctors tell us that being optimistic is good for one's health. As a money doctor, I believe that a fair dose of pessimism is good for your financial health. Sailors speak of keeping a "weather eye". You may be sailing in fair weather now, but the wise sailor always keeps one eye on the horizon.

In high school, our earth sciences teacher also taught drivers' education. This was back in the good old days when schools still offered drivers' education as a part of the regular curriculum. Mr. Hanson was famous for the "what if" game. During the course of drivers' education class he would, with no warning, pose a "what if" scenario. He would do this in the classroom as well as behind the wheel training. "What if that fellow in the Ford truck decided to pull out to pass?" "What if your tire went flat right now?" His genius was to get us in the habit of thinking about contingencies, to always be alert for the unexpected. I have played the "what if" game all of my driving life. I also have made it a habit in my financial life and the financial lives of my clients. It has prevented many accidents, both automobile and financial!

The final step is how long will I live? Obviously the longer you live, the longer the money will have to last. If we knew when we were going to die, it would make the task of maintaining financial independence much easier. In 1998, I attended a conference at the Enchantment Resort outside of Sedona, Arizona. The resort is situated in Boynton Canyon, surrounded by the beautiful red rock formations at the junction of the Sonoran Desert and the Colorado Plateau. I remarked to my associates, "This is the kind of place where you'd like to stay until you run out of money, and then just shoot yourself and be done with it!" Thankfully we haven't come to the point where that is an acceptable financial planning strategy.

However, unless we choose the time of our death, we have no idea of how long we will live. Genetics can be an indicator, but it is no guaranteed predictor. The number of our days on this earth is the ultimate uncertainty that we face as we move through our financial lifetime. Unfortunately, given the uncertainty of this world, financial independence can never be 100% guaranteed. And if an investment advisor tells you otherwise, run away as fast you can. I recall a financial planner who, during the late 1990's attracted a clientele based on the assertion that, "I can make you a millionaire in five years!" I wonder what that planner is telling those clients now.

Let me re-emphasize the point, financial independence can never be 100% guaranteed. No matter how many historical performance charts, financial analyses, research reports, computer models, or investment publications, financial independence is a journey, not a destination. The goal of the Enlightened Investor is to increase the probability of achieving and maintaining financial independence. The Enlightened Investor knows that investments are the easy part; it is the financial plans you build around them that keep you on the path of financial independence.

I often compare a financial lifetime to climbing a mountain. The analogy is useful in many ways. If I were to pose the question, "What is the highest mountain in the world?" most people would immediately answer, Mount Everest. And if I asked, "Who was the first to climb it?" more than a few people would answer, Sir Edmund Hillary. Sir Edmund and Tenzing Norgay are generally acknowledged as the first to successfully summit Mount Everest.

However, many people have no knowledge of George Mallory, a British climber who, along with Andrew "Sandy" Irvine, attempted to climb Mount Everest in 1924. They were last sighted several hundred meters from the summit. Unfortunately that is the last the world knew of them until 1999, when Mallory's body was discovered on Everest. Did he and Irvine reach the summit? We'll never know for sure. However we do know that they were not able to make it down safely.

Statistics tell us that about 70% of the fatalities in alpine climbing occur on the way down from the mountain. Why is this? Perhaps it is a combination of physical exhaustion and mental fatigue, along with a psychological letting down of one's guard after summiting.

It seems to me that the same thing is true of the climb that is our pursuit of financial independence. We spend a great deal of time and energy trying to successfully summit the peak of financial independence. The financial industry spends an inordinate amount time and treasure to focus our efforts on the accumulation of assets. However, my experience reveals that the biggest financial disasters are not on the climb to financial independence. Rather it is the dangers of climbing down the mountain of financial independence. What do I mean by this?

Many people can achieve financial independence; however they lose sight or ignore the dangers of creating and protecting an income for life; as well as the high cost of taxes and expenses of estate distribution and transfer. Financial independence is not a fixed point in time; it is a journey through a financial lifetime.

How do you go about defining your path to financial independence? An exercise that I call the *Circle of Independence* has been a great help to me on an ongoing basis. It is an exercise to help you transform the "what is" of your life into the "what should be". In Eastern religious traditions it is known as a mandala. The purpose of the mandala is that when you contemplate the mandala, which is a circle with images or symbols of personal importance, you are communicating with the unconscious ground of your being. This exercise is meant to put you in accord with your true self, in the words of Joseph Campbell, "to follow your bliss." In so doing you can break out of the "now" of your life in order to find a new path to financial independence. The *Circle of Independence* exercise can help you begin the journey.

The challenge for most of us is that we are on a financial path not of our own choosing. Our financial life is defined by someone else's expectations. We pursue a career because "that's where the money is", "my parents always wanted me to be a doctor". For many it is simply getting some kind of job. To achieve true financial independence we must find our own way. In the words of Joseph Campbell:

You enter the forest at the darkest point, where there is no path. Where there is a way or path, it is someone else's path. You are not on your own path. If you follow someone else's way, you are not going to realize your potential.

The *Circle of Independence* can be used to help you define your path to financial independence. Let's use an example of an annual *"Circle of Independence"*. The first step is to consider the "what is" of your current life. How many days do you spend working? How many days do you take vacation? How many days do you play golf, or ski, or whatever? How many days do you do volunteer work? Take an inventory of the major activities and the number of days you spend pursuing those activities during the course of a year. Granted, during most days we pursue several activities, however we want to identify the major activity of that day, and how many days it is our major activity. Our "what is" circle might look like this: 240 days work, 30 golf, 15 ski, 10 family gatherings, 40 church, 10 biking, and 20 shopping.

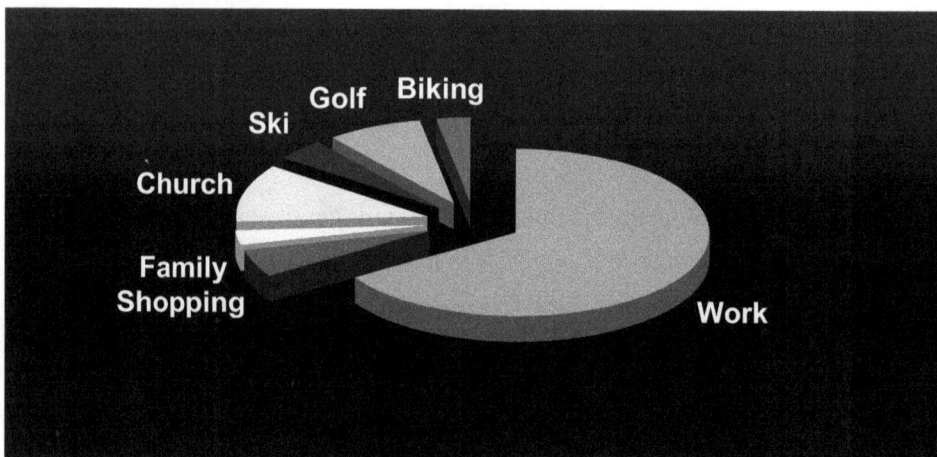

Now it is time to work on the "what should be" circle. This will take some time for reflection. The key is to imagine how you would spend your days if you had no constraints on your time whatsoever. If you could do whatever you wanted to do with your days in an ideal world, how would it look? Put it down on paper and draw your circle. Our hypothetical example might look something like this: 180 days working, 45 golf, 30 ski, 20 family gatherings, 30 gardening, 50 church, 10 biking.

When thinking about the "what should be" circle, it is helpful to think back about your ten best experiences, ten best days, ten most favorite places in the world, and ten most rewarding work experiences. In reviewing this list, it will provide you with a guide to constructing your own circle.

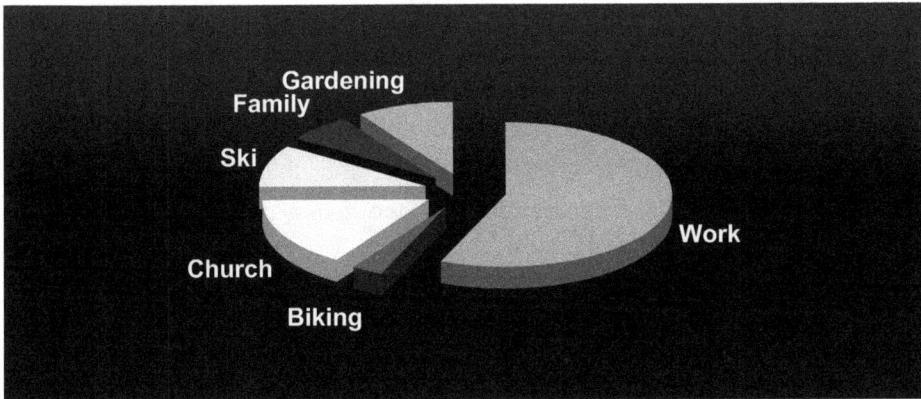

The individual in our example would obviously like to spend less time working, more time with other activities, and would like to try something new, gardening.

Having completed the "what is" and "what should be" circles, we must take time to contemplate how we can move from "what is" to "what should be". Do you have the courage of your dreams? A large part of accomplishing a goal is simply defining it. The *"Circle of Independence"* gives you a framework in which to define your life goals. Is it realistic to think that you can only work 180 days a year? Not unless you are willing to make some sacrifices.

How will you define your path to financial independence? Will it be a mindless pursuit of more income and wealth, or will it be structuring your financial life to be at the service of the other Circles of Life? Would you like to have more time to spend on outdoor activities, spiritual pursuits, family and friends? I think most of us would. The path to financial independence, if diligently pursued, is ultimately about independence itself. I recall the words of Joseph Campbell, professor of comparative mythology, when he spoke of following your bliss,

"And what then is finally the best austerity, what is the best discipline? The best discipline is to enjoy your friends. Enjoy your meals. Realize what play is. Participate in the play, in the play of life. This is known as mahasuka, the Great Delight."

The theologian Paul Tillich wrote in his *Systematic Theology, Vol. 1* that "Decision is a risk rooted in the courage of being free." Decision, risk, and freedom; in order to truly be free, we must be willing to accept risk. We must make the decision to pursue our dreams of a better life. Young Indian warriors, at the time of their initiation, were told, "As you go the way of life, you will see a great chasm. Jump. It is not as wide as you think."

The environmental movement leader, David Brower, was fond of closing his lectures with the words of Goethe, the German poet and philosopher. As we embark on the path to financial independence, the words are our clarion call to decision.

"Whatever you can do,
or dream you can do,
Begin it now!
Boldness has genius, power, and magic in it.

5 RISK AND UNCERTAINTY

"The overweening conceit which the greater part of men have of their own abilities and their absurd presumption in their own good fortune." Adam Smith

"As flies to wanton boys are we to the gods, they kill us for their sport."
King Lear, Act IV, sc. 1

"We sail within a vast sphere, ever drifting in uncertainty, driven from end to end. When we think to attach ourselves to any point and to fasten to it, it waivers and leaves us, and if we follow it, it eludes our grasp, slips past us, and vanishes for ever. Nothing stays for us. *Blaise Pascal*

I don't know which is the better attitude towards life; to expect the worst and prepare for it, or to expect the best and not to worry. The advantage of the latter attitude is that if you were fortunate enough never to be ensnared by the vicissitudes of life, all would have been beauty and light. There are those who would call such a state happiness or bliss. The disadvantage of such an attitude is that when ill fortune arrives, you are unprepared both financially and psychologically for the consequences.

We know that one of the characteristics of sane and healthy adults is that they tend to routinely overestimate the extent to which they can affect outcomes in their lives. Even when we don't have control, we like to believe that we do.

A study compared healthy, normal adults versus clinically depressed adults on their ability to accurately estimate the probabilities of their success on a moderately difficult task. The researcher expected that depressed patients would estimate the probability of success lower and less accurately than the healthy, normal adults. Her hypothesis was only partially supported. In line with expectations, the depressed patients estimated the likelihood of success much lower than the normal group. However, depressed patients' estimates were much more accurate than those made by the normal group. The conclusion is that one aspect of normalcy is to overestimate the degree to which we are in control of our lives.[xv] We commonly refer to this attribute as optimism.

It is very rare that anyone can remember the theme of the guest speaker at their college graduation. However, the words of our college commencement speaker have always stayed with me. Norman Cousins, the long-time editor of *The Saturday Evening Post*, delivered the commencement address at my alma mater St. Olaf in 1976. The theme of his address was, "nobody knows enough to be a pessimist". The wisdom of that address has stayed with me. "Nobody knows enough to be a pessimist" acknowledges that the world is an uncertain place. There is no such thing as certain knowledge. However, despite this realization, it was Cousin's contention that an optimistic outlook was a rational response to this situation. We do not know if the future will bring good fortune or ill, he maintained, therefore why not lean towards hoping for the good.

On the other hand, one could contend that "nobody knows enough to be an eternal optimist" The advantage of an "expect the worst" attitude is that you are prepared for anything that comes your way. You are ready, psychologically, emotionally, and financially for any possible contingency. The disadvantage of this mind set is that you live life always on guard. Thus, what we call happiness is hard to hold. You are pleasantly surprised when things go your way, happy for the moment, but always ready for the next turn of ill fate to come your way. Perhaps the proper path lies somewhere in between optimism and pessimism. We can refer to it as, "guarded optimism", "cautious optimism", or "hopeful pessimism".

I recently read an article posing the question, "Is Positive Thinking Destroying America?" The thesis was that America had turned from a "can do" attitude to a "hope will" outlook. The difference is subtle, but nonetheless important. It seems that over the last twenty years, everything from popular culture to religious practice has evolved into a magical kingdom where thinking something will make it so. No need to face facts and reality, I'll create my own. And because God and the universe only want good things for me, I only need to sail along.

Contrast this with earlier American optimism whereby there was a faith in a better future, however only with a clear eyed understanding that it would require work and effort, not just belief.

After coming to terms with our own mortality, the most difficult lesson that life teaches is that much of our own sense of control is an illusion. As Solon, our old friend, the lawgiver of Athens, put it to Croesus, "When you ask me about human affairs, you ask someone who knows how jealous and provocative god is. My dear Croesus, humans are the creatures of pure chance." This aspect of uncertainty makes life difficult. Western tradition, with its emphasis on reason and science, believes that there must be a cause behind everything. If something happens, something must have caused it.

However, the experience of life teaches that sometimes things just happen. Accidents, disease, market crashes, and all sorts of misfortune are facts of life. We can wring our hands at the uncertainties of life or throw ourselves into a frenzy trying to fix this broken world. Both approaches lead ultimately to frustration. The Enlightened Investor knows that the world, both financial and otherwise, is a perfect mess. Always has been and always will be. The primary task of the Enlightened Investor is to put her own life, both financial and otherwise, in order first. Only then can she look beyond to the other Circles of Financial Concern such as children, parents, community, and the world at large.

The tale of the Buddha's enlightenment is instructive. Legend has it that the Buddha's father, a grand king, upon the birth of Prince Siddhartha, the future Buddha, sought out an oracle to predict the little prince's future. The oracle declared that he would be either a great world leader or a great teacher. His father, the king, was obviously biased in which path he hoped the prince would follow. Thus he decided to give fate a helping hand. He was determined to shelter his son from all the sadness and pain of the world. He knew that if the prince experienced the sorrows and pain of the world, he would choose to be a great teacher. The little prince grew up never setting foot outside of the castle walls. And within those grand walls, the king made sure that everything the prince saw or experienced was all sweetness and light.

Eventually, the prince became curious about what was beyond the castle walls. He enlisted the help of a servant and endeavored to sneak out of the castle and walk amongst the confusion and clamor of the city. During his first trip he came upon an old man. "What's that?" asked the prince. "An old man" replied the servant. "Will I grow old?" asked the prince. "Yes", said the servant. "Take me back to the palace" said the prince. On his next trip into the city he came upon a sick woman. The conversation was pretty much the same and he went back to the palace. On his third trip he saw a corpse on the street. This was too much;

he had now seen a world of poverty, fear, pain, cruelty, and eventually death itself.

He was profoundly shaken to the root of his being by what he had seen. He could no longer ignore the realities of the world. He eventually came to his first revelation that: "All life is sorrowful." Unless one is completely oblivious to reality, we live in a world where pain, hunger, disease, grief, disappointment, and inhumanity are the rule rather than the exception. And if one was to be fortunate enough to avoid misery and suffering during life, ultimately it all comes to naught, for we all die. Granted, there are many religious traditions that would have us believe that death is the grand culmination to life, an end greatly to be desired. This indeed may be true, but actions speak louder than words, we do everything in our power and spend vast portions of our wealth, holding off death as long as we can.

Indeed, if all life is ultimately sorrowful, then how shall we live in such a world? After years of spiritual effort and reflection the Prince, the future Buddha, came to the enlightenment. How to live in a world of sorrows? By joyfully participating in such a world of sorrows. We cannot change the nature of the world as it is, he reasoned. Thus we are faced with a choice. We can say YES to the world with all its pain, fear, disease, disappointment, and death. We can strive to live fully engaged, in the midst of such sorrows. Or we can say NO and turn away from the world and withdraw.

The revelation of the Buddha is that we are faced with the world as it is. The enlightenment is to "joyfully participate in the sorrows of the world." Easily said, not so easily done. The Buddha went on to realize that the key to such joyful participation was to resist the two temptations of the world, fear and desire.

Fear: The anxiety of the "what if". What if I lose my job? What if I get sick? What if I lose all my money? The list goes on and on.

Desire: The obsession to possess or control. The imagined need to accumulate material possessions. The imagined need to make more and more money.

These temptations can wreak havoc with one's pursuit of financial independence. The Enlightened Investor knows that resisting the financial temptations of fear and desire is critical to the goal of joyfully participating in a financial world that is characterized by uncertainty at every turn.

Let's examine the ways that the financial temptations of fear and desire manifest themselves in the way we approach money. The age-old wisdom is that there are two dominant emotions when it comes to investing, fear and greed. Looking at the performance of the stock market in the late 1990's and comparing it to the market of the early 2000's, we see a textbook example of how far and how fast the pendulum can swing from greed to fear.

However, I take exception to the theory of fear and greed. I would venture that for most investors, they are motivated by two aspects of fear, rather than fear and greed. The first aspect of fear is the fear of losing it all, of becoming poor and destitute. The second aspect of fear is the fear of losing ground vis-à-vis their reference group. In other words, the fear of not "keeping up with the Jones'." Granted, there are those people who epitomize the idea of greed. We only need look at the abuses of Worldcom, Enron, etc. to see greed incarnate. However, I believe most Americans are striving for financial well-being, not inordinate wealth. And yet, the two-headed demon of fear can lead us down many false paths.

First, let's discuss the fear of losing ground. As humans, we have a tendency to compare ourselves to others. Whether it is fashion, appearance, cars, or houses, or income, we judge ourselves in comparison to others. We also judge our financial well-being in comparison to others. This is a prescription for trouble. The problem is that we never really know how much someone else earns in income or how much wealth they have. When it comes to money, appearances can be deceiving. Money is the last American taboo. We conceal our income and wealth, lest anyone else know how we are really doing. And so when we compare ourselves to others financially, we are groping among shadows. At least with cars or houses, you can see exactly what the other person has, and yet even with these things, we do not know whether they have a large mortgage or small, or whether they own the house outright; whether they lease, have a 72-month loan, or whether the car is paid off. The following is the household income received by each fifth and the top 5 percent of households in the United States for 2010 as compiled by the U. S. Census Bureau.

Lowest fifth-	$ 0	-	$20,000
Second fifth-	$ 20,001	-	$ 38,043
Third fifth-	$ 38,044	-	$ 61,735

Fourth fifth-	$ 61,736	-	$100,065
Highest fifth (80%-95%)-	$100,066	-	$180,810
Top 5 percent-	$180,810 and above		

How do you compare? Probably not as poorly as you thought. And yet we are confronted with popular media images that reflect the lifestyle of the top one percent of income earners. We see these images of the so-called "good life" and consciously or subconsciously we perceive that this is the norm. The message is, this is what everybody else has, except me. What is portrayed as normal in magazines, movies, and on television is anything but normal. Yet we are easily misled.

This uncertainty breeds paranoia which in turn leads to a "herd mentality' when it comes to money and investing. If we think everybody is rushing to buy real estate, then we better do so as well. I am reminded of the time I was salmon fishing on Lake Michigan. This was back in the days before cell phones. Marine communication was conducted on marine radios which had a limited number of channels. The group we were fishing with was constantly monitoring the channels to eavesdrop on the charter captains in order to hopefully pick up tips as to where and how deep the fish were. And of course everyone had a keen eye to keep track of where the charter boats were clustering. As a result you had this comic scenario where the charter captains would move to one part of the lake, only to be closely followed by the amateurs like us. Needless to say, we never caught very many salmon. We were just like the common investor who is always trying to catch the next hot trend.

The fear of losing financial ground is exacerbated by the belief that somebody out there knows more than you. Just as we thought that the charter captains knew where the fish were biting. In a later chapter, we will expose the fallacy of "somebody knows more than me".

There have been many psychological experiments in which the subjects are asked to perform simple tasks, such a measuring the length of line or counting the number of x's on a sheet of paper. When asked to work on these tasks alone, the subjects complete the tasks with a high degree of accuracy. However, when done in the presence of others who intentionally demonstrate the wrong answer to the subjects, the subjects are quite likely to provide the same answer themselves. The Enlightened Investor must resist the urge to financially compare himself with others. He must resist the fear of not keeping up. The

Enlightened Investor knows that the path to financial independence is a solitary path.

The other aspect of the temptation of fear is the fear of losing it all. As many investors have learned over the last several years, it is much more painful to suddenly lose 40-70% of your net worth than it is to fail to meet long-term financial goals. This is why we saw huge net redemptions of stock mutual funds in 2002 and 2008. The risk horizon of the average investor is about eighteen months. The market hit its high in March, 2000. Investors were willing to hang in there through the end of 2000 and actually through most of 2001. September 11, 2001 marked the beginning of investor capitulation. Once portfolio losses exceeded 40% and the bear market exceeded eighteen months, the combination was too much for most investors. They headed for the exits en masse.

Our fear of losing is demonstrated by a study where a group of people were told to imagine that they had $300. They had a choice between:

a) receiving another $100, or

b) A coin toss which, if they won, they would receive an additional $200. If they lost, they wouldn't receive any additional cash.

It is not surprising that almost everyone chose option (a). A bird in hand is worth two in the bush.

A second study was conducted whereby a group of people were told that they had $500 and then were given a choice between:

c) Giving back $100, or

d) A coin toss which, if they won, they would pay nothing. If they lost they would have to pay back $200.

Again, it is not too surprising that most people chose option (d).

Probability analysis reveals that all four choices are equal. They all yield an expected outcome of $400. Mathematically that may be true, but human nature prefers some choices over others. We hate to lose. When faced with a loss, we are willing to take a gamble. However when it comes to gains, we are risk averse. That is why so few people take profits when the market is going up and why so many people will sell when the market is going down. The Enlightened

Investor will resist the temptation of the fear of losing. He will understand that it is sometimes the better path to endure a procession of small losses to have the potential of ultimate gain.

The other financial temptation is that of desire. Desire can manifest itself in several ways. The first is overconfidence. According to a May 2001 Gallup/PaineWebber survey of individual investors, investors expected, on average, that the stock market would provide a mean 10.3% return over the following 12 months. However, they expected that their <u>own</u> portfolios would provide a mean 11.7% return! It brings to mind the old saying that fifty percent of people are below-average. Not when we're talking investments! In the survey everybody thought they were above-average! When it comes to investment expectations investors are living in Garrison Keillor's Lake Wobegon where "The girls are strong, the boys are good-looking, and everybody's above average!" The philosopher Nietzsche wrote, "No victor believes in chance." We can go back as far as man has been on earth and we find in written and oral history, myth, and literature stories of hubris and the inevitable tragedy of the fall.

In his <u>Theory of Moral Sentiments</u>, Adam Smith concluded that most of the world's troubles came from somebody not knowing when to stop and be content. When is enough, enough? Unfortunately the temptation of desire, as it manifests itself in investor overconfidence, rarely ever says "enough". We choose to tempt fate. This is why so many investors approach investing as they would gambling. If we have been successful in the short-run with a stock, mutual fund, or other investment strategy, we are tempted to project that short-term history into the indefinite future. We believe that the goddess Fortuna (Lady Luck) is on our side, and so we let it ride. We are mesmerized by our gains such that we are blind to the risk that a roll of "7" will take it all away in one fell swoop. No warning can rescue the person who is determined to grow suddenly rich!

The stock market is a dangerous arena in which to play this game. Consider the words of Malcolm Gladwell:

"The stock market does not behave in the way of physical phenomena such as mortality or morbidity statistics. The economist Eugene Fama demonstrated that if the movement of stock prices followed a normal distribution, you'd expect a big jump (a movement of five standard deviations from the mean), only once every seven years. In fact jumps of that kind happen every three to four years, because

investors don't behave with statistical orderliness. They change their minds, they panic, and they copy each other. Fama concluded that if you charted the market's fluctuations, the graph would have a "fat tail", meaning that the upper and lower ends of the distribution would have many more outliers than statisticians used to modeling the physical world would have imagined."[xvi]

The Enlightened Investor knows that we are never certain; therefore we must resist the temptation of desire, otherwise known as overconfidence. We are always blind to one degree or another. We see patterns where there are none. We invest in trends that are nonexistent. We believe that the trees will continue to grow to the heavens.

"The real trouble with this world of ours is not that it is an unreasonable world, nor even that it is a reasonable one. The commonest kind of trouble is that it is nearly reasonable, but not quite. Life is not illogicality, yet it is a trap for logicians. It looks just a little more mathematical and regular than it is, its exactitude is obvious, but its inexactitude is hidden, its wildness lies in wait."[xvii]

We may know a lot, but we do not know everything. As Hamlet says to Horatio, "There are more things in heaven and earth, Horatio, than are dreamt of in your philosophy." We must always be prepared to change our minds. We must act as best we can in light of what we do not know.

The other aspect of the temptation of desire is materialism. Just as obesity has become an epidemic in America, so also, we have an epidemic of over-consumption and over-spending. We know the problem very well. The Federal Reserve recently released statistics on consumer credit that illustrates the painful truth as to why most Americans have difficulty achieving financial independence. The average balance on a credit card is $8,000; the average number of credit cards of the average American household is ten. Regardless of all the low interest offers, the average credit card rate is 18.9%. It would take 25 years and 7 months to pay off $8,000 making the minimum monthly payments at an interest rate of 18%.[xviii] We have become ravenous ghosts with huge stomachs and pinpoint mouths. We cannot consume fast enough to satiate our inordinate hunger. Samuel Johnson, over two hundred years ago summarized the problem thus: "Life is a progress from want to want, not from enjoyment to enjoyment."

We like to believe that happiness does not depend on material possessions, but it is only so much talk. In survey after survey, when people are asked about what makes them happy, the answer comes back time and time again- their economic condition. It comes in ahead of even family and health. The irony of this was pointed out by Daniel Bernoulli, the Swiss scientist and mathematician. He stated, "The satisfaction resulting from an increase in wealth will be inversely proportionate to the quantity of goods previously possessed." The more and more we acquire, the less and less satisfaction and happiness we derive from it.

Equity theory puts forth the idea that we tend to be satisfied with our lives when we believe that we are getting an equitable deal from life. The theory proposes that people are satisfied when the difference between what they have and what they think they deserve is low.[xix] This all may be well and good, however; our idea of what we deserve tends to be a moving target. Harry Markowitz demonstrated that we constantly aspire to move up from our current social class.[xx] We reluctantly buy insurance to protect us from falling into a lower social class, but we enthusiastically and recklessly pursue material and financial riches in order to move up the social scale.

The United States is without a doubt, the world's greatest economic success story, but as Professor Richard Easterlin has pointed out in <u>Growth Triumphant: the Twenty-First Century in Historical Perspective</u>, rising material prosperity and economic progress is a "hollow victory". Economic growth is indeed triumphant, but to no good end. He concludes that material prosperity does not make us happier, or as he puts it, "the triumph of economic growth is not a triumph of humanity over material wants; rather, it is the triumph of material wants over humanity."

It was the historian George Santayana who coined the oft-quoted phrase, "Those who cannot remember the past are condemned to repeat it." This timeless truth has been used so many times to illustrate so many points that it has become cliché. The problem with clichés is that we hear them, nod our head in agreement, and then never give them a serious moment of reflection. In summing up our chapter on risk and uncertainty, it might be wise to revisit a little recent history.

I recently looked at a presentation that I had given back in the summer of 1998. The summer of 1998, the good old days of the never-ending bull market, right? Well not quite, at the end of the first quarter of 1998, the Dow stood at around 9000. At the end of the second quarter there were one hundred million equity mutual fund accounts with a total of $2.3 trillion in assets. It was a new record for democratic capitalism in that the $2.3 trillion represented 38.3% of all household financial assets in the United States. Optimism was rampant; money flowed into equity funds like the Amazon into the Atlantic.

However, at the end of the third quarter of 1998, the Dow had slid to 7500. This was a 17% decline from the end of the first quarter. The Russell 2000 had lost 25% of its value. How soon we forget. There was plenty of hand-wringing and gnashing of teeth among the investment community. People wondered aloud if this was the end of the great bull market.

In looking at the presentation I made back in 1998, I remembered that I reminded my audience that the situation in the market and the economy in 1998 were similar to those of 1990. In 1990 we had the build-up to the Gulf War, the S&L crisis, an S&P high in July, a sell-off of stocks in the third quarter, and a flight of capital to U.S. treasuries and money markets. Sound familiar?

What happened way back in 1990? The third quarter of 1990 marked the start of a four-year surge in stocks. From 11/90 to 10/93, the Russell 2000 was up 130%, the S&P up 68.5%.

What happened in 1998? At the end of the first quarter the Dow was around 9000, at the end of the third quarter it had dropped to 7500. And wonder of wonders, at the end of the first quarter of 1999 it had recovered to reach a high of 10,000.

What is the point of our little survey of recent history? As I write, we are climbing back from market lows of the autumn of 2008 and spring of 2009. Will history repeat itself like it did in 1990 and 1998? I have no way of knowing for certain, however I can act on probabilities. Clients that invested new money in equity markets in the summer of 2009 were surprised and delighted to see their investment increase by 50% in a few short months. Was it luck, coincidence, or probability?

What I know is that the Wheel of Fortune is much more than a mindless game show. The wheel of fortune is a metaphor for the game of life, including the game of financial independence.

As the wheel turns, which it always does, we know neither how fast it will spin nor in which direction. However we do know that we will find ourselves in one of four positions on the wheel of fortune:

At the top. . . going down. . . at the bottom. . . or going up.

What is the only part of a wheel not subject to such spinning? The center, the hub of the wheel. The question we must face is this: Knowing that the wheel of fortune has always turned, and always shall, will we be preoccupied with the wild, unpredictable spinning on the rim of the wheel? Or will we position ourselves at the still point of the immovable center?

The mythologist, Joseph Campbell tells a wonderful story about the vagaries of fortune. The story is in one of the Upanishads and it concerns the god Indra. As Campbell told the story:

"Now, it happened at this time that a great monster had enclosed all the waters of the earth, so that there was a terrible drought. Indra realized that he had a box of thunderbolts and that all he had to do was drop a thunderbolt on the monster. When he did that, the waters began to flow, the world was refreshed, and the Indra said, "My, what a great boy am I!" Indra then goes up to the cosmic mountain and decides to build a palace worthy of such as him. The main carpenter of the gods goes to work on it, and in quick order he gets the palace in shape.

But every time Indra comes to inspect it, he has bigger ideas about how splendid and grandiose the palace should be. Finally the carpenter says, "We are both immortal and there is no end to his desires. I'm caught for eternity." So he decides to go to Brahma, the creator god, and complain.

Brahma sits on a lotus, the lotus grows from the navel of Vishnu, who is the sleeping god, whose dream is the universe, the carpenter tells his story to Brahma. Brahma says, "You go home, I'll fix this up." The next morning, at the gate of the palace that is being built, there appears a beautiful blue-black boy with a lot of children around him, just admiring his beauty. The porter at the gate of the new palace goes running to Indra, and Indra says, "Well, bring in the boy." The boy is brought in, and Indra, the king god, sitting on his throne says, "Young man, welcome. And what brings you to my palace?"

"Well," says the boy with a voice like rolling thunder, "I have been told that you are building such a palace as no Indra before you ever built."

And Indra says, "Indras before me! Young man what are talking about?"

The boy says, "Indras before you. I have seen them come and go, come and go. Just think, Vishnu sleeps in the cosmic ocean, and the lotus of the universe grows from his navel. On the lotus sits Brahma, the creator. Brahma opens his eyes, and a world comes into being, governed by an Indra. Brahma closes his eyes, and a world goes out of being. The life of Brahma is four hundred and thirty-two thousand years. When he dies, the lotus goes back, and another lotus is formed, and another Brahma. Then think of the galaxies beyond galaxies in infinite space, each a lotus, with a Brahma sitting on it, opening his eyes, closing his eyes. And Indras? There may be wise men in your court who would volunteer to count the drops of water in the oceans of the world or the grains of sand on the beaches, but no one would count those Brahmin, let alone those Indras."

While the boy is talking, an army of ants parades across the floor. The boy laughs when he sees them, and Indra's hair stands on end, and he says to the boy, "Why do you laugh?" The boy answers, "Don't ask unless you are willing to be hurt." Indra says, "I ask. Teach."

And so the boy points down at the ants and says, "Former Indras all. Through many lifetimes they rise from the lowest conditions to the highest illumination. And then they drop their thunderbolts on a monster, and they think, "My, what a good boy I am!" And down they go again."[xxi]

The Enlightened Investor will seek the still point in their financial life. The still point of the knowledge that seasons come and go; we are born, grow old, and die; markets rise and fall; and that this too, shall pass. In a world of risk and uncertainty the Enlightened Investor will move joyfully down the path of financial independence knowing that the unchecked desire for earthly gains and fear of loss combine to hold us back from our real life. She also realizes that the dreams for the future must not be held hostage by the memories of the past.

6 INVESTMENT FALLACIES

"The safest way to double your money is to fold it over once and put it in your pocket."　　　　　　Frank McKinney Hubbard

"When an investor says, "I own last year's best performing mutual fund," what he forgets to add is, "unfortunately I bought it this year."
Jonathon Clements

The Enlightened Investor knows that investing can never be reduced to a science. No matter how much data is collected and over whatever period of time; no matter how intelligent and diligent the analyst, and no matter how many computer programs and systems are designed, investment results cannot be predicted. How many billions of dollars have been lost by investors who have been captivated by the siren song of market predictability?

The philosopher Karl Popper stated that there are only two types of theories:

1. Those that are known to be wrong, as they were tested and rejected. Popper referred to these as "falsified theories".

2. Those that have not yet been known to be wrong but may, at some point, be proven to be wrong.

The financial and investment industry is built on the theory that insight, intelligence, ability, and information matter in investing as they do in most other aspects of life such as engineering, dentistry, or surgery. Investment success always has a reason, but how can you know whether the money manager's success is due to his skill, or a rationalization invented after the fact, or pure unadulterated luck?

The market forecaster who is always bullish month after month, year after year, is bound to be correct at some point. And just like the broken clock that is nonetheless correct twice a day, the forecasters seize upon that fortunate coincidence to bolster their reputation, and would have us ignore all the days and months when their bold predictions did not play out. Exhibit #1, Jim Cramer of CNBC. Individuals such as he either have no memory or have no shame. Perhaps it is some of both. And yet viewers continue to tune in. I would hope that it is for pure entertainment, because his opinions are no worse and no better than anyone else's.

The question of luck in mutual fund managers' or hedge fund success has been illustrated many times by the use of a simple coin toss. There are about 10,000 mutual funds in existence today in the United States. Let us assume that every year, half of the mutual fund managers would make money and half would lose money. If the losers were tossed out of the game after every year there would be 313 managers remaining who had made money every year for five years straight. After ten years of our experiment there would only be ten managers remaining who had made money each and every year for ten years straight! We would then see these individuals' names and faces on the cover of investing magazines and see their smiling faces on the investment television channels. They would have erudite explanations for their long-term success, and yet, how would we truly know whether it just wasn't plain luck. Random chance explains their success just as well as skill. How can we really know for sure?

If we look at the actual mutual fund industry there are just about ten managers who have outperformed the S&P 500 over a ten year period. Is it skill or luck? My experience in the investment and insurance business tells me the answer is a lot more luck than skill. And yet, the entire investment industry is largely built on the false premise that money managers or investment advisors possess the singular skill to make money year after year. Perhaps you remember Peter Lynch of the Fidelity Magellan fund. He was a superstar manager for a period of years in the 1980's. The returns of the fund were compelling. Was it skill or luck? We will never know as Mr. Lynch had the good fortune or wisdom to get out while he was on top.

The investment media tempts us with theories and stories of success. The Enlightened Investor realizes that most of these temptations are fallacies. The path to financial independence is cluttered with these vendors hawking their wares. The Enlightened Investor must walk resolutely down the path to financial independence. She must ignore the cacophony. She must be able to cut through all the noise and be able to identify the signal of truth. In order to seek true financial independence she must be able to recognize these fallacies. They are:

Past performance (average annual returns versus annualized returns)

Investment returns versus Investor returns

Somebody knows more than me

Inflation and the cost of living

The effect of taxation

In the following chapters we will explore each of these fallacies and how they can inhibit a successful journey to financial independence.

7 THE FALLACY OF PAST PERFORMANCE

In his Treatise on Human Nature, Scottish philosopher, David Hume stated that "No amount of observations of white swans can allow the inference that all swans are white, but the observation of a single black swan is sufficient to refute that conclusion." You might wonder what in the world does this have do with investing. The idea of the "black swan" has recently been revived by Nassim Taleb in his book, The Black Swan. Over the last twelve years we have witnessed a number of so-called "black swan" events such as the Financial Meltdown of 2008, the internet bubble, the housing market collapse, the bankruptcies and fraud of Enron and Worldcom and others. Very few people saw these events coming. We are deceived by recent experience into believing that the future will be like the recent past. The Enlightened Investor realizes that just because ABC stock or XYZ mutual fund has increased in value every year for the last five years, there is no guarantee that it will do so next year. Just because all we've seen are white swans, we cannot say all swans are white.

Perhaps the greatest investment fallacy is the false promise of past performance. Mutual funds, as well as many other types of investments, always warn in their prospectuses and sales materials that "past performance is no guarantee of future results". They do this because FINRA and SEC require them to do so by law.

And yet, the mutual funds that have enjoyed short-term success are shameless in touting their recent returns. They prominently display their short-term performance records in the public and trade media. And unfortunately, many financial salespeople will sell the performance period that puts the particular investment in the best possible light. These performance figures are almost always expressed in terms of "average return" for a given period of time. This is fallacy #1. The fallacy is that almost all investment returns are expressed in terms of "average" annual returns, however your money and your investment return is not a function of "average" return. The money we have, and the return on our investments is instead dependent on our "annualized" return.

Unfortunately the majority of investors have no idea of the distinction between the two terms. "Average" return is also known more precisely as "arithmetic mean return" and "annualized" return is known as "geometric mean return". The distinction between the two and how that translates into an accurate picture of investment returns is crucial.

For example, consider the XYZ mutual fund. Their share price increased 100% in 1999. Unfortunately, the fund lost 50% in 2000. What is the average return for the XYZ over that two year period? (100%-50%) divided by 2 equals 25%. Not bad. Who wouldn't take a return of 25% a year? And we can be certain that XYZ fund and their salespeople will proclaim this 25% return to all who will listen. And as sure as night follows day, investors will start pouring money into the fund. However the 25% "average" return is misleading.

Let's examine our previous example in terms of "annualized" return. Shares of XYZ fund at the beginning of 1999 were priced at $20/share. As we said, XYZ fund gained 100% in 1999. Thus, at the end of 1999 the value of our shares of XYZ fund was worth $40. However, the XYZ fund lost 50% of its value in 2000. We bought into the XYZ fund at a cost of $20/share. Our share price appreciated 100% in 1999, thus our share price increased from $20 to $40 at the end of 1999. In the year 2000, XYZ lost 50% of its value. 50% of $40 is $20. Ouch! After two years of investing in XYZ fund you haven't made a dime! You started at $20/share and you are now at $20/share. And yet, XYZ fund and its salespeople will tell you that you enjoyed a 25% average annual return on your investment. The bad news is that you can't take average annual return to the bank, nor can you spend it! "Average" annual return is an artificial construct to promote investments to potential investors. It means absolutely nothing to the existing investor, nor should it mean anything to the potential investor.

What we really need to know is the "annualized" return of our investments. In the case of our example, XYZ fund had an "annualized" return for 1999 & 2000 of 0%! Granted, this example is extreme, but understanding the difference between "average" annual return and "annualized" return is critical.

"Average" return is simply the average of each of the individual annual returns. In contrast, "annualized" return is what you must earn each and every year to equal the result of your series of different annual returns. The difference is subtle, but all important. As we saw with our example of XYZ fund, the "average" annual return was 25% and the "annualized" return was 0%.

Let's examine a real life example. The Callan Periodic Table of Investment Returns is a graphic representation of the returns of nine different market indices, ranked in order of performance for any given year from best performing to the worst. The market indices represented are: Lehman Brothers Aggregate Bond Index, Morgan Stanley Capital International Index (developed stock markets of Europe, Australia, Asia, and the Far East), Russell 2000 Value, Russell 2000 Growth, Russell 2000, S&P/Barra 500 Growth, S&P/Barra 500 Value, S&P MidCap 400, and the S&P 500.[xxii]

he Callan Periodic Table of Investment Returns
annual returns for key indices (1983–2002) ranked in order of performance (Best to Worst)

1983	1984	1985	1986	1987	1988	1989	1990	1991	1992	1993	1994	1995	1996	1997	1998	1999	2000	2001
Russell 2000 Value 38.64%	LB Agg 15.15%	MSCI EAFE 56.16%	MSCI EAFE 69.44%	MSCI EAFE 24.63%	Russell 2000 Growth 29.47%	S&P BARRA 500 Growth 36.40%	LB Agg 8.96%	Russell 2000 Growth 51.19%	Russell 2000 Value 29.14%	MSCI EAFE 32.56%	MSCI EAFE 7.78%	S&P BARRA 500 Growth 38.13%	S&P BARRA 500 Growth 23.97%	S&P BARRA 500 Growth 36.53%	S&P BARRA 500 Growth 42.16%	Russell 2000 Growth 43.09%	Russell 2000 Value 22.83%	Russell 2000 Value 14.03%
Russell 2000 29.13%	S&P BARRA 500 Value 10.52%	S&P MidCap 400 35.59%	S&P BARRA 500 Value 21.67%	S&P BARRA 500 Value 6.50%	MSCI EAFE 28.27%	S&P MidCap 400 35.55%	S&P 500 0.20%	S&P MidCap 400 50.10%	S&P BARRA 500 Value 18.41%	Russell 2000 23.77%	S&P BARRA 500 Value 3.13%	S&P 500 Index 37.58%	S&P 500 Index 22.96%	S&P 500 Index 33.36%	S&P 500 Index 28.58%	S&P BARRA 500 Growth 28.25%	S&P MidCap 400 17.51%	LB Agg 8.44%
S&P BARRA 500 Value 28.89%	MSCI EAFE 7.38%	S&P BARRA 500 Value 33.31%	S&P 500 Index 18.56%	S&P 500 Index 5.10%	Russell 2000 25.02%	S&P 500 Index 31.69%	S&P 500 Index -3.10%	S&P 500 Index 46.05%	S&P 500 11.91%	S&P MidCap 400 16.91%	S&P 500 1.32%	S&P 500 36.99%	S&P BARRA 500 Value 22.00%	S&P BARRA 500 Value 32.25%	S&P MidCap 400 20.00%	MSCI EAFE 26.96%	MSCI EAFE 11.63%	Russell 2000 2.49%
S&P MidCap 400 26.08%	S&P 500 Index 6.10%	S&P 500 Index 31.57%	S&P MidCap 400 16.21%	S&P BARRA 500 Growth 3.68%	S&P BARRA 500 Value 21.67%	S&P BARRA 500 Value 26.13%	S&P MidCap 400 -5.12%	Russell 2000 41.70%	S&P BARRA 500 10.52%	S&P BARRA 500 Value 18.61%	S&P BARRA 500 -0.64%	Russell 2000 Growth 31.04%	Russell 2000 Value 21.37%	Russell 2000 31.79%	S&P MidCap 400 19.11%	S&P 500 21.26%	S&P BARRA 500 Value 6.08%	S&P MidCap 400 -0.60%
MSCI EAFE 23.69%	S&P BARRA 500 Growth 2.33%	Russell 2000 31.05%	LB Agg 15.26%	LB Agg 2.76%	S&P BARRA 500 Growth 20.87%	Russell 2000 Growth 20.17%	S&P BARRA 500 Value -6.85%	S&P BARRA 500 Growth 38.37%	S&P MidCap 400 13.95%	Russell 2000 Growth 13.37%	S&P MidCap 400 -1.54%	S&P MidCap 400 30.95%	S&P MidCap 400 19.20%	S&P BARRA 500 Value 29.98%	LB Agg 14.67%	S&P BARRA 500 Value 21.04%	S&P 500 -3.02%	S&P BARRA 500 Growth -9.23%
S&P 500 Index 22.38%	Russell 2000 Value 2.27%	Russell 2000 Value 31.01%	S&P BARRA 500 Growth 14.50%	S&P MidCap 400 -2.04%	S&P MidCap 400 20.37%	Russell 2000 16.26%	Russell 2000 -17.41%	Russell 2000 Value 30.47%	S&P 500 Index 7.62%	Russell 2000 13.37%	S&P 500 Index -1.82%	Russell 2000 28.44%	Russell 2000 16.49%	Russell 2000 22.36%	Russell 2000 8.69%	S&P MidCap 400 14.72%	MSCI EAFE -9.10%	S&P 500 -11.71%
Russell 2000 Growth 20.13%	S&P MidCap 400 1.18%	Russell 2000 Value 30.97%	Russell 2000 Value 7.41%	Russell 2000 Value -7.11%	Russell 2000 Value 16.61%	LB Agg 14.53%	Russell 2000 -19.51%	S&P BARRA 500 Value 22.56%	LB Agg 7.40%	S&P BARRA 500 Growth 10.08%	LB Agg -2.43%	Russell 2000 Growth 25.75%	Russell 2000 Growth 11.26%	Russell 2000 Growth 12.93%	Russell 2000 Growth 1.23%	S&P BARRA 500 Value 12.72%	Russell 2000 -14.17%	S&P 500 -11.88%
S&P BARRA 500 Growth 16.24%	Russell 2000 -7.30%	S&P BARRA 500 Value 29.68%	Russell 2000 5.68%	Russell 2000 -8.80%	LB Agg 11.95%	MSCI EAFE 12.43%	Russell 2000 -21.77%	LB Agg 18.00%	S&P BARRA 500 500 Growth 5.07%	LB Agg 9.75%	S&P MidCap 400 -2.92%	MSCI EAFE 18.47%	LB Agg 9.65%	MSCI EAFE -2.55%	Russell 2000 -0.82%	Russell 2000 -22.08%	Russell 2000 -12.73%
LB Agg 8.35%	Russell 2000 Growth -15.83%	LB Agg 22.11%	Russell 2000 Growth 3.58%	LB Agg -10.48%	LB Agg 7.89%	MSCI EAFE 10.54%	MSCI EAFE -23.45%	MSCI EAFE 12.13%	MSCI EAFE -12.17%	S&P BARRA 500 Growth 1.68%	S&P MidCap 400 -3.58%	MSCI EAFE 11.21%	MSCI EAFE 3.63%	LB Agg 1.78%	MSCI EAFE -6.45%	Russell 2000 Value -1.49%	MSCI EAFE -22.43%	MSCI EAFE -21.44%

What strikes you immediately, unless you are color blind, is the truth of the old sayings such as, "What goes up, must come down.", or "Whatever goes around, comes around", and "Nothing lasts forever". As is readily apparent, each asset class has its year in the sun. The problem is that no one, and I mean no one, can predict the rise or fall of any particular market segment in any given year.

I have taken the performance numbers from the Callan chart from 1982-2001 and analyzed them in terms of "average" annual return and "annualized" return. "Average" annual return is very easy to calculate. We simply add all the positive years and then subtract the negative years of a particular index, divide that sum by the number of years (20). For example, let's examine the Russell 2000 Growth Index. From 1982 – 2001 we have the following annual performance numbers: 20.98 + 20.13 – 15.38 + 30.97 + 3.58 – 10.48 + 20.37 + 20.17 – 17.41 +

51.19 + 7.77 + 13.37 − 2.43 + 31.04 + 11.26 + 12.93 + 1.23 + 43.09 − 22.43 − 9.23 = 210.72. 210.72 divided by 20 years equals 10.53% "average" annual return.

This is the number that almost all money managers will list in their advertisements. You will be impressed when they tell you they have had an average annual return of 10.53% for twenty years 1982-2001. Not bad at all! If we had started with $100 on 1/1/1982, we would have $737.96 at the end of 2001. However, as the cliché goes: "Garbage in, garbage out." You would not actually have $737.96 in your account. Your $100 would be worth only $537.12 at the end of 2001.

How can this be? The problem is that "average" annual return calculations do not accurately reflect the effects of volatility upon actual returns. "Annualized" returns however, accurately reveal the true value of investment returns. The difference in calculation stems from the fact that "average" annual return sums the twenty years of returns and then divides by twenty. "Annualized" return starts with the actual or hypothetical amount of money deposited in the investment, and then multiplies that number by each year's succeeding return. The calculation for the "annualized" return is as follows: $100.00 x 1.2098 x1.2013 x 0.8417 x 1.3097 x 1.0358 x 0.8952 x 1.2037 x 1.2017 x 0.8259 x 1.5119 x 1.077 x 1.1337 x 0.9757 x 1.3104 x 1.1126 x 1.1293 x 1.0123 x 1.4309 x 0.7757 x 0.9077 = $537.12.

One hundred dollars was invested on 1/1/1982 and it was worth $537.12 at the end of 2001. Plugging the numbers into our financial calculator, this represents an "annualized" return of 8.77%/year. Consequently in terms of "average" annual return, the Russell 2000 Growth Index from 1982-2001 had an "average" annual return of 10.53%, and an "annualized" annual return of 8.77%. This is a difference of 1.76%. The Enlightened Investor realizes that "average" annual returns are misleading and that it is "annualized" annual return that represents real return, real world, and real money.

The following chart summarizes both "annualized" and "average" annual return of the nine indices on the Callan chart in terms of percentage growth and also the growth of $100 over the twenty year period from 1982-2001.

Index	Annualized Return %	Annualized Growth of $100	Average Return %	Average Growth of $100
S&P MidCap 400	16.93	2,284	17.80	2,647
Barra 500 Value	15.20	1,693	15.91	1,961
S&P 500	15.20	1,694	16.12	1,987
Barra 500 Growth	14.85	1,593	16.29	2,046
Russell 2000 Value	14.76	1,570	14.73	1,561
Russell 2000	11.52	885	13.17	1,187
Morgan Stanley EAFE	11.02	810	13.27	1,209
Lehmann Bros. Aggregate	10.61	751	10.87	788
Russell 2000 Growth	8.77	537	10.53	738

What conclusions can be drawn from this analysis? The more volatile the investment, the greater the discrepancy between the "average" annual return and the "annualized" annual return. Unless you invest on January 1st and sell on December 31st, "average" annual return is a misleading figure. "Annualized" annual return represents the true return for a given period of time. The Enlightened Investor realizes that most performance numbers that are touted by some investment managers and financial salespeople are only a vague indicator of what the actual investor would have received.

The Enlightened Investor also realizes that making investment decisions based on past performance is a fool's errand. The biggest mistake that the average investor makes is that they confuse the future with the immediate past. To use the analogy of driving a car, most investors are steering by looking in the rear view mirror when they should be looking out the windshield at the road ahead.

8 INVESTOR RETURNS VERSUS INVESTMENT RETURNS

Since 1970 the average holding period for mutual funds has gone down from over eleven years to just over three years in 2010. By jumping from investment to investment, most investors never realize the performance they seek. Consider the period from 1984 through 2000. This was one of the greatest bull markets in history, yet many investors fared much worse because they were chasing performance. According to a study conducted by DALBAR, a financial services research firm, the S&P 500 Index returned an average of 16.29% per year for the seventeen year period ending December 2000, yet the typical equity investor earned only 5.32% per year for the same period![xxiii] This was worse than the 5.8% return provided by risk-free Treasury bills during the same period. A separate study by Financial Research Corporation reached a similar conclusion.

DALBAR updated its research through December of 2002 in "Quantitative Analysis of Investor Behavior." The report examined real investor returns from equity, fixed income, and money market mutual funds from January 1984 through December 2002. The report, based on data from the Investment Company Institute and Ibbotson Associates, concluded that the average equity investor over that 19 year time period earned only 2.57% annually. In stark contrast the S&P 500 Index earned an average of 12.22% annually during the same period. To add insult to injury, inflation averaged 3.14% during this period. The average equity investor significantly underperformed the market during these 19 years. In fact, they lost purchasing power because their average return was .57% lower than inflation itself! How can this be?

Sir Isaac Newton once said, "I can calculate the motions of the heavenly bodies, but not the madness of people." I can only imagine what he would have said in reaction to incessant performance-chasing of the modern-day investor. Whether it is in the field of biology, politics, economics, or finance; there is little evidence to support the idea that the large will keep getting larger, while the small will keep getting smaller. Kenneth Arrow, the Nobel laureate has said, "Our knowledge of the way things work, in society or nature, comes trailing clouds of vagueness. Vast ills have followed a belief in certainty." When we are enticed by short-term investment performance and consequently project that short-term trend into the indefinite future, we set ourselves up for catastrophe. If past performance can teach us anything, it is only to avoid the simple-minded idea that, when it comes to investment performance, we can learn about the future by observing the past.

We are often undone by our human nature. We desperately want to extrapolate what has happened in the past into what will happen in the future. We seek certainty; our brains are hard-wired to find it in the most questionable circumstances. The most egregious example of this behavior is the preeminence of the Morningstar ratings of mutual funds and variable accounts in annuities and life insurance.

Morningstar rates mutual fund performance in terms of a star rating that goes from 1- star through 5-star, with 5-star being the top rating. It is absolutely astounding to observe how investor and advisor behavior has been influenced by these rankings. Although Morningstar consistently states that their star ratings should not be used to predict future performance, many financial advisors and the investing public have seized upon the star ratings as a way to predict future performance based upon past performance. This misperception has been fostered by two sources.

First the "do-it-yourself" investment publications prominently display the five-star funds as those that "you must own now!" Second, investment advisors who are content to take the path of least resistance have used the star ratings as their sole screening process. Even worse, many broker/dealers, who are responsible for doing due diligence on the investments that their registered representatives sell, have prohibited the sale of any funds or variable accounts that are less than a three-star rating.

The following chart demonstrates the net inflows or outflows for mutual funds based on Morningstar ratings of the particular funds during the years of the bull market in the late 1990's and the subsequent bear market caused by the bursting of the internet bubble.

Long term net flows ($millions) by star rating, Source Financial Research Corporation

Star Rating	1998	1999	2000	2001	1qtr 2002
5	$ 85,228	$142,798	$157,906	$ 80,798	$ 45,905
4	$ 59,756	$ 54,914	$ 54,811	$ 37,653	$ 23,158
3	$ 16,175	$(77,709)	$(94,594)	$(28,405)	$(5,903)
2	$(13,760)	$(44,126)	$(32,342)	$(39,697)	$(5,641)
1	$(6,429)	$(15,777)	$(8,814)	$(11,145)	$(3,999)
Non-rated	$ 85,618	$ 97,353	$133,526	$ 77,077	$ 25,851
Total	$22,586	$157,452	$211,123	$116,282	$ 79,371

Investors desperately seek certainty. They believe they've found it with ratings such as the Morningstar system. A five-star rating is a virtual guarantee of huge inflows of cash. One-,two-, or three-star rated funds must brace themselves for a flood of investment dollars leaving the house. What is even more interesting is the fact that non-rated funds, those that have been in existence three years or less, fare better than all the rated funds except the five-star funds.

Until recently the Morningstar ratings were based on a three-year window of performance. We observed earlier, that in a three-year period, pure luck is as good an explanation of performance as is skill. Investors also lose sight of the fact that a five-star rating is not conferred for life. Mutual fund star ratings change all the time. What is five-star today can be three-star in a quarter or two. There are numerous studies that have demonstrated the under-performance of five-star rated funds in the period from the time they received their five-star rating going forward one, two, or three years. A study conducted by Pace University in New York examined 273 mutual funds that won their first five-star rating from Morningstar between 1993 and 2001. They concluded that a mutual fund's performance relative to its peers' decreases dramatically in the three years after it receives a five-star rating.

Conversely, when a mutual fund suffers a period of sub-par performance, investors head for the exits. What can explain such behavior? Simply that we hate losing a lot more than we love winning. Or put another way, loss makes us much more unhappy than gain makes us happy. For example, a purchase of a Mercedes S Class automobile feels great, but it doesn't take long before it just as well could be a Buick. However, if you were to lose the Mercedes, the loss would be much more intense than the initial pleasure. The psychologists call this loss aversion. Amos Tversky, one of the pioneers in the study of investor behavior has put it thus:

"The major driving force is loss aversion. It is not so much that people hate uncertainty, but rather, they hate losing. Losses will always loom larger than gains."

Unfortunately when it comes to investments, we tend to focus on short-term volatility at the expense of long-term returns. Psychologists who study investor behavior estimate that the negative effect of a loss is about three times the magnitude of the positive effect of a gain. If we assume that the market, either on an hourly or daily basis, is up about half the time and down the other half; any investor who is monitoring their portfolio with such frequency is experiencing three times the negative feedback compared to positive. Is it any wonder that investors panic at bad news?

Consider an investment with a 15% annual return that has 10% volatility per year. The probability of a positive return over a 1 year time frame is 93%, over any quarter it is 77%, over any month it is 67%. However, over any one day period it is only 54%.[xxiv] The bottom line is that if you are looking at your investment performance on a daily basis, there is about a 50-50 chance of an up or down day in the market. But if bad news has three times the psychological impact as good, the investor who monitors their investment performance on a daily basis is bound to driven out of the market by an overdose of negative energy. The Enlightened Investor knows that buying past performance is no guarantee of future gain.

A study of the technology mutual fund sector, from December 1996 through December of 2001, by the Leuthold Group provides stark evidence of the phenomenon. Investors had little or no interest in technology in 1997 and actually were net sellers of technology mutual funds in 1998. Large net purchases of these technology funds began in earnest in early 1999 and then absolutely exploded in the latter half of 1999 in response to the NASDAQ's surge. Purchases peaked in March of 2000 at the top of the market. While money was still flowing into technology funds, the market began to decline during the remainder of 2000. By 2001, investors were selling out of these funds in huge numbers. Research by Financial Research Corporation revealed that, on average, $91 billion of new cash flowed into mutual funds after their "best performing" quarters, but only $6.5 billion came into funds after their "worst-performing" quarters.

Chasing Performance in the Tech Sector

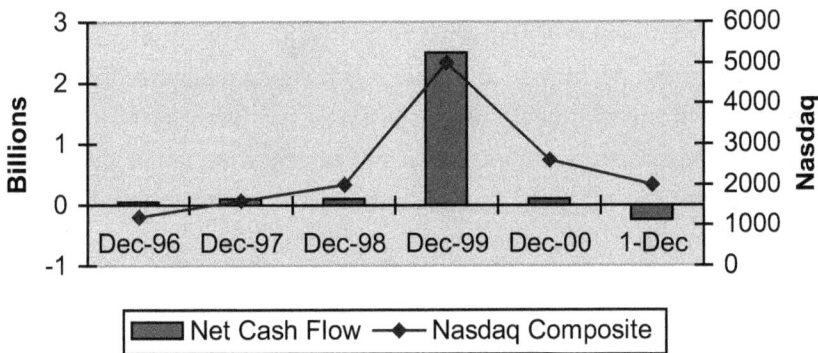

We are entrapped by fear and desire. In investment seminars I used to say that there were three reasons to consider professional management of investments as opposed to doing it yourself. They are: time, training, and temperament. Most investors don't have the time, nor do they have the training and experience, and most importantly they do not have the temperament to properly manage their own money. And of the three, temperament is the most important.

What do I mean by temperament? It is our susceptibility to the temptations of fear and desire. The Enlightened Investor knows that resisting the temptations of fear and desire in regard to money management is a never-ending struggle. It is perhaps the best argument for the use of a financial advisor. Unfortunately, many studies have indicated that investors are hesitant about paying for financial planning advice, however they have no reservations about paying anywhere from 1.00% - 3.00% for the promise of investment performance. That is why there are very few hourly fee-based financial planners and the great majority of financial planners earn their living through commissions. People are more than happy to pay through the nose for the expectation of investment performance. And when it doesn't happen, they still continue to pay!

Consider the compensation arrangement of the typical hedge fund. The fund takes a 2.00% annual fee based on assets under management regardless of whether the fund makes or loses money. Furthermore, they take 20% of the gain in an up year. Reminds me of a variation of the old coin flip proposition of "Heads I win, tails you lose." This game is "Heads I win, tails I still win." This compensation arrangement is a temptation for the managers to take excessive risk in order to achieve outsized gains. And so they have. Amongst other factors, we have this to thank for the Great Recession.

The Enlightened Investor understands that the greatest value a financial advisor can provide is not investment performance; rather it is building a plan to protect assets and investments from the inevitable black swans of financial life. An experienced financial advisor can provide the voice of reason that, when we are tempted by fear and desire, will help us resist that two-headed demon. A financial advisor can provide a light when the path to financial independence grows dark.

9 SOMEBODY KNOWS MORE THAN ME

If the name Daniel Ellsberg rings a bell, it is because of his connection with the Pentagon Papers and the Vietnam War resistance. The Enlightened Investor knows of him by way of his best-known idea, the "Ellsberg Paradox." Ellsberg spent much of his career as one of the celebrated game theorists at the Rand Institute. Most of their work involved creating and testing theories to maintain the strategic balance of the Cold War. However, his work on the "Ellsberg Paradox" is pertinent to the investment world.

The paradox arises from the results of games involving balls of different colors in containers. The most instructive is the game in which there are two containers, each of which contains one hundred balls. One container contains fifty white balls and fifty black balls. The other container contains both black and white balls; however the player has no idea of the proportion of black to white balls. For instance, there might be ten black balls and ninety white balls, or there could be seventy-five black balls to twenty-five white. The game consists of picking one ball out of either container without looking. If you are fortunate enough to pick a black ball, you win $100. The question is: Which container will you choose?

There is no compelling scientific or mathematic reason to believe that the chance of choosing a black ball is any better from one container or the other. However, Ellsberg discovered that the overwhelming majority of participants chose the container which contained fifty black and fifty white balls. The game participant would then be given another chance to win $100. This time, however, they would win the prize for choosing a white ball instead of the black.

If you, as most participants did, believed that your best chance to pick a black ball in the first go-around of the game was in the container with the 50-50 split, then it would seem reasonable that you would choose the other container to try and pick a white ball in the second go-around. And yet, the great majority of participants chose the 50-50 container for their second pick.

The "Ellsberg Paradox" theorizes that people prefer definite information over ambiguous information, such that they will not base their decisions on either the laws of probability or consistent with their own logic.

We are drawn to the illusion of definitive information like moths to the flame. The marketing function of the investment industry is built on this desire for the sure thing. Whether it is corporate officers, stock analysts, economists, money managers, or investment salespeople; they all make their living trying to convince you that they know more than you when it comes to investing your money. The very foundation of Wall Street's existence is based on the premise that these people and their supposed expertise and insight contribute extraordinary value to the investment process. The Enlightened Investor knows that these groups are evaluated and rewarded on how intelligent they sound, not on their knowledge of reality nor on their knowledge of the future. The stock trader and author Nassim Taleb put it best when he said,

"At the end of the day, market strategists know only two things: first, like everybody else, they have no idea where the market will head tomorrow. Second, that their livelihood depends upon appearing to know. It is easy to discern successful past stock-picking and market-timing strategies, but none of them work going forward."

Those who pretend to know do not know. The events in the investment world since January, 2000 have provided ample evidence of this confidence game. Consider the crisis in corporate governance in the early 2000's.   The following are a few examples from the corporate dishonor role:

Adelphia: Alleged to have failed to properly disclose $3.1 billion in loans and guarantees to it founder's family. From 1/14/00 to 6/20/02 its share price fell 99.75%.

Computer Associates: Alleged to have artificially inflated revenue and improperly rewarded top executives. Share price fell 73.58%.

Enron: Admitted it improperly inflated earnings and hid debt through business partnerships. Share price fell 99.80%.

<u>Dynegy</u>: Alleged to have used its "Project Alpha" transactions to cut taxes and artificially increase cash flow. Share price fell 64.97%.

<u>Global Crossing</u>: Alleged to have sold its telecom capacity in a way that artificially boosted its 2001 cash revenue. Share price fell 99.87%.

<u>Worldcom</u>: Used questionable methods to book sales, classify assets, and account for debts it couldn't collect. Share price fell 96.60%.

<u>MicroStrategy</u>: Settled without admitting wrongdoing in an SEC suit accusing it of backdating sales contracts to meet quarterly financial estimates, among other improper revenue-recognition practices. Share price fell 99.07%.

Add to the list Xerox, Tyco International, Reliant Resources, Qwest Communications, PNC Financial Services, Conseco, Network Associates, Kmart, Lucent Technologies, ImClone Systems, Martha Stewart, Halliburton, and on and on.[xxv]

In fact, the number of publicly traded companies that were forced to restate their earnings went from 3 in 1981 to a record of 158 for 2001. Lynn Turner, who served as Arthur Levitt's chief accountant at the SEC, estimates that investors lost a hundred billion dollars owing to faulty, misleading, or fraudulent audits in the six years preceding Enron's crash.[xxvi] Meanwhile, according to the *Financial Times*, senior executives and directors of the twenty-five largest business failures during those years cashed in $3.3 billion in salary, bonus, and stock options. According to Graef Crystal, author of <u>In Search of Excess: The Overcompensation of American Executives</u>, in 1973 the average C.E.O. of a large American company made about forty-five times the average pay of workers. In 1991 it had risen to a hundred and forty times, and as of 2001 it had ballooned to five hundred times the average pay of workers!

The primary reason behind these abuses was the phenomenon of stock options. The use of stock options was supposed to have motivated corporate executives to build businesses that would create long-term value for shareholders. The reasoning was that if the executive had a large stake in the company, he would act more like a proprietor rather than a bureaucrat. Unfortunately, the reliance upon stock options encouraged executives to utilize fraudulent accounting practices to manipulate stock prices to their advantage.

And it didn't matter whether the company was profitable or not, the top executives still profited handsomely. It was heads they win, tails they win.

David Yermack, an economist at New York University, published an article in 1997 which revealed how companies manipulated stock options for the benefit of executives. He discovered that companies who anticipated bad earnings would delay the issuance of stock options until after the quarterly earnings announcement. Thus, the stock price would fall after a disappointing earnings report and the executive's stock option strike price would be much lower than had they granted the option prior to the disappointing earnings. Conversely, he discovered that companies that had good earnings to report would grant stock options immediately preceding the earnings announcement. As a result, the strike price of the options would be locked in at a lower price before the stock price would rise in response to the good earnings report.

The New York brokerage firm, Sanford C. Bernstein, concluded that if the companies in the S&P 500 had been required to expense stock options between 1995 and 2000, their profitability would have decreased from an annual rate of nine percent to only six percent. In response to these abuses of stock options, late in the summer of 2002, 89 companies voluntarily vowed to expense options to make their earnings more realistic. However, according to a study by Oxford Metrica, a management consulting firm, the number of companies volunteering to expense stock options dwindled to a trickle in the fourth quarter of 2002. Twenty companies took the pledge in October, 2002, four more in November of 2002, and only three in December of 2002. It would seem that the movement to reform stock options was like a summer thunderstorm in the desert, intense but brief.

And as the cycle of greed continued to spiral out of control, corporate executives turned to accounting sleight-of-hand to keep the game alive. Until recently, most investors had the mistaken belief that accounting and the reporting of corporate earnings was a tightly regulated process with little room for misrepresentation. As the bull market roared on, corporate executives, in response to their own greed and to the rising expectations of Wall Street analysts, began to use questionable, and in some cases, outright fraudulent accounting practices.

For anyone who wants to do their own research on the validity of financial reports, the book "Financial Shenanigans: How to Detect Accounting Gimmicks and Fraud in Financial Reports", is a valuable guide. The author, Howard Schilit, is the founder of the Center for Financial Research & Analysis. In his book he listed the seven major accounting tricks that companies use to inflate earnings. They are: 1) recording revenue too quickly or of questionable validity; 2) recording false revenue; 3) increasing income with onetime gains; 4) shifting current expenses to an earlier or later period; 5) improperly reducing liabilities or failing to record them outright; 6) shifting current revenue to a late period; and 7) shifting future expenses to the current period as a special, onetime charge to earnings.

In the words of Hamlet, "To be honest as this world goes is to be one man picked out of ten thousand." Unfortunately, it wasn't the first time, nor was it the last time that corporate executives lie, cheat, and steal. In his book The Great Crash of 1929, John Kenneth Galbraith provided a clear explanation for the phenomenon of corporate malfeasance.

"At any given time there exists an inventory of undiscovered embezzlement. This inventory-it should perhaps be called the bezzle -amounts at any given moment to many millions of dollars. In good times people are relaxed, trusting, and money is plentiful. But even though money is plentiful, there are always people who need more. Under these circumstances the rate of embezzlement grows, the rate of discovery falls off, and the bezzle increases rapidly. In depression, all of this is reversed."

Anyone who has watched Wall Street was not surprised at the revelations concerning the cozy relationship between stock analysts and the investment bankers. There has been a long history of imbalance, clearly pointing to bias, in the number of buy recommendations compared to sell recommendations. During the Internet boom of the late 1990's, that ratio increased to an estimated ratio of 100 to 1, up from the historical average of 6 to 1. Logic would tell you that if an analyst were truly looking for "undiscovered gems", you would expect relatively few "buy" recommendations among the stocks that the analyst covers. The fact that "buys" vastly outnumber "sells" is a clear indicator that something is amiss.

According to New York's then Attorney General Eliot L. Spitzer, Merrill Lynch's internet analysts had never issued a sell recommendation during the run up in internet stocks in the late 1990's. Spitzer's investigation revealed that internet stocks that were publicly promoted with a buy or accumulate recommendation were called "horrible", "a piece of crap" or a "powder keg" in internal communications. In fact, one analyst stated, "We see nothing to turn this around, near-term," of a stock that he had given a positive rating to the public.

The internet analysts and the abuses of stock options by corporate executives are two excellent examples of the problem of asymmetric markets. University of California, Berkeley economist George Akerlof won the Nobel Prize for this theory of information economics. His theory of asymmetric markets states that if one side of an economic transaction, for instance the seller of a stock, has more information than the buyer; the seller will have the upper hand in the transaction and thus the ability to distort the transaction to their favor. These distortions ultimately work to destroy wealth because they create suspicions, either founded or unfounded that markets are not fair. Thus, fewer parties are willing to engage in trades, whether it is stocks or used cars.

Conflicts of interest abound in corporate executive suites, on Wall Street, and in the accounting industries. We act surprised when these conflicts are exposed as a result of a bear market or whistle-blowers, yet we all know more than we now care to admit. The conflicts stare us straight in the face. By the late nineties it was clear to anyone who took a moment to look, that the game was rigged; research analysts recommending companies in order to win their investment banking business, accounting firms signing off on questionable audits in order to keep the lucrative consulting business, and boards of directors signing off on outrageous executive compensation packages. In 1998, *Business Week* ran a cover story entitled "Wall Street's Spin Game" in which they stated, "The analyst today is an investment banker in sheep's clothing." However, during the bull market of the late '90's, nobody really cared about the conflicts as long as they were making money on their investments.

In December of 2002, then New York Attorney General, Eliot Spitzer announced a settlement with ten Wall Street firms which entailed approximately $1.4 billion in fines. It stipulated that the firms provide independent research to investors in addition to the firm's own analysts, prohibits the firms from distributing Initial Public Offering (IPO) stocks to top executives or directors of public companies, and separate the ties between investment banking and investment analysts.

On the face of it, this was a positive development. However, the fines were a mere slap on the wrist for these companies. It was akin to getting a parking ticket for causing a fatal traffic accident. The agreement did not include punishment of any Wall Street analysts or executives that supervised them, nor did the firms either admit or deny charges that they had misled investors. Wall Street may have cleaned up its act for a short time, however it didn't take them long to figure out new methods to game the system. The financial crisis of the autumn of 2008 and the resulting Great Recession that followed is just the worst so far in the continuing cycle of Wall Street gaming the system, looking to the government to bail them out when their bets go south, and then crying foul when regulations are proposed to prevent the behavior from recurring.

The Enlightened Investor, despite so-called reforms, will cast a skeptical eye towards "expert" opinion. She will understand that Wall Street's objective is to move money and collect fees. Their interest in the individual investor, despite their protestations to the contrary, is way down their list of priorities. Consider that in their agreement with the state of New York, they did not admit to misleading investors, even though there is a mountain of evidence that they knew exactly what they were doing. As has been pointed out many times since the Great Recession, not one of the perpetrators has gone to jail for the crimes committed against America. And although fines have been levied against a number of the Wall Street firms and banks, it is done without the institution admitting any guilt.

The other aspect of this debacle is that we were willing, perhaps even anxious to be deceived. As we discovered earlier with the Ellsberg Paradox, people prefer definite information over ambiguous information, even if the definite information is tainted. In my high school debating days, I realized an essential truth, "A proposition, no matter how absurd, if advocated vigorously and intelligently, will often carry the day." Or, as Mark Twain put it, "Everyone knows that the truth is not hard to kill, but a lie well-told, is immortal!"

George Lowenstein, an economics professor at Carnegie Mellon University devised an experiment which demonstrates our willingness to be deceived. He and his colleagues Don Moore and Daylian Cain divided subjects into two groups. The first group, the Estimators were asked to look at several jars of coins from a distance and then estimate the value of the coins in each jar. They were compensated according to the accuracy of their estimates. The other group, the Advisors, was allowed close proximity to the jars and they were to provide the estimators advice on their estimates. The advisors were told that their compensation was based on how high they could get the estimators to guess. Thus, the Advisors had an incentive to give bad advice.

As a result, when estimators had the advice of the Advisors, their guesses were much higher than when they made the guess based on their own observation. The amazing thing about the experiment is that when the Estimators were informed of the Advisors' conflict of interest, they didn't care. They continued to make higher guesses. The disclosure of the conflict of interest didn't make them any more skeptical.[xxvii]   The Enlightened Investor must understand that our desire for concrete investment information leads us astray.

We suffer from a glut of information. There are too many people trying to sell too many bad ideas to investors. Ever since the invention of the telegraph, the transmission of information has been instantaneous. The revolution in communications has not been in the quality of the information delivered, rather the volume delivered. Communication technology has surpassed our human capability to accurately analyze and digest it. In the cacophony of market and investment news, is it any wonder that many corporate executives, analysts, money managers, or investment advisers are tempted to exaggerate, or outright lie, in order to be heard above the din. As a result, the quality of investment information has suffered. It has become trivialized and temporized, here today and gone tomorrow.

The information you want is not the information you need, and the information you need is not the information that you can get. The philosopher Montaigne said, "Ignorance, aware of itself, is the only true knowledge."   The Enlightened Investor knows that the search for the truth must be built upon skeptical faith, rather than blind confidence. Unfortunately, the technology of falsehood and deceit has exceeded the evolution of wisdom.

As a result of the accounting, analyst, and CEO scandals, the investment industry has taken to the remedy of full disclosure. They now disclose their conflicts of interest in the hopes that confessing their sins will absolve them of having to actually reform the system.   In Professor Lowenstein's experiment, the quality of the Advisors' advice to the Estimators actually got worse when the conflict of interest was revealed. As Lowenstein remarked, "It's as if people said, 'you know the score, so now anything goes,'"[xxviii] Full disclosure of conflicts of interest will do nothing to reform the system.

10 INFLATION AND THE COST OF LIVING

The effect of inflation on future purchasing power is often used to make the case for investing heavily in equities, even during retirement. The argument is straightforward, since 1944 inflation has averaged 4.4%. What you could buy for a dollar in the 1990's, cost 37 cents in 1975, 21 cents in 1960, and 13 cents in 1946! Perhaps the most dramatic illustration is that for many retired Americans, they paid more for their most recent automobile than they did for their first house.

Based on the average rate of inflation since 1944, the cost of living has doubled every 16.4 years. If we look at life expectancy charts, it is very likely that the average American will spend 25-40 years in retirement. At present the average age of retirement in the U.S. is 63. Consider the fact that a husband and wife both age 63, one of them will in all likelihood live to age 95! Thus, the argument is made that the average American retiree will see the cost of living double, not once, but twice during their retirement. If this is true, the retiree who is comfortable with $50,000/year at age 63 will need $200,000/year at their age 95. Do you have a plan for tripling your income during the course of your retirement?

It is true that the cost of living increases over time, yet this argument exaggerates the amount of income that a retiree will need to keep pace with the increase in the cost of living. In the United States, the most common measure of inflation is based on the Consumer Price Index (CPI). The CPI is used extensively to adjust incomes, lease payments, retirement benefits, alimony, and tax brackets. Because the CPI is based on the buying habits of the proverbial "average" consumer, it may or may not be an accurate reflection of the cost of living for a particular family. The CPI divides the consumer market basket into eight major groups of goods and services. Each group is assigned a percentage that the average consumer would spend as a part of their overall income. The categories are:

1.	Food and beverage	15.7%
2.	Housing	40.9%
3.	Apparel	4.4%
4.	Transportation	17.1%
5.	Medical care	5.8%
6.	Recreation	6.0%
7.	Education and communication	5.8%
8.	Other goods and services	4.3%
	Total	100%

To the extent that a family's expenditures do not match up with the "average" will determine whether their true cost of living is greater or less than the CPI. For example: many retirees own their home free and clear. Their housing costs probably do not account for 40.9% of their expenses. Therefore the inflation in home prices or rent is irrelevant to their true experience of the cost of living.

The emphasis strictly on the rate of inflation and cost of living ignores the real question: How much income do you need to be satisfied? The truth is, the older we get the less we need. The Enlightened Investor knows that the older we get, financial independence becomes less dependent on objective levels of income and wealth. For the most part, the wealth management business has completely ignored the subjective factors of financial independence. There has been considerable research that indicates that older people perceive the world as more equitable than their younger counterparts. In large part this accounts for the fact that older people are more likely than young and middle-aged people to be satisfied with the income and financial assets available to them, despite the fact that in objective terms, older people are financially less well off than their counterparts.[xxix] Eighty-five percent of older Americans report that they are "satisfied" or "very satisfied" with their income and financial status. Furthermore, their satisfaction is not affected by changes in the level of income or financial assets available to them.[xxx]

Whereas the young and middle-aged tend to compare themselves in economic achievement with the most financially well-off, older adults tend to compare their situation to those of other older adults. The truth is that most people lower their aspirations as they get older. We not only settle for less, we genuinely want less, thus we will not be purchasing consumer goods, automobiles, houses, etc. as often as we did when we were younger. Income and financial assets account for only 25% of the perceptions of financial well-being of older people, as compared to 75% of the total population.[xxxi]

The Enlightened Investor understands that the issue of inflation is not as dire as the wealth management community would have us believe. Does the cost of living go up over time? Certainly it does. However, as we grow older we will neither want nor need to consume as much as we did when we were younger. The only exception to this would be in the event that a retiree needs an extended period of medical care, commonly known as long-term care. Without a doubt, the greatest risk to financial independence for retirees is the expense of providing long-term care, either in-home, assisted living, or a skilled nursing facility.

The specter of rampant, runaway inflation has been used as a rationale for investing heavily in equities since the double-digit inflation of the 1970's. However the world has fundamentally changed since those days when there was a huge demand because of the coming of age of the Baby Boom generation. Demand outstripped supply in all areas of economic life during those years and real income growth was rising dramatically. Now we live in a time when real incomes have not grown in real terms for most Americans, and as a result of the housing market collapse and unemployment, the capacity of the economic machine to supply goods and services far outpaces the demand. When supply exceeds demand, it is difficult to make the case that inflation is around the bend.

11 NET TAX RATE VERSUS MARGINAL RATE

The final investment fallacy that the wealth management community promotes is the detrimental effect of taxation on investments by using marginal tax rates instead of net tax rates to calculate potential tax savings from certain investment or wealth management strategies. First, let's define the difference between marginal and net tax rates. Marginal tax rates are the different tax rates that are applied to different levels of income. If we look at federal income tax rates the percentages start at 10% and progress up to 35%. If you are in the top income tax bracket for federal taxes, it does not mean that you are paying 35% on all your income. No, the 35% rate is only applied to the amounts over $156,000.

Your net tax rate is the actual percentage of your income that you pay in taxes. For example, if your income was $100,000 your federal income tax bill would be $20,000. Net tax is a simple calculation. Divide your amount of tax by your income ($20,000 divided by $100,000 = 20%) Your net tax rate is 20%.

Invariably, when investment advisors are selling tax-deferred or tax-free investments, they will calculate the tax savings by using the highest marginal tax rate of 35%. This grossly over-estimates the potential tax savings of the particular investment or strategy.

Don't get me wrong, I think tax-deferred and tax-free investments are great strategies to achieve and maintain financial independence; however the Enlightened Investor will not be fooled by exaggerated claims of tax savings. When analyzing the potential benefit of a tax strategy or of a tax-deferred or tax-free investment, always insist upon using your net tax rate rather than the highest marginal rate.

12 PERENNIAL INVESTMENT WISDOM

How many investment ideas, strategies, theories, and outright shams have been promulgated in the course of human history? Perhaps not as many as the grains of sand on the beaches or drops of water in the ocean, but a sizeable number nonetheless. One only need watch CNBC for a day, or read Money magazine and they will provide the investor more ideas, tips, and advice than they could implement in several years' time. In response to such a glut of "get rich now" schemes, the average investor takes one of two courses: 1) recklessly pursuing the "idea du jour," or 2) throwing in the proverbial towel and capitulating at the onslaught of ideas.

When it comes to investing, people tend to be bi-polar: They are greedy to be rich or they are afraid to be poor. Both fear and desire can reside in the same psyche, one or the other holding sway at any given time. The Enlightened Investor comes to realize that neither course is a path to financial independence. In this section we will explore several investment strategies that have stood the test of time. While no investment idea or strategy is infallible, these strategies have provided investors with disciplined approaches which increase the probability of financial success. It is important to understand that they do not guarantee success. The beauty of these ideas is that they can reduce the possibility that an inevitable, unforeseen financial event will destroy their financial life. These strategies are not overly-complicated. The best ideas usually aren't. By utilizing one or more of these ideas, which I refer to as perennial investment wisdom, the Enlightened Investor can simplify her financial life. No longer does she need to waste her time listening, wondering, and worrying about every investment idea that comes her way. No longer does she need to spend the time endlessly worrying about her financial future. Instead, she can let these strategies work while she engages in other, more meaningful pursuits.

Diversification

"My ventures are not in one bottom trusted,
Nor to one place; nor is my whole estate
Upon the fortune of the present year;
Therefore, my merchandise makes me not sad.
The Merchant of Venice Act I, Sc. I

Diversification, the bedrock of a successful investment strategy, cannot be more succinctly and eloquently summarized than in the words of Antonio, Shakespeare's merchant of Venice. At the beginning of the play, Antonio is boasting of his business acumen. To paraphrase him, "I haven't put all my eggs in one basket!" His merchandise is not confined to one particular bottom (boat) sailing the Mediterranean, his boats are not bound for the same port, and his business is not dependent on whether this particular year is good or bad.

If Antonio were a modern day investor his boast would go something like this:

"I do not have all my money in one particular investment, nor have I put all my money in this year's 'hot' sector. I am investing for the long run. Therefore, I am not worried about my portfolio."

Over 400 years ago, Shakespeare captured the essence of diversification in four short lines. It took until the late 20th century for the science of mathematics and power of computers to validate what has been known for centuries.

However, the Merchant of Venice teaches another timeless lesson. Namely, that the unthinkable can, and does happen. Not long after Antonio's boast, he is informed that all of his boats have been lost at sea. He has lost everything. Diversification is no defense against the catastrophic event. It is, however, the best working hypothesis we have for long-term investment success.

Mark Twain, tongue-in-cheek, spoke of another approach when he quipped, "Put all your eggs in one basket, and then watch the damn basket!" This makes eminent sense if you run your own business, but for the investor seeking financial independence, one of the goals must be to establish many different kinds of financial baskets.

And yet how many thousands of investors have been lured by the siren song of the "sure thing". Most people know of Mark Twain the author and humorist, however not many people are aware of Mark Twain the investor. His financial life is instructive as to what not to do. Mark Twain aka Samuel Clemens lived a truly American life. Growing up in Hannibal, Missouri, he rose from modest means to become America's favorite humorist and author, and arguably the creator of the greatest American novel, Huckleberry Finn. At a relatively early age he was celebrated and had become financially independent because of the success of his books and his lecture tours. And yet fame and fortune weren't enough to satisfy him. This was the Gilded Age, the age of Carnegie, Vanderbilt, and the other robber barons of the last part of the 19th century. Mark Twain aspired to such fabulous wealth himself. A blinding lust for fortune was a part of his nature just as much as his desire for fame. He speculated, and as a result suffered, as instinctively as he wrote.

He thought he had found his chance with the invention of the Paige Compositor. As a writer, and as a printer in his youth, Twain knew the laborious process of setting type. This typesetter, the Paige Compositor, held the promise of a much more efficient way to set type that would revolutionize the world of printing newspapers. Unfortunately, the Paige Compositor was one of the most complicated pieces of equipment ever devised. Success always seemed just a refinement or a re-design away. Twain poured his entire fortune into the Paige Compositor. Unfortunately, the Paige Compositor was a failure. It proved to be too complicated, subject to constant breakdown.

The Paige typesetter led Twain to the edge of bankruptcy. As a result he spent ten years of his life traveling around the world delivering his lectures in order to pay off his creditors in full. He had put all of his eggs in one basket, and no matter how closely he watched them, they didn't hatch. His experience led him to comment, "Vast wealth, acquired by sudden and unwholesome means is a snare. It did us no good, transient were its feverish pleasures; yet for its sake we threw away our sweet and simple and happy life- let others take warning by us."

Let's examine the problem of putting all your eggs in one basket using a different analogy from the world of sports. Imagine watching a baseball game. The team in the field has its nine fielders in the usual positions. The team at bat sends five straight batters to the plate who straightaway hit singles to left field. How would we react if the manager of the team in the field directed the right- and center-fielders to reposition themselves in left field alongside the left-fielder, and then instructed the first- and second-basemen to move over to the left side of infield with the shortstop and third-baseman? Most fans would be dumbstruck at this stupidity. We would be unmoved in our low opinion even after the post-game interview when the manager stated his case. "I was reacting to past performance. There were five hits in a row to left field; any body could see the trend. It was obvious." It was obvious until the sixth batter hit it into the right field corner.

Except in the rarest circumstances, the players in the field stick to their respective positions in the infield and the outfield. Why? Because anyone who knows baseball, or any sport for that matter, knows that "anything can happen". That's why they play the game. In sports, we instinctually know that past performance does not guarantee future results. Why do we find this to be so difficult when it comes to investing?

There are essentially three methods which investors can attempt to achieve investment success. The first is security selection, picking the right stock, bond, or mutual fund. The second method is market timing, choosing the right time to be invested in a stock, bond, or mutual fund. The third is diversification, allocating investment dollars amongst a number of asset classes. As we mentioned in an earlier chapter, much of the investment industry is focused on convincing us that security selection or market timing is the way to investment success. So which is it, security selection, market timing, or diversification?

In 1986, Gary Brinson, L. Randolph Hood, and Gilbert Beebower published a study entitled, "Determinants of Portfolio Performance" and in 1991 a follow-up entitled, "Determinants of Portfolio Performance II: An Update. They attempted to determine which of the three aspects of investment strategy, security selection, market timing, or diversification (also known as asset allocation) was most important in overall investment success. In their study, they compared the quarterly returns of ninety-one pension funds in the United States from 1974-1983. Their conclusions were revolutionary; they found that an amazing 93.6% of portfolio success was attributable to investment policy. In other words, success was predicated on how the pension fund managers diversified their investments amongst the different investment alternatives available to them. They also concluded that the particular security selected within an investment class was only responsible for 4.2% of portfolio success, and that market timing accounted for only 1.7% of portfolio success.[xxxii]

Portfolio Success

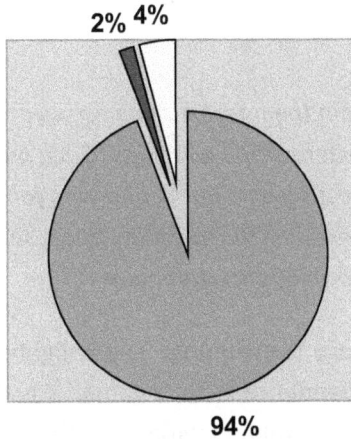

2% 4%

94%

□ Diversification ■ Market Timing □ Security Selection

In 1991, Brinson, Hood, and Brian Singer updated the original study released in 1986. This time they evaluated the quarterly returns for eighty-two pension funds in the United States over a ten year period 1978-1987. The results were essentially the same. They found that 91.5% of the portfolio success for these pension funds was attributable to their investment policy in regard to diversification. Market timing and security selection were once again negligible factors in overall portfolio success.[xxxiii]

Furthermore, John Bogle, the Chairman and founder of the Vanguard Group of mutual funds, commissioned an internal study by the Vanguard Group to test the Brinson group's conclusion. Instead of analyzing pension fund results, they used the performance of a group of balanced mutual funds for a period 1987-1996. This study concluded that 88.7% of the fund's success was attributable to the investment strategy of diversification. Given the wide range of these studies in terms of time periods, number of pensions funds and mutual funds analyzed, and the similarity of their finding, the Enlightened Investor would be well-advised to go with the odds and use diversification as the keystone of her investment strategy.

Diversification in investing is like match play in amateur golf. The surest way to lose a match is to try to hit the ball too hard, or to try to make the perfect shot. The best way to win a match is to put the ball in the fairway and then put it on the green. You don't win so much as you avoid losing. But how can this be? This flies in the face of the American myth of giving 110%, going for broke, giving it your best shot, playing to win. Consider the words of economics' professor Edward Miller,

> *"Occasional large gains seem to sustain the interest of investors and gamblers for longer periods of time than consistent small winnings. Such a response is typical of investors who look upon investing as a game and who fail to diversify. Diversification is boring. Well-informed investors diversify because they do not believe investing is a form of entertainment."[xxxiv]*

Sometimes not losing is the best strategy for winning. The Enlightened Investor realizes that the path to financial independence is not a game. You don't have to try to hit the grand slam, the cross-court forehand winner, or the 340 yard drive. Consistently putting the ball in play is the key to diversification.

Warren Buffett has stated that a successful investor:

1) Does not require a superhuman I.Q.

2) Does not require rare business insight.

3) Does not require insider information.

4) <u>Does</u> require a sound intellectual framework for making investment decisions.

5) <u>Does</u> require the ability to keep emotions from eroding that framework.

Diversification provides such a framework. In an uncertain world, diversification gives us the best chance of achieving financial independence, not only because it works, but it requires little time and thought, thus freeing you to do to other more important things with your life.

Let's take a look at three different investment strategies for investing $200,000 over a 20-year period from 1982-2001. For purposes of our illustration, we will divide the market into six indices which represent small- to large-cap, growth to value, international, and fixed-income styles. The indices are: MSCI EAFE,

Russell 1000 Growth, Russell 1000, Russell 1000 Value, Russell 2500, and Lehman Brothers Aggregate Bond.

The first scenario represents the "performance chaser". Our investor invests $10,000 at the end of every year into the best-performing market segment of that particular year. At the end of 2001, the account was worth $620,460.

The second scenario is the "contrarian". She invested $10,000 at the end of every year in that year's worst performing market segment. At the end of 2001, her account was worth $738,804.

Our third scenario is the "diversifier" who invested $10,000 per year, investing equally in each of the six market segments every year, year-in, year-out, regardless of performance that year. At the end of 2001 the account was worth $864,868![xxxv]

Power of Diversification

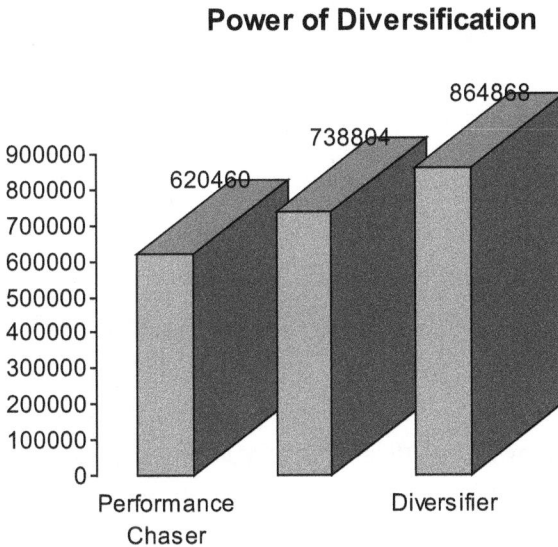

Another example of the power of diversification can be found by using the data in the Callan Table referred to earlier. This particular example contains nine indices, instead of the six previously over a twenty year period from 12/31/1981 – 12/31/2002. We have three hypothetical investors, the "performance chaser", the "contrarian", and the "diversifier".

Each of them invests $10,000/year into the indices for twenty years. The "performance chaser" invests his $10,000 each year into the best performing index of the previous year. The "contrarian" invests her $10,000 into the previous year's worst performing index. The "diversifier" invests his $10,000 equally ($1,111.11), in all nine indices every year regardless of the previous year's performance. The results are illustrated in the graph below.

Power of Diversification

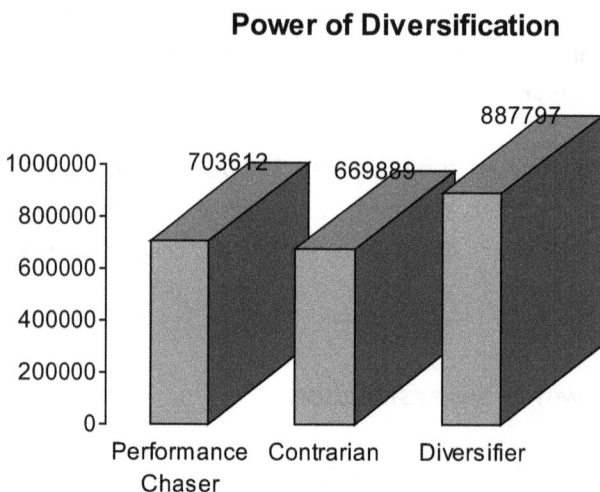

The "diversifier' comes out ahead again. Surprisingly the "contrarian", who buys low, finished the worst of three in this example. Although the Enlightened Investor knows that diversification is as close as we mortals can come to investment certainty, she also knows that diversification is not a guarantee against a loss. For example, in 2001, the average of all nine indices was -4.74%.

Let's take a look at diversification from another angle. Investor A has been frightened by the bear market and has put his nest egg of $100,000 into a guaranteed investment at a fixed rate of 6% for 25 years. (If only there was such an investment!) At the end of the 25 years, his nest egg would be worth $429,187.

Investor B, an Enlightened Investor, understands the value of diversification. She decides to invest $20,000 into each of five different investments. Over the next 25 years, the five different investments had radically different performance. The first $20,000 was a total loss, it is worth $0. The second $20,000 had no loss or gain at all, it broke even. The third $20,000 managed a return of 5%/yr., the fourth $20,000 earned 10%/yr., and the final $20,000 earned 12%/yr.

Investor B

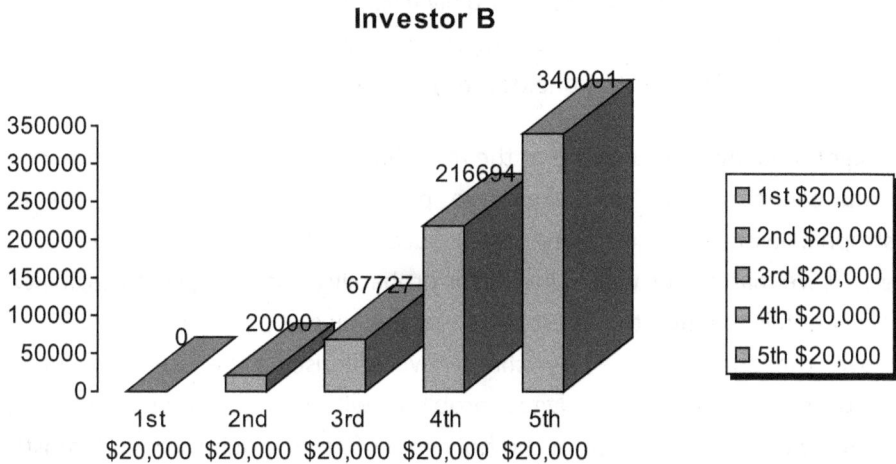

As you can see from the chart, $60,000 of our Enlightened Investor's investment had returns dramatically below her expectations. However, $40,000 of her investment did quite well. The result: a combined total value after 25 years of $644,422! Nearly 50% more than Investor A's fixed investment at 6.00%. The point needs to be made that there is nothing wrong with a fixed-income investment. In our example it is highly unlikely that one could find a fixed-income investment that would return a guaranteed 6% for 25 years. But if this was possible and financial independence was achievable with $429,187, it might be the best choice.

Chasing market performance or attempting to predict market changes can never be substitutes for a disciplined, long-term, diversified investment strategy. We need only to look back at the Callan Periodic Table of Investment Returns to see how various market performances can vary dramatically one year to the next. Markets are rarely calm; they are always in a state of flux. When tempted by the "sturm und drang" of market conditions, the Enlightened Investor will look far down the path of financial independence, and avoid the obsession of looking at her shoes.

The Enlightened Investor knows that financial independence is a function of time and investment return. She also knows that there is no reason to take more risk than is necessary to achieve financial independence. As stated in an earlier chapter, the goal of making as much money as possible from investing, and the goal of financial independence, are mutually exclusive. You can choose one, but you can't have both. If you are shooting for the highest investment returns, you will expose yourself to risk that one day may turn your riches into rags.

The Enlightened Investor knows that the most fundamental principle of investing is: You cannot expect to make large profits without taking the risk of catastrophic losses. Shakespeare put it succinctly in King Lear, "Striving to better, oft we mar what's well." Invest for probability, insure against possibility. Diversification is the investor's best bet to let the laws of probability work in her favor over the long run. In a later chapter we will discuss the issue of insuring against possibility. One of the biggest problems with the investment industry is that they hold out the promise of the holy grail of getting rich through fantastic investment returns, and almost totally ignore what should be their responsibility to investors, namely to help them achieve financial independence by reducing risk whether it be market risk, inflation risk, liquidity risk, interest rate risk, credit risk, or mortality and morbidity risk.

In point of fact, many investment advisors present diversification as if it were a way to make stocks the risk equivalent of long-term default-free bonds. They are fond of using charts, sometimes posted prominently on their office walls, to illustrate the long-term growth of stocks. The most familiar of these charts is the Ibbottson chart which shows the growth of $1 invested in various assets classes such as large-cap stocks, small-cap stocks, bonds, and U.S. treasuries. It is a very dramatic chart. For instance it shows that $1 invested in 1926 is worth hundreds, if not several thousand dollars some seventy years later. However, one the problems with such a chart is that there aren't many people that have a seventy-year investment horizon. Diversification is not without some risk. To understand the nature of such risk, consider an investor with $1,000 in his account. He has a 50-50 chance of earning 20% or losing 10% each year. If we define risk as the probability of losing money in any given year, the risk declines as the time frame increases. In this instance, our investor has a 50% probability of losing money in the first year, but only a 25% probability of losing over a two-year time frame.

However, if we define risk as the amount of money that the investor may lose, the risk actually increases as the time frame increases. For instance, in our example, our investor may lose $100 after one year ($1000 – 10% = $900), but might lose $190 if he had two straight years of loss ($1000 – 10% = $900 – 10% = $810). The following diagram illustrates the potential gains or losses over the two year time frame.[xxxvi]

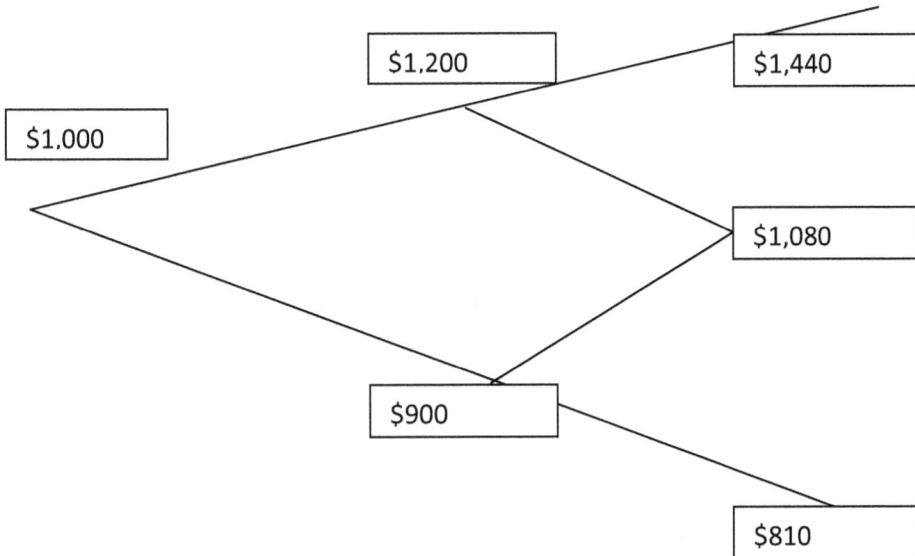

	$1,200	$1,440
$1,000		
		$1,080
	$900	
		$810

Source: Meir Statman, "The Psychology of Risk and Taxes" 1999

As noted at the beginning of the discussion on diversification, it is the investor's best bet for long-term investment success. It minimizes the probability of a catastrophic loss, however it does not protect against the possibility of loss. The brutal bear market that started in March, 2000 and the Great Recession that began in Autumn of 2008, demonstrated that a diversified portfolio is no guarantee against loss. Diversification should be the foundation of a personal investment strategy. However, it requires additional perennial investment techniques to make it less prone to the possibility of dramatic loss. We will discuss these techniques in later sections of the book.

Asset Allocation

We must take a moment to discuss asset allocation. Unfortunately, diversification and asset allocation have come to be synonymous in the language of the investment advisor. Some would say asset allocation is diversification taken to its highest and most scientific potential. Others confuse asset allocation with market timing. It is neither diversification nor market timing, although it incorporates elements of both.

Asset allocation or modern portfolio theory sprang onto the investment landscape almost twenty years ago. It was developed by Professor Harry M. Markowitz in his publication, *Portfolio Selection and Efficient Diversification of Investments.* The essence of his theory, (and let us not forget that it is a theory, not a scientific fact), is that the type or class of investment owned was far more important to overall investment return than the investment itself. According to Markowitz, 90% of investment return is driven by asset allocation and only 10% by individual investment selection. The goal of asset allocation is not to achieve the highest possible return, but rather to maximize return for a given amount of risk taken.

In developing asset allocation models, past history, the risk/reward relationships among asset classes and prospective returns on the investments are analyzed. The computer determines the statistical probability of future returns. Finally the past history, future estimates, and probable accuracy of those estimates are subjected to computer modeling to determine the percentage of money that should be allocated to any given investment class within the overall portfolio. For example, it may indicate that the portfolio should be allocated 60% to stocks, 30% to bonds, and 10% to cash.

Asset allocation is not market timing. Asset allocation combines different classes of investment assets to assemble a portfolio which may make occasional shifts in allocation percentages or investment classes over time due to changes in economic, market, or investor goals. Market timing, by contrast, makes large moves in and out of markets, and sometimes shifts completely in or out of investment asset classes. Asset allocation can be compared to continental drift theory, slow movement over time. Market timing, on the other hand, is like an earthquake, a sudden and dramatic movement of the landscape.

Asset allocation may be considered a variation of diversification; however it is not diversification in its purest sense. Asset allocation does make shifts based on economic or market conditions. True diversification will ignore these temporary shifts in order to stay the course. The only change in a diversification strategy is when investor goals change.

Asset allocation was, and continues to be the hot topic in investment circles. Investment advisors have used it to attract and retain clients by leading them to believe that asset allocation is a miracle theory to allow you to "have your cake, and eat it too." After all, what could be better than a science-based, computer-modeled prediction of where you should put your money? If it worked, nothing could be better. However, as I said earlier, it is a theory, not a fact. Asset allocation as a theory suffers from two major flaws:

1)   Survivorship bias. In compiling historical data about investment performance, the losers never show up. Investments that have gone bankrupt aren't taken into account because they no longer exist. We can look at the historical record and it does suggest excellent investment returns, but it only reflects those economies and companies that prospered and survived, we generally have no record of those that failed.

2)   The other major flaw of asset allocation is its primary assumption that you can determine an investment asset class's future volatility, in other words, its risk exposure, if you know future uncertainty.[xxxvii] Asset allocation theory is based upon the false premise that if you know how markets will react and interact into the future, you can construct a portfolio that minimizes risk for a given return. The problem is that the future is uncertain, the unexpected will always happen. It is not a matter of if, but when. Past performance and history may be a guide, but it is not a clear window onto the future.

Asset allocation theory is not the first, nor will it be the last, investment theory that purports to remove all risk from the investing enterprise. The Enlightened Investor would be wise to heed the words of Peter L. Bernstein when he says,

"Nothing is more soothing or more persuasive than the computer screen, with its imposing array of numbers, glowing colors, and eloquently structured graphs. As we stare at the passing show, we become so absorbed that we tend to forget that the computer only answers questions; it doesn't ask them. Whenever we ignore that truth, the computer supports us in our conceptual errors. Those who live only by the numbers may find that the computer has simply replaced the oracles to which people resorted to in ancient times."[xxxviii]

Dollar Cost Averaging

Dollar-cost-averaging is an investment strategy that entails investing the same dollar amount over a period of time, typically on a monthly basis over a 6- to 18-month time frame, as opposed to investing a lump sum at a particular time. The same dollar amount is invested each period regardless of whether the investment share price has gone up or down. Thus the investor will buy more shares when the price is low and fewer shares when the price is higher. Dollar-cost-averaging is typically used by investors who have a sum of money in one investment such as a money market account and want to move that money into another investment such as an equity mutual fund. It is also used as a strategy for very long-term investment plans such as a 401(k) or a monthly investment program to save for retirement.

Dollar-cost-averaging is a strategy that invokes a strict rule that mandates that a specified dollar amount be invested at specified points in time regardless of underlying investment performance. It is an investment strategy for investors who are afraid that the market may crash at some point in time, but understand that they have no way of knowing for certain whether that crash is more or less likely now, two months from now, or at some other time. This strategy provides a way to avoid one of the most common investor mistakes, namely investment regret.

Investment regret is the frustration that arises after the fact when an investment decision results in a loss. The consequence of such regret is a tendency for investors to stop investing all together, or to take more risk to attempt to recoup their losses. This tendency is illustrated by the following example in which participants are faced with a choice of two losses, one of which is small, but certain loss; and the other choice which is either no loss at all or a much greater loss. The choices are:

Choice #1:   A certain loss of $1,000, or

Choice #2:   A 30% chance of losing $4,000, and a 70% chance of losing nothing.

Most people will choose Choice #2, even though the probable loss is greater (30% x $4,000 = $1,200). People become extreme risk-takers when they are faced with the possibility of loss. One of the defects of human nature is that we do not find it easy to cut our losses. However, there is a point where the loss becomes so large and the potential for further loss becomes so great, that the investor will capitulate and take a certain loss. This is exactly what happened in July, 2002 as investors redeemed billions of dollars in stock mutual funds to reposition into bonds or money market funds. They had taken severe losses over the preceding two years, but most had hung on to their stock funds. However, in the summer of 2002 the market slid to retest the lows it had hit after 9/11. This proved to be too much, a bridge too far for many investors. Faced with the possibility of truly staggering losses, investors bailed out. In fact, investors withdrew a record $52.61 billion out of stock mutual funds in July, 2002. In retrospect, a mistake of epic proportions.

The perennial wisdom of dollar-cost-averaging is that it helps to avoid investment regret by imposing a framework of systematic investing, regardless of whether the markets are going up or down. The decision of how much to invest and when is taken out of the hands of the individual. The Enlightened Investor understands that she is often her own worst enemy. Most of us do not have the strength or discipline to resist our impulses. As we have witnessed during the bear markets of 2000-2002 and 2008-2009, three years of losses can turn investors with a thirty-year time frame into investors with a one week time frame.

Having a system such as dollar-cost-averaging can impose the rules we need as a second line of defense when self-control fails. Dollar-cost-averaging can make the most irrational investor a paragon of rational behavior. We must note however, that dollar-cost-averaging cannot reduce the overall market risk of investing. Someone who had dollar-cost-averaged into the market for the thirty-years prior to March, 2000 would still have seen their investments shrink during the crash of 2000-2002. What it does accomplish however, is to reduce the element of investment regret that arises when we put all of our money into an investment, only to see that investment crash shortly thereafter, i.e. the internet bubble. The perennial wisdom of dollar-cost-averaging is that it is far better to be approximately right than to be precisely wrong.

Now that we have established the rationale for dollar-cost-averaging, exactly how does it work and what is the best time frame in which to dollar-cost-average? As we noted earlier, dollar-cost-averaging is an investment discipline that invests an equal dollar amount on a regular, periodic basis. Typically the time frame is once per month. By investing an equal dollar amount, you are buying more shares when the price is lower and fewer when the price is higher. Over time, dollar-cost-averaging offers the opportunity for a lower average price per share than the average market price per share. By way of illustration, which of the following scenarios would you choose for an ideal market into which to dollar-cost-average $100 per month over a six-month period?

Example #1

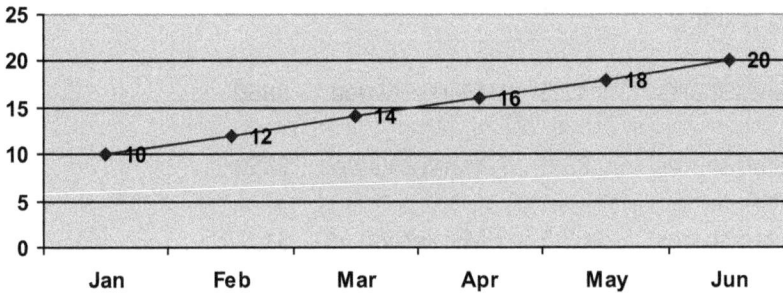

Example #2

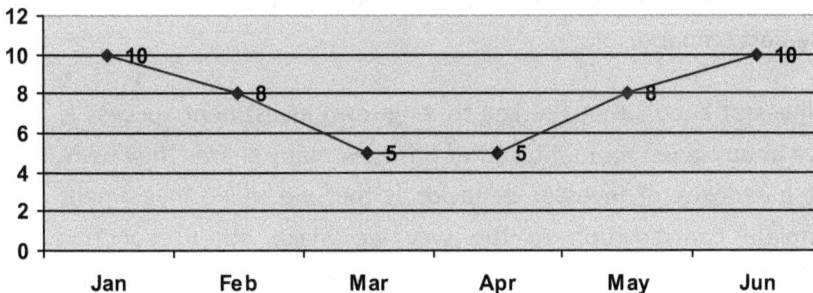

Example #3

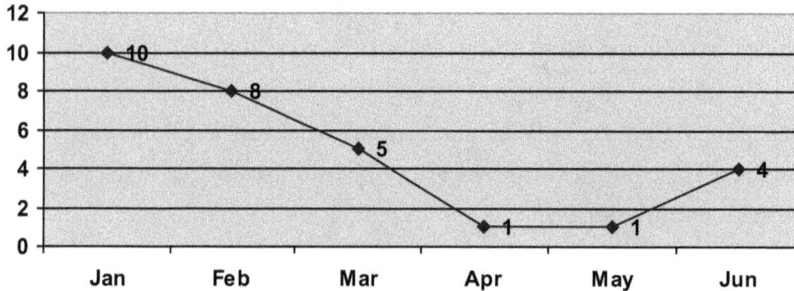

If we had started our dollar-cost-averaging program on January 31 and had invested $100 at the end of each month, as of July 1 each example would have had the following results:

#1:   Accumulated shares   42.5   Market Value: $850

#2   Accumulated shares   85.0   Market Value: $850

#3   Accumulated shares   267.5   Market Value: $1,070

On the face of it, most people would prefer the share price trend of example #1, a steadily rising share price. Example #2 sees the stock price fall but eventually recover to its original price. Example #3 is the least appealing with a dramatic fall and then a slight up tick in the last month. But as so many aspects of life, appearances can be deceiving. For the dollar-cost-averaging investor, example #3 turns out to be the best scenario.

The Enlightened Investor knows that the key to long-term investment success is not the share price at any given moment; rather it is how many shares they own. One of the great paradoxes of investor behavior is that we make investment decisions in complete contradiction to the way we make other economic decisions. Consider the act of buying soup in the grocery store. Which is the better deal, three cans of duck soup for one dollar or two cans for a dollar? All other things being equal, this is what is known as a no-brainer. Most of us love a sale, except when it comes to investing. Bear markets offer the chance to invest at sale prices, bull markets offer investments at full retail. The advantage of dollar-cost-averaging is that it is a systematic, disciplined method of investing which takes advantage of sale prices on investments. When the price is down, you are buying more shares. When the price is up, you buy less. The Enlightened Investor knows that investing is like duck soup, three for a dollar is better than two! Dollar-cost-averaging is an excellent investment strategy to avoid the risk, and the consequent regret, of investing a lump sum and then watching the value of that investment decline soon thereafter.

But what then is the best time frame over which to dollar-cost-average? Six months, twelve months, two years, longer? Mathematics professor Bill Jones conducted an analysis of dollar-cost-averaging out of a money market account into an equity fund over 6-,12-,18-,24-, and 36-month time frames. He compared this to moving a lump-sum from a money market into the stock fund. He measured stock returns by using the total return of the S&P 500 including reinvested dividends. Money market returns were estimated using 3-month treasuries. His analysis was conducted using historical returns from 1953-1996.

The goal of dollar-cost-averaging is to avoid the possibility of investing your money only to see its value drop dramatically shortly thereafter. It is not a strategy to achieve higher returns; rather it is a risk management strategy. It is a strategy which attempts to avoid a worst case scenario. Therefore we will use Professor Jones' definition of effectiveness based on the amount of protection dollar-cost-averaging provided in the worst 50 cases out of the 500 or so analyzed. His analysis revealed:

Six-month dollar-cost-averaging beat lump-sum 46 times out of 50. In these 50 cases, the lump-sum lost over 7.3%. In 34 cases, the six-month dollar-cost-averaging beat the lump-sum by 5% and in 11 cases by 10%

Twelve-month dollar-cost-averaging beat lump-sum 48 times out of 50. In those 50 cases, lump-sum lost over 8.2%. In 40 cases, the twelve-month dollar-cost-averaging beat the lump-sum by 5%.

Eighteen-month dollar-cost-averaging beat lump-sum 47 times out of 50. In those 50 cases, lump-sum lost over 3.6%. In 34 cases, the eighteen-month dollar-cost-averaging beat the lump-sum by 5%.

Twenty-four month dollar-cost-averaging beat lump-sum 41 times out of 50. In 33 cases by 5%.

Thirty-six month dollar-cost-averaging beat lump-sum 36 times out of 50. In 30 cases by 5%.[xxxix]

Based on this analysis, dollar-cost-averaging over a 6- to 18-month time frame appears to offer the best trade-off between minimizing the risk of substantial loss versus maximizing overall return. For those investors willing to tolerate a little more uncertainty, the 6-month dollar-cost-averaging would appear to offer the best scenario.

One final word on dollar-cost-averaging, as a long-term investment strategy it makes eminent sense, however it runs counter to our nature and impulse. Psychologists have demonstrated that laboratory rats have been found to continue longer in a particular behavior if they are rewarded on a random schedule than if they are rewarded every time a desired action is performed.[xl] No offense intended, yet in this regard our behavior as investors is not that different from that of the lab rats. We are seduced by the temptation of the big payoff and bored with the month-in and month-out monotony of consistent investing. The Enlightened Investor must understand that investing is not gambling.

Constant Ratio Rebalancing

Constant ratio rebalancing is the third manifestation of perennial investment wisdom. The idea has been around for over fifty years, but only in the last decade or so has it gained some measure of popularity, particularly within variable annuities which offer a large number of investment sub-accounts and can automatically incorporate rebalancing on a tax-deferred basis, as part of the overall investment plan.

The rationale for rebalancing is that the risk and return characteristics of an investment portfolio change over time due to the volatility of markets. For example, someone who began with a diversification strategy of 60% equities and 40% fixed-income in 1977 would find that twenty-five years later their portfolio was comprised of 84% equities and only 16% fixed-income. If they were forty years of age in 1977, they would be 65 in 2002 and either retired or close to retirement. A portfolio of 84% equities and 16% fixed-income is extremely aggressive for someone that age. Constant ratio rebalancing is a critical and useful strategy for those nearing, or in retirement. The benefit of constant ratio rebalancing is that it reduces the probability of extremely negative returns. It must also be mentioned that it also reduces the probability of highly positive returns. But this is a trade-off that many investors should be willing to make. I'm sure there are many investors who would have been thankful to have a rebalancing program in place at the start of the bear market of 2000. The reason is that periodic large losses in a portfolio can have a disastrous effect on annualized return.

Technically this is referred to as the asymmetry of compounding. For example: a loss of 50% requires a gain of 100% just to break even. Many investors do not have the time or patience to recover from such a decline. Because of this, it may well be worth it to sacrifice the potential of a tremendous gain to reduce the possibility of a tragic loss.

Constant ratio rebalancing is quite simple, straightforward, and effective in reducing market risk. The first step in the process is to select a percentage mix of asset classes that fits with your overall investment goals. For ease of understanding, let's use an example of an investment portfolio that is split 50-50 between stocks and bonds. The second step is to determine the period of time for rebalancing. Typically it's either quarterly, semi-annually, or annually. The final step is to rebalance back to the original 50-50 split at the end of the selected time period. Let's refer to our example. We have $50,000 in bonds, and $50,000 in stocks for a total portfolio value of $100,000. We will choose an annual rebalancing. One year later our bonds are up 20% and our stocks have declined by 10%. The bond component is now worth $60,000 and the stock worth $45,000.

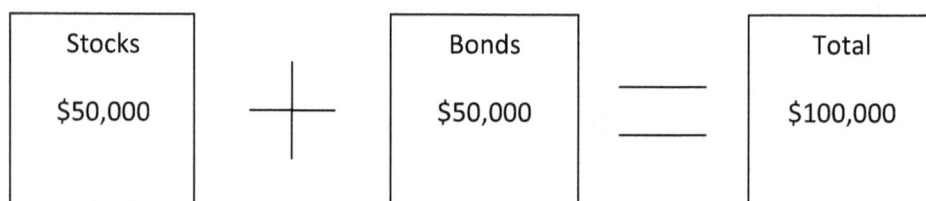

Stocks		Bonds		Total
$50,000	+	$50,000	—	$100,000

One Year Later

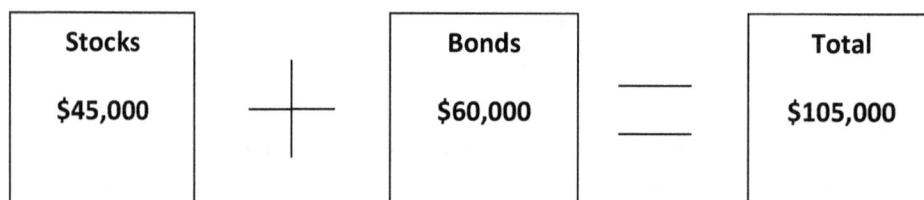

Stocks		Bonds		Total
$45,000	+	$60,000	—	$105,000

We now want to rebalance back to a 50-50 balance within the entire portfolio. The total value is $105,000. 50% of that is $52,500. In order to rebalance, we will need to sell $7,500 of the bond component and buy $7,500 of the stock component. In so doing, we now have $52,500 in each. What have we accomplished? We have sold some of the best performing component (sell high), and we have purchased additional amounts of the worst performing component (buy low). This is the holy grail of all investors, to buy low and sell high.

Stocks		Bonds		Total
$52,500	$+$	$52,500	$=$	$105,000

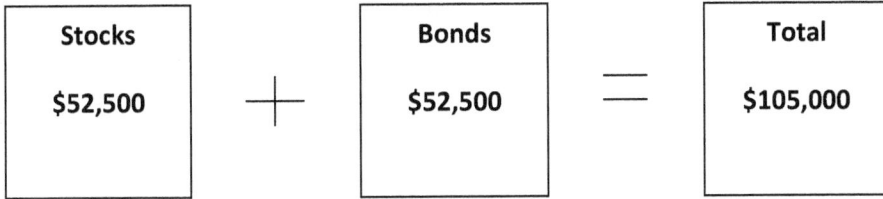

Rebalancing is not an absolute guarantee of being able to buy low and sell high. For example, all components of your portfolio may drop in value. However, it is a time-tested strategy to remove emotions as to when to sell or when to buy. It is a disciplined approach to reduce volatility. We know that markets are uncertain. If you do not rebalance a portfolio, eventually the percentages of your diversified portfolio may be completely different than your original percentages and as explained earlier, it can result in a time bomb waiting to explode.

Rebalance Frequency	Portfolio Growth	Compound Return	Standard Deviation	Sharpe Ratio
Monthly	$151,414	11.48	11.56	1.04
Quarterly	$153,017	11.53	11.52	1.05
Semi-Annual	$152,242	11.51	11.58	1.04
Annual	$155,905	11.61	11.63	1.05
Never	$151,553	11.49	14.49	0.86

Source: Ibottson and Associates

This is a powerful example of the benefits of constant ratio rebalancing. All four rebalancing strategies resulted in more money over twenty-five years. Granted, the difference in compound return is minimal, but the real benefit is in the category of portfolio volatility. Based on the measurements of standard deviation and the Sharpe Ratio, the rebalanced portfolios were able to achieve their returns with substantially less volatility.

The final question in our discussion of constant ratio rebalancing is: Which time frame is the best for rebalancing? From our example we see that annual rebalancing provided the greatest return of 11.61%. All of the rebalancing portfolios had nearly identical volatility profiles. In my experience, I would concur with the conclusion of our historical example. Annual rebalancing provides the best trade-off of risk versus return.

A final thought on rebalancing. One must be aware, or beware, of transaction costs and taxes associated with a rebalancing program. Every time there is a rebalance, it may trigger commissions for trading stocks or bonds. In a taxable account, it may trigger income and/or capital gains taxes. Of course, the tax consequences of rebalancing can be deferred within a qualified plan such as an IRA or 401(k), a variable annuity, or variable life insurance. Attention must be paid, because in a currently taxable account, the taxes and transaction costs associated with rebalancing could offset the potential benefits.

Stop Loss

The investment industry tempts us with a constantly shifting array of investment strategies, the "sure-bet du jour". Whether it is from Wall Street, CNBC, <u>Money</u> magazine, mutual fund companies, investment newsletters, stockbrokers, or Charles Schwab; there is an endless array of strategies that promise to work investment magic. They range from fundamental techniques, technical analysis, macro- or micro-analysis, and in some cases, psychic projection. And you can be sure that there will be a compelling argument as to how and why their particular strategy works.

I have always been fascinated by the gullibility of the investing public in their willingness to buy in to such nonsense. The Enlightened Investor, upon learning of the most recent strategy, will always ask herself, "If this strategy is so great, why is this company or individual sharing it with me?" If, in fact, a new investment strategy would work (which is doubtful), the surest way to lose any edge over the market is to let others in on the idea.

The first rule of human nature is that when push comes to shove, self-interest is the only interest. If *Money Magazine* or CNBC or whoever has the greatest new idea, they would use the strategy exclusively for their own account and amass a fortune, quit their jobs, and buy their own private island. The Enlightened investor must always be skeptical. When presented with a "hot tip" or "new idea" the Enlightened Investor must always ask herself, "Perhaps they let me in on the new idea only to use it as a motivating tool to accomplish the ultimate goal, to sell me something, or to keep me watching and reading." As Warren Buffett has quipped, "A fool and his money are invited everywhere." The Enlightened Investor realizes that the cost of missing a potential "new investment strategy" pales in comparison to the cost digging your way out of all the garbage that the investment industry piles onto investors in the guise of the "new idea" or the "new trend."

Let's turn our attention to another example of perennial investment wisdom, the stop loss order. Stop loss orders are a simple, yet successful, investment strategy; however most investors fail to take advantage of it. A stop loss order is an order to sell a stock if its price falls below a specified price. For example: I buy XYZ, Inc. at $50/share. I can enter a stop loss order for $40/share. Thus, if XYZ stock drops to $40/share, a market order to sell will be entered once the stock hits $40/share. It is important to note that the stop loss order does not guarantee that you will be able to sell at $40/share because it is a market order, which specifies that the trade will be executed at the best possible price. If the stock is really taking a dive or if the market is in free fall, you'll definitely sell, but it may be at some price below your stop loss order.

The Enlightened Investor knows that success in investing is more often than not, a function of minimizing losses rather than attempting to maximize the gains. A stop loss order is like insurance, you hope that you won't need it; nevertheless if an investment starts falling, you have some protection. And unlike most insurance policies, you don't have to pay a premium! The stop loss order costs nothing to place.

We discussed earlier the psychological reality that losses are felt much more keenly than gains. This hinders many investors from selling at a loss. At some point however, usually when the investment has lost 50% or more of its value, investors can't take it anymore and sell out. The decision to sell an investment is an emotionally difficult decision. We are torn between patience which says, "Give it another chance, it will eventually come around." and panic which cries out, "Sell now!" Patience causes us to procrastinate, giving the stock another day, another week, another month to turn around. In meantime, the losses continue to mount. The attitude that a falling investment can't go any lower is an exercise in self-delusion. We only need look at the experience of the market in the early 2000's and 2008-2009 to be reminded that investments can sometimes wilt away to nothing.

The advantage of the stop loss order is that it removes emotion from the decision-making process. It is automatic. Selling is triggered at a pre-determined price, which was determined by a rational process, not in the heat of the moment. For instance, instead of waiting until the stock has fallen 50-70%, a stop loss order could be preset to sell once the price declined 20%. Anybody can buy an investment, It is the easiest part of investing. However, few investors have the discipline to sell either to avoid a huge loss or to take profit. Most wait until it is too late when the price has fallen dramatically or the profit has disappeared.

The other advantage of the stop loss order is that you don't have to monitor your investment on a daily or hourly basis. I have seen cases where the effective use of stop loss orders has enabled a portfolio to post a profit, despite gains on only 20% of trades. The reason is that the losses on the 80% of trades were limited by stop loss orders, while the gains were allowed to ride, eventually outpacing the losers. Hedge fund manager Nassim Taleb summarizes the strategy when he writes, "I use statistics and inductive methods to make aggressive bets, but I will not use them to manage my risks and exposures. Trade on ideas based on some observation, including past history, but make sure the costs of being wrong are limited."[xli]

Also, remember that the use of a stop loss order does not prevent you from buying the stock back at bargain prices if you still believe in the long-term prospects of the stock. Furthermore, stop loss orders are not just used as a way to prevent large losses. It can also be used as a strategy to lock-in profits. In these situations it is referred to as a trailing stop. The idea is quite simple, instead of setting the stop loss order at a percentage level below your purchase price, you set the percentage based on the highest share price achieved.

For example: You purchased ABC shares at $50/share and set a trailing stop at 20%. One month later the share price has appreciated to $80/share. Your trailing stop order would lock-in at $64/share ($80 – ($80 x .20) = $64). If, in the following months the stock started falling and eventually fell to $64/share, your trailing stop order would kick-in at $64/share and your shares would be sold at the best possible market price. If the order filled at $64/share, you would have locked in a $14 gain per share by use of the trailing stop.

Our discussion begs the question: "What is a proper stop loss percentage?" There are many views on this issue. A common approach is to set the stop loss 10%-20% below the purchase price. One must be careful to set the stop loss order to compensate for normal intra-day price fluctuations. Short-term volatility is normal and one does not want to get closed out due to such fluctuations. My personal opinion is that for the long-term investor, setting a stop loss at 20% seems reasonable. The usefulness of stop loss or trailing stop orders is to prevent catastrophic losses. It is important to re-emphasize that these strategies are risk management strategies. There certainly may be occasions when the use of a stop loss order sells you out of a stock, only to see the price rebound shortly thereafter. The Enlightened Investor will remember that in a world of uncertainty, one must minimize down-side risk, sometimes at the expense of short-term gain.

At this point, some of you may be saying to yourselves, "Stop loss and trailing stops are all well and good, but we invest in mutual funds." It is true that stop loss and trailing stops cannot be used in the typical mutual fund. It is one of the disadvantages to investing in a mutual fund. There is no automatic way to lock in a sell price to either minimize loss or lock in gain. The only way to do so is to monitor your fund on a daily basis. And even then, buy and sell prices are only calculated at the end of the trading day.

Mutual Funds, Exchange-Traded Funds, and Separately Managed Accounts

In light of the crushing bear markets of the last decade, the inability to use stop loss or trailing stop orders is a disadvantage which may make a traditional mutual fund the investment choice of the past, not the future. The future of investing may be in a new type of mutual fund called an Exchange Traded Fund, and for those who can afford it, the Separately Managed Account.

Mutual funds exploded in popularity in the 1980's and 1990's. They became the investment of choice for most American investors. In fact, Morningstar currently tracks more than 10,000 mutual funds. The appeal of the mutual fund was that for a very small amount of money, you could invest in the great companies and financial instruments of the U.S. and the world. Furthermore, it offered the advantage of professional management and some degree of diversification. As the bull market roared on, investors were oblivious to the deficiencies of traditional mutual funds. However, the bear market of 2000-2002 exposed the disadvantages of mutual funds, and subsequent investigations revealed significant conflicts of interests among fund managers, directors, and their largest shareholders.

There are four disadvantages to traditional mutual funds:

The first disadvantage is that they cost too much. The average expense ratio of a domestic stock fund is more than 1.5% per year. Bond mutual funds average around 1.0%. In an investing environment, where by most estimates, the return will be below 10% for the foreseeable future, every dollar counts. For example: Compare the returns of a high cost mutual fund that averages 8.00% per year after expenses to a low cost fund that averages 9.50% per year after expenses. If the investor began with an initial investment of $10,000 the results would be:

	High Cost Fund 8.00% net return	Low Cost Fund 9.50% net return
10 years	$21,589	$24,782
25 years	$68,485	$96,683

After twenty-five years, a 1.5% difference in annual expenses translates into a difference of $28,198! Study after study has demonstrated that the costs of investing in mutual funds such as management fees, commissions, 12b-1 fees, etc. have a significant negative effect on net returns. The good news for investors is that there are now alternatives to traditional high-cost mutual funds that are less expensive. We will discuss them later in this section.

The second disadvantage is that you have no idea what stocks or bonds are held by the mutual fund. Funds are required by law to post their holdings only twice a year.   And by the time the semi-annual and annual reports are assembled, printed, and distributed, they're outdated material. There has been a recent push for more disclosure of fund holdings, yet the mutual fund industry has resisted this effort with all their lobbying might. I would not expect this to change anytime soon.

The third disadvantage is that mutual funds only post their price once a day, after the market close. As we noted before, this prevents the use of stop loss or trailing stop orders.

Finally, mutual funds can be a tax quagmire. In order to offer the small investor instant diversification among thousands of securities, mutual funds must pool investor dollars. Since this pool already exists, the new investor is buying into a fund with securities that have an original cost basis that may extend back many years.

The potential tax problems with mutual funds deserve an in-depth exploration. Consider one of the most popular mutual funds, the Vanguard S&P 500 Index fund which began in 1976. The Vanguard S&P 500 is an example of an extremely low turnover fund, and yet it could cause significant adverse tax consequences. As of the end of December, 2000, Morningstar reported that the potential income tax exposure was 46%! Consider a worst-case scenario in which there were massive redemptions of the fund or it decided to close and distribute assets to investors.

If you had invested $10,000 into the Vanguard S&P 500, the original cost basis of the underlying stocks in the fund was $5,400. In a worst case scenario, this would mean potential 1099 income of $4,600. Depending on whether your gain was characterized as short-term (maximum 35% federal rate) or long-term (15% federal rate) capital gains you would be faced with a tax of $690 on the low end or $1,610 on the high end.

The other aspect to the problem of built-in gains is when a mutual fund manager buys and sells securities during the year it often generates short-term capital gains. This has become a problem over the last decade as many mutual funds reported turnover rates well in excess of 100%. This means that they were buying and selling securities at a feverish pace in search of market-beating returns. Unfortunately, these short-term capital gains are reported on Form 1099, which must be declared and subject to ordinary income tax rates. The popular term for this phenomenon is "phantom gains". You don't make any money, yet you have to pay tax.

Consider the following example. You invested $10,000 in XYZ Technology Fund in January, 2010. As of December 31, 2010, your $10,000 was now worth $7,500. You had a loss of $2,500. Adding insult to injury, the fund managers sold stocks in the fund's portfolio which generated short-term capital gains. These gains are divided amongst the shareholders of the fund and at the end of January, 2011 you receive a Form 1099 from XYZ Technology Fund which states that your share of short-term capital gains was $2,000. Assuming you were in a 35% federal income tax bracket, you were faced with an additional $700 in income tax! Your investment had lost $2,500 and yet you have to declare an additional $2,000 in 1099 income. Such is the double whammy of mutual fund taxation.

Furthermore, if XYZ Technology Fund had instead generated a short-term capital loss instead of a short-term gain of $2,000, the short-term loss would not pass through to you the individual investor to offset other income. The fund must defer this loss and carry it forward until it can be used against net income. Heads I win, tails you lose! Is it any wonder that many investors feel like they are Alice in Wonderland when it comes to taxation of traditional mutual funds?

In addition to the inherent disadvantages of traditional mutual funds, in 2003 thanks to the efforts of then New York Attorney General Eliot Spitzer, it was revealed that some of the most prominent mutual fund families had engaged in late trading and market timing to the detriment of a majority of their shareholders. In perhaps one of the most prominent cases, Attorney General

Spitzer announced a $40 million settlement against hedge fund Canary Capital Partners for late trading and market timing of funds run by Bank of America and those of several other companies. The funds permitted the Canary hedge fund to engage in late trading and market timing in exchange for other business from Canary. Late trading is illegal and market timing violates securities regulations if the fund company tells its investors that it prohibits the practice, as the fund families in question most certainly did.

Unlike stocks or bonds, whose price changes throughout the trading day, mutual fund shares are priced only once per day, based on the value of the underlying fund's assets when the market closes at 4:00 PM EST. Therefore, in order to get the price as of the particular day's close, an investor must place an order prior to the close. Orders placed after the close are filled at the following day's closing price.

In the Bank of America and Canary hedge fund case, Canary was allowed by Bank of America to buy and sell Bank of America fund shares after the 4:00 PM close. This was illegal and an unfair advantage since Canary could profit from late news that would affect the fund price either up or down the following day. Attorney General Spitzer remarked that it was like betting on a horse after the race was already run.

Bank of America was not alone in allowing preferred customers to late-trade. Strong, Janus, Invesco, and Putnam were among the well-known mutual fund families that had allowed late trading. The mutual fund scandals mirrored the previous corporate malfeasance scandals of Enron, Tyco, Worldcom, Global Crossing, et al. The Board of Directors of these companies, as well as the mutual fund companies, had become cozy with senior management and unaware of what was really going on within the funds they were supposed to oversee. Unfortunately, the temptation of easy money has corrupted many within the mutual fund industry.

 Are there an alternatives for the investor that seeks easy accessibility and diversification, without the adverse taxation of traditional mutual funds, and possible conflict of interests? Yes there is, and the alternatives are Exchange Traded Funds and Separately Managed Accounts.

Exchange-Traded Funds

The first alternative is Exchange-traded funds (ETF). Exchange-traded funds made their debut almost two decades ago, however because of the bull market of the 1990's, they did not gain much attention. Investors were getting double-digit annual returns with their mutual funds and didn't pay attention to the disadvantages of traditional mutual funds. Since the market crash of 2000, Exchange-traded funds have gained attention and have become the most potent rival to traditional mutual funds.

Exchange-traded funds consist of a group of securities, just like a traditional mutual fund. Until recently Exchange-traded funds were strictly equity portfolios comprised of various indices such as the Dow Jones, NASDAQ 100, S&P 500, etc. However, we now have several Exchange-traded funds that track various bond indices, as well as several actively-managed exchange-traded funds.

Exchange-traded funds offer investors four advantages over traditional mutual funds. They have lower expenses, purity of asset class, tax efficiency, and the ability to trade like stocks.

In regard to expenses, the average Exchange-traded fund has an expense ratio of 15 basis points (0.15%). Compare that to the average equity fund expense ratio of 150 basis points (1.5%). Consider that the nation's premier bond mutual fund, **Pimco Total Return A**, has an expense ratio of 90 basis points (0.9%), and **ACM Income Fund**, one of the most widely held closed-end bond funds, has an expense ratio of 231 basis points (2.31%). In contrast, **iShares**, a group of Exchange-traded funds advised and marketed by Barclays Global Investors, has an expense ratio of only 15 basis points (0.15%). Clearly Exchange-traded funds offer an advantage over many traditional mutual funds in regard to expenses.

The second advantage of Exchange-traded funds is their transparency and purity of asset class. With an Exchange-traded fund, you can see exactly what stocks are in the portfolio at any given time, compared with traditional mutual funds which are only required to list their holdings on a semi-annual basis. Exchange-traded funds typically are comprised of a specific market index such as the Dow Jones, S&P 500, Lehman 20+ year treasury, etc. If your goal is diversification, you know exactly what asset class your particular Exchange-traded fund is investing in. Contrast this with the tendency of some traditional mutual funds to drift from one style to another and one asset class to another in search of short-term investment returns.

For example: the Fidelity Magellan fund was one of the largest, if not the largest mutual fund for many years. When Peter Lynch was managing the fund it was primarily a small-cap, growth-oriented fund. Because of his success, the fund took in billions of dollars. As it grew larger and larger, it was forced to buy bigger companies until it ended up as a large-cap fund. There was a point in time where the Fidelity Magellan fund was invested primarily in bonds as Jeffrey Vinik, the fund manager at the time, made an aggressive bet on market trends. His bet didn't pay off and he resigned as a result. After his departure, the Fidelity Magellan fund essentially turned into an S&P 500 clone.

The reason for such style drift is that mutual fund investors are extremely fickle. Investors chase recent performance. The best performing funds see a huge influx of investor dollars in the year following top performance. Laggards see money drain out like a breached dam. Many fund managers, in a frantic search for short-term performance, stray from their funds stated investment objectives. For the investor that invests based on a solid plan of diversification, such style drift may be disastrous. He may have had five funds in his portfolio, each with a stated investment objective that was unique. It was not unusual to find that in the mad rush for short-term returns, that all five funds were investing in similar securities. The advantage of Exchange-traded funds is that style drift, especially for Exchange-traded funds that track market indices, is not an issue. An investor can assemble a diversified group of Exchange-traded funds and have the assurance that the diversification will be maintained.

The third advantage is tax efficiency. Since most Exchange-traded funds are based on various indices, they trade less and have a lower turnover ratio than traditional funds. Thus the creation of short-term or long-term capital gains is kept to minimum.

The other aspect to tax efficiency is that Exchange-traded funds are issued in "creation units", which are individual baskets of all the securities the fund owns, weighted exactly like the underlying index. Shares of Exchange-traded funds can thus be purchased and sold just like a stock or bond. When these creation units are redeemed, the shareholders get securities instead of cash. This creates a tax advantage over traditional mutual funds.

When a traditional mutual fund sells shares of the stocks it owns in the fund, it sells those with the highest cost basis first. For example: Suppose that the fund had purchased shares of XYZ Corporation over several years. Some of the shares were purchased at $20/share, others at $35/share, and others at $45/share. If the fund manager decides to sell some of XYZ Corporation at $65/share, she will choose to sell the shares that have the highest cost basis, the shares that were purchased at $45/share. The reason for this action is to reduce the current capital gains tax. However the disadvantage of this strategy is that the shares that were purchased at $20/share and $35/share are still in the fund and the capital gain on these shares must be paid at some future date. As a result, when you buy a mutual fund, you may ultimately end up paying a share of someone else's capital gains.

Exchange-traded funds handle this transaction in such a way as to maximize tax efficiency for the shareholder. Individual shareholders buy and sell Exchange-traded fund share through institutions. When the institution redeems shares in an Exchange-traded fund, it takes back stock, not cash. And the Exchange-traded fund will give the institution the lowest cost-basis stock and retain the higher cost-basis stock in the fund. Therefore when you purchase shares of an Exchange-traded fund, the percentage of embedded capital gains within the fund will typically be much smaller than a traditional mutual fund.

The final advantage of Exchange-traded funds is that they can be traded just like stocks and bonds. This enables the investor to utilize stop loss and trailing stop orders to minimize downside risk automatically. Along with low cost and tax efficiency, I believe this risk management capability is the most significant feature of Exchange-traded funds.

As mentioned earlier, there are more and more Exchange-traded funds being created every year. However, the most widely-held Exchange-traded funds are summarized below:

SPDR's

Standard & Poor's Depository Receipts, commonly referred to as "spiders", is a group of Exchange-traded funds that track a variety of Standard & Poor's indices.

Vipers

Vanguard Index Participation Receipts are Exchange-traded fund versions of several Vanguard index funds.

Qubes

This is an Exchange-traded fund that tracks the Nasdaq-100 index. Qubes are by far the most heavily traded Exchange-traded fund.

Diamonds

The Diamonds Trust Series I tracks the Dow Jones Industrial Average.

iShares

A group of Exchange-traded funds advised and marketed by Barclays Global Investors.

HOLDRs

Holding company depository receipts is an Exchange-traded fund marketed by Merrill Lynch. HOLDRs focus on narrow industry groups. Each HOLDR initially owns 20 stocks and is unmanaged. They can only be bought and sold in 100-share increments.

Separately Managed Accounts

Separately Managed Accounts have many of the same advantages of Exchange-traded funds. However they have two distinct disadvantages. First, the minimum dollar amount per manager is around $100,000 for stocks and $300,000 for bonds. If one wants to diversify using several managers it would therefore require a minimum portfolio of about $800,000 or more. Clearly this is a benchmark that puts Separately Managed Accounts out of reach of the average investor. The second disadvantage is that they are much more expensive than Exchange-traded funds.

One of the advantages of Separately Managed Accounts is in terms of tax-efficiency. The cost-basis of each security that is purchased for a client portfolio is established when purchased, thus the Separately Managed Account has no embedded gains which can result in the phantom income problem we discussed in relation to traditional mutual funds.

It also offers several strategies for taking advantage of losses. Mutual funds typically use the average cost per share method of determining basis, whereas the Separately Managed Account can identify a particular block of stock purchased at a particular price. For example: If we purchased 100 shares of XYZ Corporation at $50/share, 100 shares at $100/share, and 100 shares at $150/share, and at some point wanted to sell 100 shares when the market price was $110/share, we could identify the 100 shares we purchased at $150/share to produce a loss of $40/share.

The other technique is "doubling up". Doubling up allows the portfolio manager to maintain a position in a specific stock, while at the same time recognizing a loss for tax planning purposes. This technique is quite straightforward, the manager purchases an equal number of shares compared to the current position in the stock. After 30 days, in order to avoid wash sale rules, the original shares are sold in order to produce a loss, meanwhile holding on to the higher cost-basis shares.

Separately Managed Accounts have seen tremendous growth in assets under management in the last several years. As we have discussed, they offer distinct tax advantages over traditional mutual funds. However because of their high minimums, their use will be confined to investors with significant wealth.

Tax Diversification

John Maynard Keynes once said, "The avoidance of taxes is the only intellectual pursuit that still carries any reward." I'm sure this remark was delivered tongue-in-cheek, however for the Enlightened Investor; it is a strategy well worth pursuing on the path to financial independence. First we must differentiate between tax avoidance and tax evasion. Tax avoidance is utilizing the tax code to legally avoid paying taxes. Tax evasion is illegally evading taxes. As Keynes said, tax avoidance is a pursuit that has its rewards; on the other hand, tax evasion usually results in punishment. One is worth the pursuit, the other not.

James Madison, fourth president of the United States, and one of the authors of the *Federalist Papers* wrote, "The tax code should not be so verbose that no one will understand it, nor should it be so long that no one will read it." It is regrettable that Congress has never heeded his admonition. At present, the tax code is comprised of twenty-seven volumes of 47,000 pages in length. When it comes to taxes, what you don't know can definitely hurt you! When it comes to taxes, people don't make mistakes because they necessarily want to, rather they make mistakes because they just don't know any better.

There are generally three categories of investment taxation. 1) Currently taxable, either as ordinary income, dividend, or capital gains; 2) tax-deferred; and 3) tax-free. It is virtually impossible for investors to avoid taxation with most investments; it is rather a matter of when the tax must be paid.

The most prominent exception to this rule would be municipal bonds. Typically the interest on municipal bonds is free of any federal tax and possibly free of state tax. Although the gross rate of return on municipal bonds is typically lower than other taxable bonds, the fact that they are tax-free makes the net return quite attractive. For investors in a high tax bracket, tax-free municipal bonds may make sense as a part of a diversified portfolio.

Most investors, however, either want or need a higher rate of return than municipal bonds can offer. In these situations, tax-deferral is a method of delaying the payment of taxes to some point in the future, which can result in better long-term performance. The beauty of tax-deferral is that you can take advantage of triple compounding: you earn interest on your principal, you earn interest on your interest, and you earn interest on the taxes you otherwise would have had to pay. Examples of tax-deferred investment vehicles are IRA's, qualified pension plans such as a 401(k), annuities, and life insurance.

The power of tax deferral and the power of time combine to provide an excellent tool to help achieve financial independence. Let's look at an example to illustrate the concept. We will start with a $50,000 investment and assume an 8% annual return with an effective tax bracket of 31% over a thirty year period. The chart illustrates the power of tax deferral over time. At the end of thirty years, the tax-deferred account would be worth $503,130. Alternatively if taxes were paid on the interest every year, the investment would only be worth $250,620, 50% less than the tax-deferred account.

This is all well and good, however critics of tax-deferred investments point out that the tax has to be paid at some point. This is most certainly true, eventually tax must be paid on the gain. The final column on the chart illustrates a worst-case scenario whereby the investor paid tax on the entire amount of gain at the end of thirty years. The tax-deferred account is worth $503,130. This represents a deferred gain of $453,130. If this were taxed at 31%, it would result in a tax of $140,470. This would leave the investor with $362,660 after-tax. This is $112,040 more than the investor would have had if he had paid tax on the interest every year.

Power of Tax Deferral

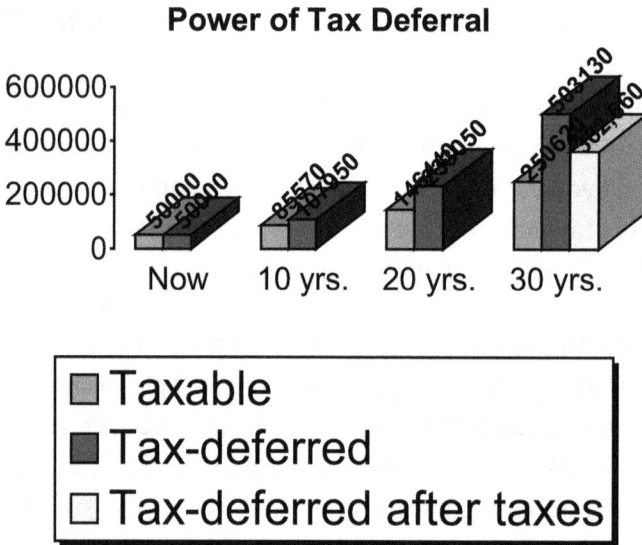

Our hypothetical example illustrates the tremendous advantages of tax deferral. Now let's get more specific. What effect can taxes have on an investment in stocks as measured by the S&P 500, bonds as measured by the 20-yr. U.S. government bond, and cash as measured by the 30-day U.S. Treasury Bill? Our timeframe is from 1926 – 1999. Ibbotson Associates calculated the tax using the actual 1926-1998 marginal tax rates for a single taxpayer earning $75,000 in 1989 dollars every year. No state taxes are included in the calculation.

Returns Before and After Taxes

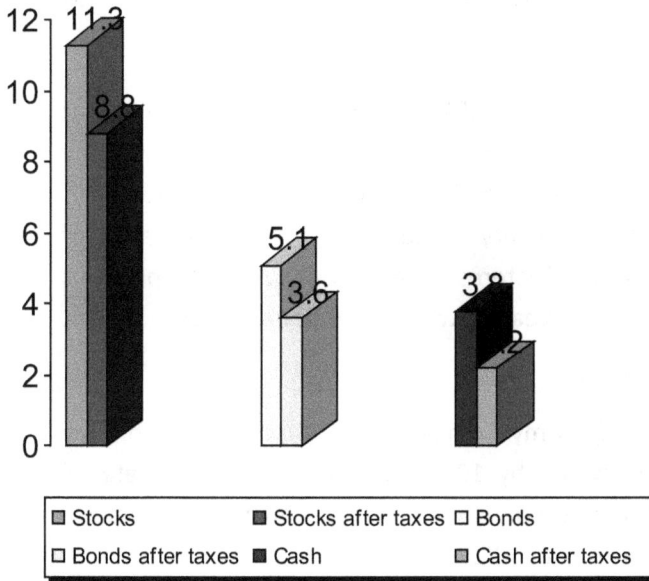

Source: Ibbotson and Associates

The average return on stocks from 1926 through 1999 was 11.3%. However, the return drops down to 8.8% after taxes. Likewise with bonds, the average return was 5.1%, after tax it fell to 3.6%. Finally cash delivered an average return of 3.8%, after tax it was 2.2%. The difference between the gross return of the S&P 500 of 11.3% and the after-tax return of 8.8% may seem insignificant, however as I mentioned earlier, the power of tax deferral coupled with the power of time can be truly amazing.

Consider that $1,000 invested at 11.3% over a 74- year period results in $2,758,304, whereas the same $1,000 invested at 8.8% over a 74-year period results in $513,497! Granted there will be very few of us that will invest over a 74-year time frame, yet it is hard to deny the advantage of tax deferral. Even over a 20-year period, an average return of 11.3% on a $1,000 investment is worth $8,509 compared to an average return of 8.8% which is worth $5,402.

In working with clients, I have used the following form to help them understand the power of tax deferral in their pursuit of financial independence. It utilizes the "rule of 72" to provide a simple, straightforward illustration of the power of tax deferral.

First, let's review the "rule of 72". The "rule of 72" is a mathematical oddity that allows you to calculate how many years it will take to double your money at any given interest rate. For example, if I can earn 8% on my money, the 'rule of 72" tells me that I will double my money every 9 years. It is simply a matter of dividing the number 72 by the assumed interest rate. The result of the previous calculation is 9, which is the number of years it will take to double your money at an 8% rate of return.

Another example: if I can get 10% on my money, I know that I will double my investment every 7.2 years (72 divided by 10 = 7.2 years). The Tax Deferral Worksheet allows you to do a simple comparison of a taxable investment versus a tax-deferred investment using the "rule of 72".

Let's look at a very conservative example. Mrs. Smith has $100,000 to invest. By examining her tax returns over several years, we know that she has an effective tax rate of 20%. She expects an average return of 6% per year. We now proceed to the left column of the worksheet, "Taxable". If Mrs. Smith is earning 6% per year in a taxable investment, it translates into a net return of 4.8% after taxes (6.00% - 20% = 4.80%). In order to find out how many years it will take to double her money, she divides 4.8 into 72. The result is 15 years. Mrs. Smith is 60 years old, thus we double her investment every 15 years. At age 75 her $100,000 is worth $200,000. At age 90 it is worth $400,000.

We now move to the left column, "Tax Deferred". If Mrs. Smith doesn't have to pay current taxes her gross return of 6.00% is also her net rate of return. Utilizing the "rule of 72", she divides 6 into 72 which equals 12. At a tax-deferred return of 6.00%, she will double her money every 12 years. She is still 60 years old and at age 72 her $100,000 will be worth $200,000. At age 84, $400,000, and if she lived to age 96 it would be worth $800,000.

What is your tax rate? **20%**
What rate would you like to earn? **6%**
How much can you invest? **100,000**

Client Name	Rule of 72	
Mrs. Smith		Years to double money
	Net rate of return	72

Taxable	Tax Deferred
$ **100,000** at **6** % at **20** % tax rate	$ **100,000** at **6** % at **0** % tax rate
20 % tax on **6** % = **4.8** % NET	**0** % tax on **6** % = **6** % NET
15 Years	**12** Years
4.8 % ⌐ 72	**6** % ⌐ 72

Taxable		Tax Deferred	
Age Today **60**	$ **100,000**	Age Today **60**	$ **100,000**
Age + **15** **75**	**200,000**	Age + **12** **72**	**200,000**
90	**400,000**	**84**	**400,000**
		90	**567,000**

		567,000
	Principal −	**100,000**
		467,000 Taxable Gain
	Tax **20** % −	**93,400**
		373,600
$ **400,000** After Tax	+ Principal	**100,000**
		473,600 After Tax

You will notice that we stopped at age 90. By utilizing some simple arithmetic, we can calculate that she will have $567,000 at age 90. We did this so Mrs. Smith could make an "apples to apples" comparison with the "taxable" account. At age 90, Mrs. Smith has $400,000 in the "taxable" account and $567,000 in the "tax-deferred" account.

However, we must take into account the taxes that Mrs. Smith must pay on her gains in the "tax-deferred" account. For our illustration we will assume a worst-case tax scenario where she would take distribution of the entire $567,000 in one year. The calculation of the tax is as follows: She now has $567,000, $100,000 of which is her original investment which is therefore not subject to tax. We subtract the $100,000 which leaves us with a $467,000 gain subject to a 20% tax.

20% of $467,000 is $93,400 which leaves an after-tax gain of $373,600. We add back her original investment of $100,000 for a grand total of $473,600 after-tax.

By utilizing tax-deferred investing, Mrs. Smith ends up with an additional $73,600 more than she would have had with a currently taxable investment, $473,600 versus $400,000. Furthermore, we must remember that we are illustrating a worst-case tax scenario. With most tax-deferred investments, Mrs. Smith would have the option of withdrawing less than the total amount in one year. Thus she would have the ability to spread out the tax which might prevent her from climbing into a higher marginal tax bracket.

The Enlightened Investor understands that the longer she can defer paying taxes on investments, the faster she can travel on the path to financial independence. The miracle of compound interest combined with tax deferral is perhaps the most powerful of the perennial investment strategies we have discussed. This does not imply that we should only use tax-deferred investments. Just as diversification makes eminent sense when investing; so too does the concept of tax diversification. The Enlightened Investor will take advantage of taxable, tax-deferred, tax-deductible, and tax-free investments to build a tax-diversified portfolio. By creating different baskets of assets that have different tax characteristics, it is possible to develop a flexible plan of withdrawing income that can reduce overall taxes.

The following form is an excellent tool to begin the process of tax diversification. It divides investments into four categories of tax treatment: Taxable, Tax-free, Tax-deferred, and Tax-deductible. As you work your way through the form, you list the value of each asset and also list the amount of income per year if you are drawing income from that asset. Then it is simply a matter of totaling the value of assets in each tax classification. While there is no hard and fast rule concerning the percentage of assets that should be in any tax classification, the Enlightened Investor will seek tax diversification to the extent that it fits within her overall plan.

Tax Allocation Worksheet— Current

Taxable

	Value	Income
Savings/ checking		
CD's		
T-Bills		
Mutual funds		
Bonds		
Other		

Tax-Free

	Value	Income
Roth IRA		
Muni bonds		
Life ins. cash value		
Other		

Tax-Deferred

	Value	Income
Variable annuities		
Fixed annuities		
Bonds		
Other		

Tax-Deductible

	Value	Income
401(k)		
403(b)		
IRA's		
Other		

	Value	Income
Taxable		
Tax-Free		
Tax-Deferred		
Tax-Deductible		

Tax Credits

The final tax reduction strategy is the use of tax credits. In my seminars I ask the question, "How many of you would like an extra vacation each year compliments of the IRS?" Of course you would. Tax credits offer the opportunity to keep some of the taxes that would otherwise go to the IRS in your own pocket.

Tax credits are much more valuable than tax deductions. Tax credits are a dollar-for-dollar reduction in the tax that you pay. For example, if my federal income tax liability is $8,000 and I have $3,000 of tax credits, my tax liability is reduced dollar-for-dollar to $5,000. Through the use of tax credits, instead of your $3,000 going to the IRS, you keep the money.

Tax credits are not a tax "loophole". They are mandated and authorized under Section 42 of the IRS code and federal law. They are issued by the Treasury Department for taxpayers that invest in private, low-income subsidized housing. Unlike corporations, which have unlimited use of tax credits, individual taxpayers are limited in the amount of tax credits they can utilize to reduce taxes. The limits are determined by your marginal federal income tax bracket.

To calculate the maximum annual federal tax credit allowed for individuals, you multiply the investor's marginal federal tax bracket by the highest $25,000 of taxable income as follows:

Marginal Tax Bracket		Taxable Income		Annual Credit Allowance
15%	X	$25,000	=	$3,750
25%	X	$25,000	=	$6,250
28%	X	$25,000	=	$7,000
33%	X	$25,000	=	$8,250
35%	X	$25,000	=	$8,750

Another advantage of tax credits is that they may be used to reduce taxes on net passive income. Additionally, tax credits are prefunded to eligible properties for ten full years which means that the investor will be able to use the annual tax credits for ten full years.

For example: Someone in the 33% marginal tax bracket would be eligible to generate a total of $82,500 of tax credits over a ten year period. Many clients use tax credits to offset the taxes they have to pay on IRA distributions. Using our previous example of an investor in a 33% tax bracket, if he were to take $25,000 in annual distributions from his IRA, he would be subject to $8,750 in income taxes on that distribution. If instead, he utilized tax credits up to his maximum, he could offset that $8,750 in tax with $8,750 in tax credits. By utilizing tax credits to offset taxes on IRA distributions, this individual would have been able to take $250,000 out of his IRA and not have paid any tax on the distributions!

The use of tax credit programs are not suitable for many investors, however in the right circumstance they can provide a powerful benefit to the individual investor as well as to society as a whole.

13 THE OPPORTUNITIES AND CHALLENGES OF A FINANCIAL LIFETIME

As we progress through our financial lifetime and travel the path to financial independence, most of us will encounter financial challenges along the way. Some of these challenges we all must face. Others, depending on how our lives play out, we may not have to confront. These challenges can either be stepping stones to opportunity or they can present insurmountable roadblocks to financial fulfillment. The choice is ours.

In the following chapters, we will discuss the great financial opportunities and financial challenges that most Americans will confront at some point during their financial lives. Whether the particular situation will be seen as a challenge or whether it will be seen as an opportunity is entirely a function of the action or non-action of the individual. As with most things financial, those who plan and take action early will open the door to opportunity and financial independence. Those who procrastinate or ignore these issues may be confronted by challenges that may be difficult to surmount. The choice is yours.

Retirement

The major premise of this book is that financial independence is a goal that can, and must, be defined by each individual. As stated earlier, financial independence is when you have enough capital and assets working for you, to create the income you want for as long as you will need it, such that work is optional and retirement is affordable. For most Americans, financial independence and retirement are synonymous. If I am retired, therefore I must be financially independent. However, it is critical to understand that financial independence gives you the option of retirement, not the necessity or finality of retirement. In many ways, the late twentieth century conception of retirement is fast disappearing. The prevailing perception that we must try to get to retirement as fast as we can, quit working forever, and live happily ever after is no longer realistic for most Americans. Furthermore, the idea of permanently retiring at a relatively young age may not be the best prescription for long term health.

The concept of retirement as a condition of permanent leisure is a relatively new phenomenon. Retirement as it is usually portrayed in the media didn't exist prior to the early 1900's. It was only with the advent of Social Security and defined benefit pension plans that the popular notion of retirement became a possibility for most Americans. In 1945, the average American spent eighteen years in school, forty-seven years working, and five years in retirement. In an era when most of the jobs involved some degree of physical labor, many workers couldn't continue to work even if they wanted to because their bodies just couldn't handle it. In addition, there were huge numbers of young people entering the workforce that needed jobs.

By the time of the decades following the 1950's, old age was no longer synonymous with poverty. Social Security, Medicare, defined benefit pension plans, and a robust American economy had transformed older age into a time of unprecedented wealth and income.

Contrast this with today's realities. Baby Boomers and following generations will have an entirely different experience of retirement than did their parents and grandparents. This person will spend twenty-five years in school, thirty years working, and thirty or more years in "retirement". Most of the jobs in the present-day workforce do not involve physical labor, and there are not as many young people entering the workforce. Faced with these realities, the idea of completely retiring may be a short-lived phenomenon of the late twentieth century. In fact, if current trends continue, only a small percentage of baby boomers will have the ability to retire without working. It very well may be true that only one generation in American history will be able to enjoy the dream of retirement without financial care or worry. They have accomplished this by drawing upon five sources of income. The following graph illustrates the percentage of total income for Americans age 65 and older.

Components of Total Income in 2000

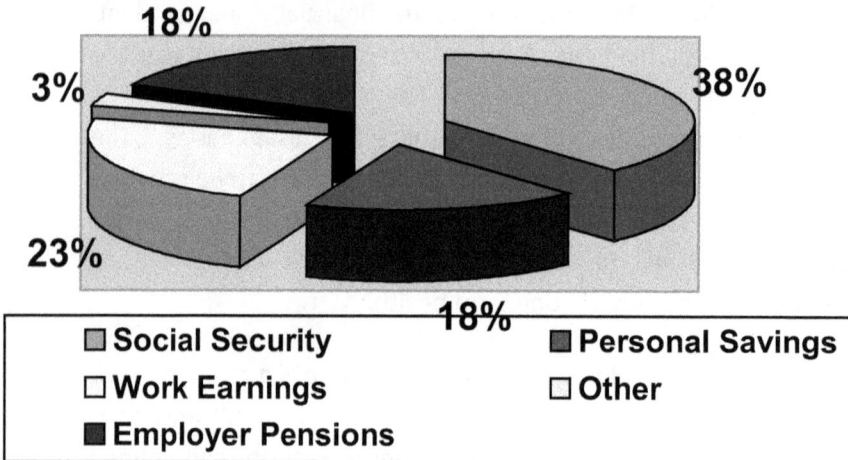

18%

3%

38%

23%

18%

■ Social Security   ■ Personal Savings
□ Work Earnings   □ Other
■ Employer Pensions

Source: Social Security Administration, 2002

For all the talk from the investment industry about investing to achieve a comfortable retirement based on personal savings, the reality is far different. Consider that Social Security still provides almost 4 out of every 10 dollars of income paid to Americans age 65 and older. Employer defined benefit pension plans account for about 2 out of every 10 dollars. Only about 2 out of every 10 dollars come from personal savings and investments. Approximately 6 out of every 10 dollars of income for Americans 65 and older are provided by the government or their former employers. In working with a predominantly retired clientele, I know that if it were not for Social Security and defined benefit pensions, most of these clients would not have adequate retirement income to last the remainder of their days.

If these statistics weren't eye-opening enough, consider that Social Security is almost the sole source of retirement income for one-third of Americans 65 and older. For 1 in 5 of these Americans, Social Security is their entire income! The following graph illustrates the percentage of Americans 65 and older deriving a given percent of their income from Social Security.

Role of Social Security, 2000

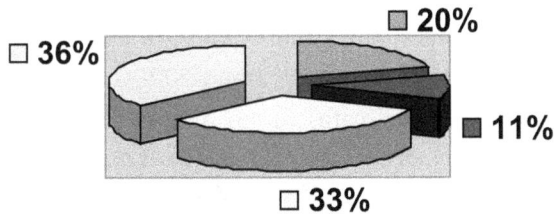

| ■ 100% of income | ■ 90-99% of income |
| □ 50-89% of income | □ less than 50% |

Source: Social Security Administration, 2002

Fully two-thirds of Americans age 65 and older rely on Social Security for half or more of their retirement income. Is it any wonder that politicians proceed with fear and caution when discussing Social Security? It seems obvious that Social Security will remain an essential, if not primary, source of retirement for several generations of Americans to come. And yet we know that Social Security faces a financial challenge because of the reality of demographics. In 1950, average life expectancy in the United States was 69 which was only two years more than the median retirement age. By the year 2000, average life expectancy had risen to 76.5 years while the median retirement age fell to 62. In 1950, there were 7 workers paying taxes for every Social Security recipient, today there are 3.9 workers per Social Security recipient, and by the time the last of the Baby Boomers retires in 2030, it is estimated that there will be only 2.2 workers for each recipient of Social Security benefits. If nothing is done by way of reforming the system, the cost of benefits will exceed the taxes collected in 2017, and it will be fiscally insolvent by 2041.

According to Jeremy Siegel, author and Wharton finance professor,

The picture is not pretty. Although the retirement age has dropped five years since 1950 to its current level of 62, it will have to increase steadily to age 69 years by 2030 in order to feed, clothe, and pay for the medical care of the retiring boomers. The increase in retirement age outpaces the expected increase in life expectancy, so that for the first time in modern history future generations will not only have to work longer but will have a shorter period in which to enjoy the fruits of their labor.[xlii]

We have seen many reform proposals over the last several years, most prominent among them the proposal to allow some percentage of Social Security taxes to be invested in individual accounts in either the stock or bond markets. If there was any silver lining in the bear markets of 2000- 2002 and 2008-2009, it is that the market crash has exposed the potential catastrophe of allowing people to risk their Social Security benefits in the market. We simply need look at how people have reacted with their own money to understand that private Social Security accounts would be a disaster-in-waiting.

If this scheme were allowed, at some point in the future we would witness large numbers of Americans who had invested poorly or had the ill fortune of bad timing, facing retirement with very little in personal savings and even less in Social Security benefits. What goes missing in any discussion of Social Security reform is the fact the Social Security is not an investment plan. It is an insurance program. We pay a premium, namely the payroll tax, in order to insure that Americans don't retire destitute. It is an insurance policy for social stability. And we have seen from the statistics, that if not for Social Security, a comfortable retirement would not be an option for a majority of Americans.

If we look at the top 20% of American income earners age 65 and over, the primary reason they are in the top 20% is because they continue to work either full- or part-time. Their share of income from work earnings is much higher than the lower 80%. The reality, even for Americans 65 and older, is that in order to maintain affluence, you must continue to work! The message to those younger than age 65 is that unless you change your attitude and approach to money, much of your retirement will be spent working either part- for full-time to maintain your standard of living.

For example, statistics from the Social Security Administration reveal that 44% of Americans age 65-69, 26% of Americans age 70-74, 14% of Americans age 75-79, and 7% of Americans age 80-84 are still receiving income from working.

Income from work, by age

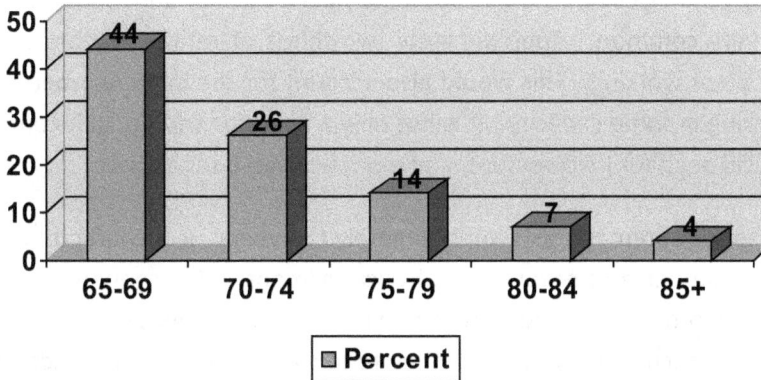

Source: Social Security Administration, 2002

These percentages are much higher than most casual observers would have thought. Obviously, as we age our health and mobility may decline such that we may not be able to work. However, I believe there is another explanation for this trend towards continuing to work in our later years. We tend to imagine retirement as one long monolithic experience, yet the reality is that there are three distinct phases of retirement.

The first phase of retirement generally lasts ten to fifteen years. Retirees are no longer working full-time and are confronted with large amounts of leisure time. It is like a second childhood, only without parental supervision and with a lot more money! And because of this new-found freedom, many retirees find that their annual spending equals, or in some cases exceeds, their pre-retirement spending. They have a lot of things that they want to do, and now they have the time to do them. I have seen many retirees who are shocked when they look at how much they have spent in the first several years of retirement. And in many of these situations, one or both of the spouses will take on part-time employment to earn extra income or to help pass the time. After all, how much golf can you play without becoming totally bored? As an aside, on many occasions I had the opportunity to play golf with my father and his retired friends. It never ceased to amaze me how quickly they played. They play so much golf that it is no longer a game; it has become a habit or ritual. It is hit and drive the cart, hit and drive the cart, putt and drive to the next tee. It has become an activity to merely help pass the time. Golf on automatic pilot!

It is this over-abundance of time and the lack of meaningful activity that causes many retirees who shift from full-time work to full-time leisure to become ill, both physically and psychologically. Post-retirement heart attacks and bouts with depression are very common. Approximately two-thirds of retirees report that they are unhappy not working. This would also account for the large numbers of retirees still working in some capacity. It is not only a need for additional income; it is a psychological need for involvement, and a physical need for activity.

The second phase of retirement lasts approximately ten years. It is characterized by an increasing number and severity of physical ailments. Consequently, the activities of retirees in this phase are slowed down dramatically. As a result of not being able to do as much as they used to, they tend to live on much less income than they did in the first phase. There is also a psychological factor that affects activity in this phase of retirement. As the retiree enters this phase, there is a profound desire to stick "close to home". They are drawn back to the comfort and pleasures of community, friends, and family.

In the book Black Elk Speaks, Black Elk, the Sioux elder, is asked about the center of the spiritual world. He replies, "Harney Peak", the highest summit in the Black Hills of South Dakota and sacred place of the Sioux. Yet he went on to add, "But the spiritual center is anywhere you want it to be." This is perhaps the realization that many people embrace as they age. Or as Dorothy states in the Wizard of Oz, "There's no place like home."

The third and final phase of retirement is defined by the failing health of the retiree. This results in the need for increased medical and perhaps nursing home care. Wants are minimal during this phase and with the exception of medical care expenses, income needs are minimal. However, nursing home and medical expenses in the last years of life can wreak havoc on any semblance of financial independence. It is generally acknowledged that almost two-thirds of an individual's lifetime medical expenditures come in the last year of life.

It is the looming uncertainty of severe illness or incapacity that has resulted in an overwhelming majority of older adults to admit that they are afraid their financial resources will not be able to meet their future income needs. Furthermore, there is no relationship between income levels and anxiety over potentially inadequate financial resources in the future. In other words, rich or poor, it makes no difference, the uncertainty of running out of money before one runs out of time knows no difference between rich and poor. According to the U.S. Census Bureau, net worth of households increases as people age, reaching its highest point on average between the ages of 65-69. However, after that point, net worth of households tends to decrease.

Net Worth of Households, 1995

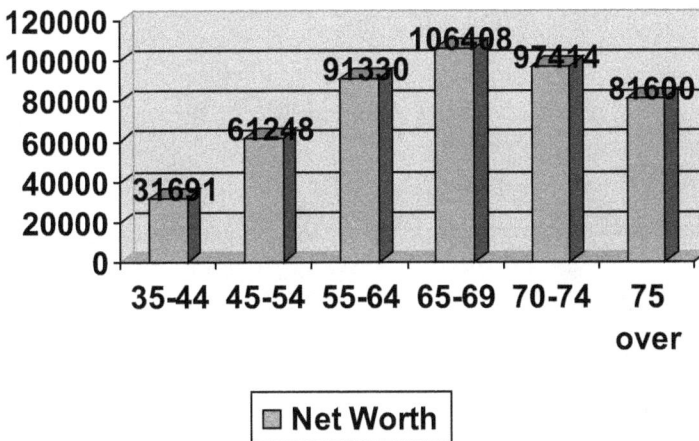

Source: U.S. Census Bureau

The anxiety over running out of money before running out of time is well-founded. It can and does happen. As Americans continue to live longer lives, mortality is decreasing, but morbidity is increasing. We live longer, but in our older age we will be susceptible to many more periods of illness and incapacity, both short-term and chronic. And yet despite this anxiety, older Americans are much more satisfied with their financial condition than are younger Americans.

Why is this so? The obvious reason, as we mentioned, is that they have more financial resources than their younger counterparts. The other not so obvious reason is that financial satisfaction is a function of two variables: how much you have, and how much you want.

As we age our wants tend to align with the financial resources we have available to us. Another interesting aspect of this satisfaction is that numerous social surveys have demonstrated that a majority of older adults view themselves as better off than most of their peers. The belief that older people are poor, sick, and lonely helps older adults to feel good about what they see as their own relatively advantaged status. It appears that older people seek out opportunities to compare themselves favorably to their age peers.[xliii] Sociologists call this the "poor dear syndrome". When we are younger, we tend to compare ourselves financially to those who are wealthier and earn more income, whereas as we grow older we tend to compare ourselves to those less well-off. Perhaps this is a finely-developed coping strategy, or perhaps it is the result of wisdom gained through experience of life.

In looking at our financial lifetime, if we were to chart our financial desires against our financial resources it would look something like this:

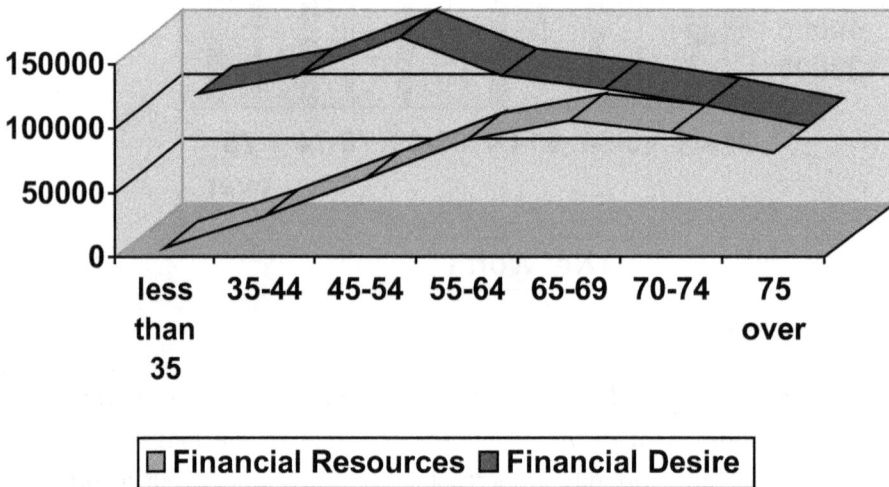

Ellen Glasgow, the novelist stated: "A tragic irony of life is that we so often achieve success or financial independence after the chief reason for which we sought it has passed away." Or perhaps, putting an optimistic spin on things, it is our saving grace. The Enlightened Investor knows that one of the keys to financial independence is to bring our financial desires in line with our financial resources. Unfortunately, the more successful the individual has been in social and economic terms, the more resistance they have to lowering aspirations.

People with high levels of education and income refuse to "give up" or "give in". However, the Enlightened Investor knows that it is not a matter of "giving up" or "giving in". It is an issue of being held hostage by the two temptations of fear and desire. Does our refusal to "give up" stem from a fear of the consequences? Are we unwilling to let go of our unfettered desire?   Would it not be better to seek an alignment in concert with our hopes of a life lived in balance and meaning? We are not "giving in" or "giving up"; we are truly "stepping up"! Stepping up to the potential of turning dream circles into reality.

Aware of the three phases of retirement, the Enlightened Investor will prepare three budgets for retirement. A first phase budget that will be 80-100% of pre-retirement expenses, a second phase budget that will be 50-75% of pre-retirement expenses, and a final phase budget that would be the very lowest amount the retiree could live on and still be assured of shelter, food, and care.

Let's look at a hypothetical retirement scenario. The first step is to take a detailed account of expenses. These include all fixed and discretionary expenses. We will assume that for our example, the need is $75,000 per year.

Once you have determined the expense side of the equation, the second step is to determine how much you can expect to receive in guaranteed income. This is income from such sources as Social Security or a defined benefit pension plan. In other words, income that is not subject to either investment or interest-rate risk. For a current Social Security benefit statement based your earnings history, you can contact the Social Security Administration at 800.772.1213 and request Form ssa-7004, Request for Earnings and Benefit Estimate Statement or you can go to their website at www.ssa.gov. For an estimate of defined benefit pension income, you can contact the employer. If you will have any other sources of guaranteed income such as an annuity, you would also add this into the total. For our example we will assume that we can count on guaranteed income of $50,000 per year.

The third step in the process is to include an inflation factor. The table below contains the factors that can be used depending on how many years you have until your anticipated retirement. The factors are based on an assumed average inflation rate of 3.0% per year. Multiply your retirement budget by the inflation factor below. The result is an estimate of annual expenses at your anticipated retirement.

	5 yrs.	10 yrs.	15 yrs.	20 yrs.	25 yrs.	30 yrs.	35 yrs.
Years		*Until*		*Retired*			
Inflation Factor	1.2	1.3	1.6	1.8	2.1	2.4	2.8

In our example, we will assume that we have twenty years until retirement. We would multiply our retirement budget of $75,000 per year x 1.8 = $135,000.

The fourth step is to subtract your guaranteed income from your anticipated inflation-adjusted expenses. This is the amount of annual income you will need to provide from your investments. In our example, $135,000 - $50,000 = $85,000.

The fifth step is to take the amount determined in the step #4 and multiply it by 17. It is estimated that at least $17,000 in investments will be needed to produce $1,000 of retirement income adjusted for a 3.0% inflation factor. In our example, we would multiply $85,000 x 17 = $1,445,000.

The sixth step is determining the value of investments that are specifically earmarked for retirement. This would include such things as 401(k) s, IRA's, annuities, etc. For our example, let's assume we have $300,000 in accumulated assets that we plan to use for retirement. We will apply an appreciation factor to our assets which will give us an approximation of what our retirement assets will be worth when we actually retire. The table below provides the appreciation factor based on the assumed rate of return and the number of years until retirement.

Appreciation Factor

Yrs. until retired	6%	7%	8%
5	1.3	1.4	1.5
10	1.8	2.0	2.2
15	2.4	2.8	3.2
20	3.3	3.9	4.7
25	4.3	5.4	6.8
30	5.7	7.6	10.1

In our example, we have twenty years until retirement and we've chosen to use a conservative growth assumption of 6% per year. That table gives us an appreciation factor of 3.3. We multiply our current retirement investments of $300,000 x 3.3 = $990,000. This is the projected value of our current investments in twenty years. The seventh step is to subtract our projected retirement assets of $990,000 from our target retirement assets of $1,445,000. This equals $455,000.

The eighth and final step of our calculation is to multiply the result in step seven ($455,000) by the investment growth factor found in the table below. We have twenty years until retirement and again using a conservative investment growth rate of 6% per year, the table gives us a growth factor of 0.0175. $455,000 x 0.0175 = $7,962. This $7,962 represents the minimum additional amount that we would need to invest per year in order to achieve your retirement goal. In the calculation of investment growth factors, we assume that annual retirement savings will increase by 5.00%

Investment Growth Factors

Yrs. until retired	6%	7%	8%
5	0.1568	0.1531	0.1495
10	0.0600	0.0572	0.0545
15	0.0306	0.0284	0.0264
20	0.0175	0.0159	0.0144
25	0.0107	0.0095	0.0083
30	0.0068	0.0059	0.0050

This eight step calculation can provide a starting point on your path to financial independence. Of course it is predicated on the assumptions that are used. In our example we used an investment growth rate of 6% per year and a projected retirement date of twenty years. Will our investments grow exactly 6% per year? If there is one thing I can guarantee, it is that over a twenty year period, they certainly will not. There are many things that can change as we move along the path to financial independence. Who knows what lies ahead? We may decide to retire in fifteen years, or we may become unemployed or disabled and have to delay retirement to twenty-five years instead of twenty years. It is critical to monitor progress at least annually to make sure that the retirement plan keeps pace with changes in our financial life.

Is it possible to guarantee that we will not run out of money before we run out of time? We know there are no ultimate certainties; however the Enlightened Investor can structure her financial resources such that the probabilities of financial independence are enhanced while the possibility of financial catastrophe is minimized. This is the best that we can do given the realities of the world. But in so doing we can hopefully reduce, if not eliminate, the gnawing anxiety of "Will I have enough money?"

We invest for retirement with one purpose, to create a stream of future income. The value of any investment earmarked for retirement is the income it can produce at some point. Remember our definition of financial independence; when you have enough capital and assets (investments) to create the income you want for as long as you will need it, such that work is optional and retirement is affordable. When it comes to retirement, it is income that is the key consideration. If you have a lot of wealth, but that wealth cannot produce an adequate income, it serves no purpose. As we move closer to retirement, we have to turn our attention from accumulation of assets to distribution of income.

In America, we tend to focus on how much somebody is worth in terms of total assets, i.e. "he's a billionaire". However, in other parts of the world if you were to pose the question "How much is he worth?" the answer would be framed in terms of how much income he can count on per year. The Enlightened Investor knows that assets and investments are merely the means, and that it is a reliable stream of income that is the end of the quest for financial independence.

We have explored a planning process that can be used to help determine how much additional money must be invested to meet your own individual retirement goal. For our purposes, let's assume that we were fortunate enough to weather the vicissitudes of investment performance, employment, health, and life in general, such that we found ourselves able to retire when we had planned with the amount of money that we had hoped. We would have successfully traveled the accumulation phase on the path to financial independence.

At this point we begin the distribution phase of the journey. This is by far the trickiest part. The primary concern of this phase is the question we posed earlier, "Will I run out of money before I run out of time?" The dilemma is this: if we withdraw too much of our investments or our investment returns are poor, we will run out of money; or if we withdraw too little or investment results exceed expectations, we unnecessarily lower our standard of living.

In working with retirees, their financial goals for the distribution phase of their financial lives typically takes one of two forms. They want to maintain a modest, yet acceptable lifestyle such that their net worth will continue to grow. They are looking for ways to maximize their wealth in order to provide a comfortable reserve in case of emergencies, and to leave a legacy to family and/or charities.

The other group is looking for ways to maximize their income such that they can enjoy the highest standard of living in retirement as possible. They may not have the bumper sticker that says, "I'm spending my children's inheritance", but that is their frame of mind. Most retirees choose to err on the side of caution. And in light of the market crashes of 2000-2002 and 2008-2009, it would be the prudent thing to do.

In either case, they are looking for an answer to the question, "How much can I withdraw from my personal investments, given the uncertainty of markets, interest rates, and life itself? Until recently, the best any advisor could do was to make assumptions as to the average growth rates of either stocks or bonds, or the assumed interest rates of fixed investments; and then project investment returns based on that rate, year in and year out over the life expectancy of the retiree. The fatal flaw of this technique is that average rates of return are misleading. We know that rates of return, whether from stocks, bonds, or fixed investments such as CD's are subject to wide fluctuation over time. Furthermore, we know that history is not an infallible guide to future performance.

The Achilles' heel of this approach is that the volatility of an investment portfolio in the early years of retirement can have a dramatic effect on the ability of the investments to provide needed income in later years. If the investment portfolio has better than expected performance in the early years, it turbo charges the portfolio's ability to weather sub-par performance in later years. Conversely, if the investment portfolio suffers worse-than-expected performance in the early years, the portfolio may never recover. Unfortunately there are thousands of recent retirees who were devastated by the market crash of 2000 and/or 2008 who have suffered a real-life lesson in investment volatility. Many of them have had to cut their standard of living or go back to work. The issue of prime importance to a retiree is not where their investments end up, but rather the path they take to get there.

There is a new planning tool which can help answer the question of, "How much can I withdraw?" It is called a Monte Carlo simulation. The Monte Carlo simulation takes information such as how much money will be withdrawn from the retirement portfolio, when the money will be withdrawn, expected inflation, historical returns of various asset classes, and whether the account is currently taxable, tax-deferred, or tax-free. The Monte Carlo simulation takes all of this information and uses what is called a "random number generator" to calculate thousands and thousands of possible outcomes of a given portfolio over time. What the Monte Carlo simulation provides is the ability for a retiree to examine the effect that investment volatility can have on the probability of success of a given withdrawal rate. It is important to realize, that just like other planning tools, it cannot guarantee results. It provides the probability of success based on past history. As such, it is a tool to assist the retiree and the financial advisor in structuring retirement portfolios such that they have the best chance to fulfill their purpose. Retirement income planning is an art and a science. When investors or their advisors delude themselves into thinking that it is possible to make the process 100% science, they set themselves up for failure.

We have explored several planning tools that can help you "put your arms around the problem" of how much retirement income can be generated from a portfolio without exhausting it before death. Based on my experience there are several additional rules of thumb that can be used as a guide. Many of these are common sense, however as they say, "To expect common sense in others is to show a distinct lack of it yourself!"

*   Retirees who want their withdrawals to increase with inflation must accept reduced withdrawals in the first several years of retirement.

*   Incorporating bonds or fixed investments such as CD's or fixed annuities can increase the probability of long-term success for reasonable withdrawal rates.

*   Investing in stocks or stock funds provides the ability to outpace the cost of living and therefore the ability to sustain higher withdrawal rates.

*   As a general rule, retirees should withdraw income from currently taxable investments first. Since these investments generate taxable income or capital gains whether you spend them or not, it makes sense to draw upon these assets first. The exception to this rule would be in situations where the retiree plans to pass the asset to heirs or to gift it to charity. Because of the step-up in basis at death or the income tax deduction for charitable gifts, it may make sense to hold onto these investments until death or until they are gifted.

*   Since tax-free investments such as municipal bonds are free from state and/or federal taxes, they also represent a consistent source of retirement income.

*   Tax-deferred investments such as annuities, IRA's, or qualified pension money would be last in line for withdrawing retirement income. Since these investments are tax-deferred, the longer you can let them accumulate, the greater the growth potential. Also recent tax law changes have enabled beneficiaries of IRA's to enjoy tax-deferral through the so-called stretch-out provisions. In this regard, it is

critical to review the beneficiary and contingent beneficiary arrangements on any IRA's in light of the new regulations.

* The last basket of assets that the retiree should draw upon is the Roth IRA. Roth IRA's combine the best of both worlds, they offer tax-free growth, and all contributions and earnings are distributed tax-free, provided that the account has been held for at least five years or the owner is age 59-1/2, whichever is longer.

The Enlightened Investor must remember that the only true safety in regard to retirement income is the guarantee of purchasing power. But in this world of uncertainty, is this possible? The American generations that came of age during the Great Depression and World War II were able to achieve safety through Social Security and defined benefit pension plans offered by their employers. Social Security is a guarantee of income provided by the government of the United States. Its promise is as safe as any promise can be in a world of uncertainty. Defined benefit pension plans are retirement plans that are provided to employees of corporations, unions, or government whereby the income benefit is a function of the number of years the individual worked for the organization and the final income of the individual. Based on this calculation, the individual receives a stipulated retirement income for the rest of his, and possibly his beneficiary's life.

Both Social Security and defined benefit pension plans offer the possibility of income streams that could not be outlived. The investment risk was borne by the organization providing the defined benefit pension plan, and the government had the ability to tax in order to provide the Social Security benefit. Add Medicare and Medicaid health benefits and you have a package of benefits that has come as close as anything can to providing absolute income security in retirement. Is it any wonder that with such guarantees, these generations of Americans were the only generations in the history of the world that could realize the dream of a comfortable and secure retirement?

The situation for Baby Boomers, Generation X, Echo Boomers, and the Millenial generation will be different. Less than 30% of American workers now have the luxury of a defined benefit plan. In all likelihood, these generations will face retirement without a defined benefit pension benefit, and a Social Security benefit that will not be as generous as in the past. What then to do? The answer for many of these future retiree's will be found in the use of annuities. Annuities may be able to replace the defined benefit pension plan as a retirement income stream that cannot be outlived.

The New World of Annuities

Most annuities have traditionally been purchased because they offer the ability to defer current taxation on investment growth. The tax-deferral feature is especially attractive to middle- and older-age individuals who may have investments that generate interest, dividends, or capital gains, and who let the interest, dividends, and capital gains accumulate instead of taking it in the form of income. Even though they are not spending the returns on their investment, if it is invested in a currently taxable investment such as a mutual fund, certificate of deposit, or bonds, they have to pay current income, dividend, or capital-gains taxes. The annuity allows the deferral of current taxation to some point in the future. This aspect of the annuity is referred to as the accumulation or deferral phase. As we discussed in an earlier chapter, tax-deferral can be a powerful tool in building wealth.

The other aspect of the annuity is referred to as the payout or distribution phase. The owner of an annuity has three options in the payout phase, 1) they can either surrender the contract for its value, 2) they can take periodic or systematic withdrawals, or 3) they can annuitize the contract into a stream of payments over a given number of years or over their and/or their beneficiary's lifetime. It is the ability to annuitize over a lifetime that allows an annuity to promise an income that you can't outlive. With many Americans no longer enjoying the guaranteed income of defined benefit pension plans, the advantage of creating an income you can't outlive will prompt many retirees to use annuities, in addition to create a foundation of income for their retirement years. The writer Dorothy Parker once quipped, "The two most beautiful words in the English language are, "Check Enclosed." The Enlightened Investor will look for opportunities to create guaranteed checks for retirement, and create as many of them as possible.

Upon surrender of an annuity, the owner is liable for tax on the gain in the contract. For example: If someone had invested $100,000 into an annuity and some years later surrenders the annuity for its current value of $300,000, he would be liable for income taxes on the $200,000 of gain. However, if he instead chooses to annuitize the annuity, the tax treatment of the gain will be more favorable. Each payment will be considered a partial return of the initial investment and a partial distribution of the gains. This allows the individual to spread out the taxation over a number of years.

An annuity is a type of insurance contract. It can either be a fixed annuity or a variable annuity. With a fixed annuity, you deposit your money into the contract; in return the insurance company offers a fixed rate of return for a certain number of years. A variable annuity, however, offers you the opportunity to allocate your dollars into any of a number of investment subaccounts such as stock and bond funds. This allows you the ability to seek higher rates of return. This comes at a cost, however. Management fees, similar to those charged by mutual funds, are assessed which results in higher costs for these type of annuities. Furthermore, your money is subjected to market risk. There is no guaranteed rate of return for dollars invested in the subaccounts. Annuities also have surrender charges, which means that you are obligated to keep your money in the contract for a certain numbers of years. If you withdraw more money from the contract than is allowed, a surrender charge is assessed.

Another type of annuity which has been promoted in recent years is known as an equity-indexed annuity. This type of annuity promises the best of all worlds, principal and minimum interest guarantees, along with the possibility of participating in the gains of stock market index such as the S&P 500. These annuities are extremely complicated and surrender periods as long as fifteen years or more. Investors who may be tempted by equity-indexed annuities should proceed cautiously. History has shown that they promise much more than they actually deliver, and because they are not regulated securities, the obligation of full disclosure is nonexistent.

It is not my purpose to go into a detailed explanation of annuities. That task would very well take a book of its own; however annuities offer a number of other benefits in addition to tax-deferral and the ability to create lifetime income. Money invested in fixed annuities or the fixed account of a variable annuity offer a high degree of safety and protection against market losses. Most annuities offer a guaranteed death benefit which guarantees both principal and gain in the event of death. For example: The individual invests $100,000 into a variable annuity contract. He chooses a number of stock subaccounts. He enjoys the fruits of a bull market and sees his annuity grow to a value of $300,000. However, one year later, a bear market has reduced the value of his annuity to $200,000. If he were to die, his beneficiary would receive, not the current value of $200,000, but rather the high-point value of $300,000.

Many variable annuities now offer what is known as a guaranteed living benefit. This guarantees some level of guaranteed growth or income, regardless of what the market does. For example: The annuity contract may guarantee that the value of your investment will increase by a guaranteed 5% per year. At some point in time, you will have option of taking the current market value of your annuity, or an income based on the guaranteed increase of 5% per year. The cost for this type of benefit is relatively expensive, however in light of the bear markets of 2000-2002 and 2008-2009; many investors are willing to pay for such a guarantee. Also these guarantees come with many underlying stipulations as to how and when you can exercise the guarantee.

Unlike mutual funds, stocks, or bonds, annuity subaccounts allow the investor to transfer money tax-free between different investment accounts within the annuity. And although annuities have surrender charges, most offer the ability to access some percentage of the account each year without surrender charge. Finally, annuities avoid the cost, delay, and publicity of the probate process. At death, the money is paid directly to the beneficiary of the annuity.

Another aspect of annuities is worth discussing. Because they allow tax-deferred accumulation, the IRS code provides for a 10% penalty tax, in addition to income tax on the gain, for distributions from an annuity prior to reaching age 59-1/2. There are exceptions to this penalty for distributions made because of death or disability. Also, the Tax Reform Act of 1986 created another exception to the 10% penalty tax on premature distributions. It is commonly referred to as a 72(q) distribution. It allows an exception if distributions are taken from the annuity in "substantially equal periodic payments", made at least once a year over the life expectancy of the owner of the annuity, or the joint life expectancy of the owner and the beneficiary.

In the event of financial emergency or early retirement, 72(q) distributions can create a stream of income for the annuity owner. It is important to note that distributions will still be subject to regular income tax. Once someone decides to take distributions via 72(q), the payments cannot be modified or discontinued for reasons other than death or disability before the later of age 59-1/2, or the fifth anniversary of the date of the first payment. For example, if an individual decided to take 72(q) distributions from her annuity at age 52, she would have to continue taking those payments for at least seven years until she was older than 59-1/2. If instead, the individual was age 58 when beginning a 72(q) distribution, she would have to take payments for five years until she was age 63. The key is that payments must continue for the <u>later of</u> age 59-1/2 or five years. After this, the individual can discontinue or modify the payment stream. In an era of financial uncertainty, this flexibility is an important and beneficial feature.

The IRS allows three methods of determining the payment amount under a 72(q) distribution. The first is life expectancy of either the annuity owner or the annuity owner and the beneficiary. The calculation is relatively straightforward; the value of the annuity at year end is divided by the life expectancy. As a person ages, their life expectancy decreases, thus the life expectancy method results in a smaller payment at the beginning of the distribution period and increases as the owner ages. Until recently, very few annuity owners who used a 72(q) distribution chose the life expectancy method. There are several reasons. First, most people who take a 72(q) distribution need money for some purpose, early retirement, new home, medical expenses, extended travel, etc. They typically are looking for the largest payment possible right from the beginning. As we pointed out, the life expectancy method starts small and typically grows larger. The second reason that life expectancy is seldom used to calculate 72(q) payments is that the payment from year to year can fluctuate based on the investment results of the previous year. Typically, an annuity owner is looking for a predictable stream of income.

The second method of determining the 72(q) payment is amortization. This method does, in fact, create a predictable stream of payments that will be equal. The calculation uses the life expectancy of the annuity owner or the joint life expectancy of the owner and beneficiary as of the date distributions begin, assumes growth at a reasonable interest rate based on the "applicable federal rate" as reported by the IRS every month. For example, a 50 year old with an annuity value of $100,000, an assumed interest rate of eight percent, and a life expectancy of 33.1 years, would receive $8,679 per year using the amortization method.

The third and final method of determining the 72(q) payment is annuitization. The payment amount is determined by dividing the annuity's account value by an annuity factor derived using a reasonable mortality table and a reasonable interest rate assumption as of the date the payments begin. This method typically results in the largest initial payments, and based on recent IRS private letter rulings, may allow the flexibility to revalue account balances and redetermine the interest rate factor annually.

As discussed in an earlier chapter, in the late 1990's many Americans, emboldened by the raging bull market, decided that they could retire in their early- to mid-fifties by utilizing 72(q) distributions from their non-qualified annuities and by using 72(t) distributions from their qualified IRA's and 401(k)'s. 72(t) distributions for qualified money are the counterpart to 72(q) distributions for non-qualified annuities. The rules and methods of determining payment are virtually identical. These people chose either the amortization or the annuity methods because they resulted in the highest payment right from the start. The disadvantage is that they were required to take that amount until the later of age 59-1/2 or five years.

However, during the bull market no one was concerned because the assumption was that the market would continue to generate double-digit returns forever. Unfortunately, the years 2000-2002 saw market declines of 40%-80%. Many of the early retirees found themselves between the proverbial rock and a hard place. Their account values had dropped dramatically and they were locked into taking large payments each year. Many were faced with the prospect of their accounts being entirely depleted within several years.

In 2002 the IRS, in Revenue Ruling 2002-62 gave some relief to those who had begun taking distributions from a "qualified retirement plan" prior to age 59-1/2. It allows a one-time change from either the amortization or annuitization method to the life expectancy method. The good news is that by using the life expectancy method, the retirement account will never be depleted; however the bad news is that it will result in lower annual payments. It is important to note that the ruling allows a one-time election to change that cannot be reversed. Also it applies only to qualified retirement plans and not to 72(q) distributions from non-qualified annuities.

The moral of the story is that 72(t) and 72(q) distributions can be a great financial planning strategy in the right circumstances, however, the Enlightened Investor will resist the urge to pursue investment or financial strategies that can blow up due to the unexpected event. She will be steadfast in her determination to hope for the best, but to prepare for the worst.

For many years, annuities were disparaged by the financial press. Annuities were too expensive, the only reason advisors sold them was because of attractive commission payouts, etc. Since the experience of the bear markets of 2000-2002 and 2008-2009, and the terrible equity markets of the last decade, these critics have reconsidered. The unbridled optimism of the investing public during the 1980's and 90's has been replaced by fear of loss and uncertainty.

In the late 1990's, the firm I worked with developed the first variable annuity product that contained an income guarantee feature. It provided a guarantee that the insurance company would pay 7.00% of the guaranteed principal per year and the payment would continue for 14.2 years, regardless of what the market value of the investment had done.

For example, if someone had an investment value of $100,000, the insurance company would guarantee payment of $7,000/yr. for 14.2 years. If in the third year, the market value of the investment dropped to $60,000 and never rose, the insurance company would continue to make the $7,000/yr. payment until the owner had received a total of $100,000. The cost of this protection was ½ percent of the account value each year.

We introduced this income protection feature at the top of the stock market bubble in 1999. Advisors would ask incredulously, "Why would anyone want this?" The assumption underlying the statement was that markets would only go up, and the possibility that markets could fall or remain dormant over an extended period of years was impossible.

It was only a couple of years later before all variable annuities were competing to see who could offer the most attractive income guarantees. Advisors were selling billions because clients loved the idea of being able to invest for growth, while having the protection of a guaranteed income stream in case markets did not cooperate.

In this new investment world of great uncertainties, the opportunity to create guaranteed income makes annuities a valuable tool to help assure financial independence.

IRA Distributions

Besides the equity in their homes, most Americans largest asset will be in the form of an Individual Retirement Account (IRA). When Congress first established IRAs some thirty years ago, I am sure they never imagined how successful IRAs would become. It was envisioned that retiree's would draw down their IRAs over time to create retirement income. In the event that retirees did not need to draw upon IRA assets for income, Congress mandated that at a certain age, 70-1/2, IRA owners would have to take distributions of some size each year. Up until recently, the rules and regulations regarding IRA distributions were a complicated tangle and a potential income and estate tax trap for the unwary. Fortunately, in 2002 the IRS issued final regulations regarding IRA distributions which greatly reduced the complexity. It has made the process simpler; however there are still traps for the unwary. The following discussion is intended as a basic guide to assist investors with their IRA planning.

There are four important time periods in regard to IRAs: 1) before age 59-1/2, 2) Between the ages 59-1/2 and 70-1/2, 3) Age 70-1/2 and older, and 4) After death.

IRA Period #1 – Before Age 59 ½.

We have already discussed IRA distributions prior to reaching age 59-1/2. The rule is straightforward. Premature distributions are subject to income tax and also a 10% penalty tax. However there are exemptions. We have previously discussed the use of 72(t) distributions which allow the IRA owner to take distributions in substantially equal payments over a period of time. There are several other exemptions available. They are:

Total Disability. The definition of disability is based upon the Social Security definition which is very narrow in its scope.

Medical Expenses which exceed 7.5% of adjusted gross income.

College tuition expenses for the IRA owner or family members.

The purchase of a first home. This is subject to a lifetime maximum of $10,000.

Payment of medical insurance premiums after receiving unemployment compensation for more than 12 weeks.

Distributions paid to a beneficiary due to death of the IRA owner.

IRA Period #2 – Age 59 ½ to 70 ½.

This period from age 59-1/2 to 70-1/2 is sometimes referred to as the "penalty-free" period. There are no requirements that distributions must be taken nor are there any penalties for withdrawals. Withdrawals are taxed at ordinary income tax rates. Funds in the IRA continue to grow tax-deferred if not withdrawn.

If the IRA owner dies before age 70-1/2, the spouse has several options in regard to distribution. The spouse can roll the IRA into his or her name and defer minimum distributions until his or her age 70-1/2. The spouse can also name new beneficiaries. The spousal rollover is by far the most flexible, and in most cases, the best choice for post-death distributions.

If the spouse chooses not to rollover the IRA but instead leaves it in the name of the deceased spouse, there are several distribution options. 1) The spouse must take distribution of the entire IRA by December 31st of the year that includes the fifth anniversary of the death of the IRA owner. 2) The spouse must begin taking minimum distributions over his or her life expectancy beginning by the December 31st of the year following death. 3) The spouse must begin taking minimum distributions no later than the December 31st of the year the deceased owner would have reached age 70-1/2. The minimum distributions would be calculated based on the surviving spouse's life expectancy.

IRA Period #3 – After Age 70 ½.

This is by far the most critical and complicated of the periods. The most important date within period #3 is the Required Beginning Date (RBD). The RBD is defined as the April 1st of the year after you attain age 70-1/2. An IRA owner must start taking minimum distributions from IRAs no later than the Required Beginning Date. This can be a trap for the unwary. The first element in this process is to properly determine your RBD. The key date is the April 1st of the year following age 70-1/2. For example: If Bob's birth date is 6/30/1936, he will be age 70-1/2 on 12/30/2006. Therefore his RBD would be 4/1/2007. On the other hand, Bob's wife Jill was born one day later on 7/1/1936. She will reach age 70-1/2 on 1/1/2007 and therefore her RBD will be one year later on 4/1/2008.

The other trap is that even though your RBD may be 4/1/2007, you are required to take a minimum distribution in the year you turned 70-1/2 which is the year 2006. Thus, if you did not take a minimum distribution by the end of 2006, you would have to take two minimum distributions in 2007. Unfortunately, many IRA owners do not understand this and as a result fail to make the proper minimum withdrawal in the first year. Failure to withdraw the proper amount of minimum required distribution from an IRA is no laughing matter. The penalty is one of the harshest in the tax code. Internal Revenue Code 4974(b) states that if the IRA owner fails to withdraw the minimum required distribution on a timely basis, an excise tax of 50% of the shortfall is imposed on the owner.

For example: If the required minimum distribution for an IRA owner was $10,000 in 2003, however the IRA owner only withdrew $6,000, the consequences would be severe. The owner would pay a 50% penalty on the shortfall of $4,000. That would result in a $2,000 penalty tax. In addition they would be subject to income tax on the entire $10,000 required minimum distribution amount. If they were in a 20% tax rate, that would be an additional $2,000 in income taxes. The bottom line is that they would be liable for a total of $4,000 in taxes on a $6,000 withdrawal. The message is clear; it is a good idea to take your required minimum distribution! It is also a good idea to seek the advice of a qualified financial advisor in the year before you turn 70-1/2 to discuss the issues surrounding required minimum distributions.

Fortunately, determining the amount of minimum required distribution necessary in any given year after the IRA owner reaches age 70-1/2 is much easier than it used to be. In April of 2002, the IRS published new rules governing required minimum distributions. The rules became effective as of January 1, 2003. The IRS has recognized that Americans are living longer and therefore they have adjusted the distribution table which is used to calculate IRA required minimum distributions. The result is that for most people the mandatory withdrawal will be less, meaning that more of their IRA accounts will continue to grow tax-deferred. One question that many IRA owners ask is, "Can I take out more than the required minimum in any given year?" The answer is "Yes you can." After age 59-1/2 you can withdraw as much as you want from your IRA without penalty.

The new calculation for required minimum distributions is very simple. You determine your IRA account balance as of 12/31 of the previous year. You divide that number by the factor in the IRS Uniform Distribution Table. The table runs from age 70 to age 115. Under the new rules, everyone will use this table to determine their required minimum distribution. The only exception is where the spouse is ten years or more younger than the IRA owner. In that case, they will use their joint life expectancy. Another important fact is that you always look backwards to determine the account balance, but always look forward for age.

IRS Uniform Distribution Table

Age	Distribution Period	Age	Distribution Period	Age	Distribution Period
70	27.4	86	14.1	102	5.5
71	26.5	87	13.4	103	5.2
72	25.6	88	12.7	104	4.9
73	24.7	89	12	105	4.5
74	23.8	90	11.4	106	4.2
75	22.9	91	10.8	107	3.9
76	22	92	10.2	108	3.7
77	21.2	93	9.6	109	3.4
78	20.3	94	9.1	110	3.1
79	19.5	95	8.6	111	2.9
80	18.7	96	8.1	112	2.6
81	17.9	97	7.6	113	2.4
82	17.1	98	7.1	114	2.1
83	16.3	99	6.7	115	1.9
84	15.5	100	6.3		
85	14.8	101	5.9		

Let's look at an example. If the IRA owner is 75 years old as of 12/31/2003, his factor from the table is 22.9. If the account balance in his IRA was $400,000 as of 12/31/2002, he would divide $400,000 by 22.9 which would equal $17,467. This would be his required minimum distribution for 2003. If he were 80 years old instead, his factor would be 18.7 and he would divide $400,000 by 18.7 which would equal $21,390.

If the IRA owner is 115 years old the factor is 1.9, and no matter how long he lives, the factor will continue to be 1.9. Under the new rules, you will never outlive your IRA if you only take required minimum distributions.

Another question that frequently arises is, "If I have more than one IRA, can I take the combined required minimum distributions for all my IRAs out of just one of the IRAs?" The answer is, "Yes you can." The IRS issued Notice 88-38 which allows the owner to withdraw combined required minimum distributions for multiple IRAs from only one of the IRAs. Conversely, the owner may take the required minimum distribution from each respective IRA that she owns if she so chooses.

The new rules have also clarified how financial institutions must report certain information to the IRS and IRA owners. Each year, starting in 2003, financial institutions must notify IRA owners age 70-1/2 or older that they need to take a required minimum distribution. Furthermore, starting in 2004, they are required to issue form 5498 to notify the IRS that the IRA owner is subject to required minimum distributions for that year.

IRA Period #4 – Distribution at Death

How an IRA gets distributed at the death of the owner is by far the most complicated aspect of IRAs. The new IRS rules have made the process simpler, but it is far from uncomplicated. Perhaps the biggest change in distributions to beneficiaries as a result of the new rules is the fact that beneficiaries can be changed at any time prior to death of the IRA owner. Prior to the new rules, once an IRA owner reached his required beginning date of the April 1 following age 70-1/2, he was unable to change the beneficiary designations in effect prior to that time. This led to many unfortunate situations wherein family and financial situations had changed, yet the IRA owner was unable to change the beneficiary to reflect such changed circumstances.

In other situations beneficiary designations were set up improperly and not discovered until after the IRA owner's required beginning date. The IRS finally realized the problem and changed the rules to allow a change in beneficiary at any time up until death. This was a welcome change, however care must still be taken to make sure that an IRA owner's beneficiary designations are set up properly to reflect their desires and to take maximum advantage of the tax-deferral available through what has come to be known as the "stretch" IRA.

Another major change in the IRS rules was that the identity of the IRA owner's "designated" beneficiary is not finalized until the September 30 following the year of the IRA owner's death. On the face of it this may sound strange, however it does allow for post-death planning to make sure that IRA assets are distributed efficiently and effectively. Once the IRA owner dies, additional beneficiaries cannot be named, however the existing beneficiaries both primary and contingent can use planning tools such as disclaimers and distributions to maximize the value of the IRA and to accomplish important estate planning goals.

IRA beneficiaries can be classified in three categories: Spouse, Non-Spouse (children, grandchildren, and qualified trusts), and Non-Qualified Entities (estate, non-qualified trusts, and charities). The type and number of distribution options available at death will depend on the category of the beneficiary.

In our discussion of post-death distributions, we must distinguish between death prior to the IRA owner's required beginning date, and death after the required beginning date.

IRA Owner Dies Before the Required Beginning Date

If the spouse is the sole designated beneficiary, she has three options which we discussed previously: 1) she can roll the IRA into her own IRA within 60 days of IRA distribution and she is then treated as the owner of the IRA, 2) She can choose to keep the IRA in the name of the deceased spouse and take required minimum distributions over her life expectancy as determined by the uniform table. She must take her first distribution the later of the end of the year she turns 70-1/2 or the end of the year after her spouse's death, or 3) she must withdraw all of the IRA assets by the December 31st of the 5th year after her spouse's death.

If a non-spouse is the sole designated beneficiary, they have two options available: 1) he must begin taking required minimum distributions by the December 31st of the year following the year of death of the IRA owner. The distribution period will be determined by the life expectancy of the sole beneficiary, or the life expectancy of the oldest beneficiary where there are multiple non-spouse beneficiaries, or the life expectancy of the oldest qualified-trust beneficiary. Life expectancy is determined based on the designated beneficiary's birthday in the year after the year in which the IRA owner died, and reduced by one each year thereafter. The first distribution must be taken in the year after the year of the IRA owner's death. 2) All IRA assets must be withdrawn by the December 31st of the 5th year after the IRA owner's death.

If a non-qualified beneficiary such as the IRA owner's estate, a non-qualified trust, or a charity is named there is only one option available. All IRA assets must be withdrawn by the December 31st of the 5th year after the IRA owner's death. A trap for the unwary is that if there are multiple IRA beneficiaries in different categories, the IRS will use the most unfavorable category for purposes of determining distributions at death. This arises most frequently when an IRA owner names a charity as a partial beneficiary of an IRA. Even though the spouse may be a 90% beneficiary and the charity only 10%, the IRS will determine that the IRA must be distributed by the end of the fifth year. In effect, the spouse will not have the other two options available to her.

As mentioned earlier, the new rules allow for post-mortem planning which can avoid the previous scenario. The new rules state that the designated beneficiary(s) will be determined as of the September 30th following the year of death of the IRA owner. In our example, we would distribute the charity's 10% share before the September 30th deadline, leaving the spouse as the sole beneficiary. She would then be the designated beneficiary and would have all three spousal options available to her.

Another planning trap involves the use of trusts as beneficiaries. The new rules distinguish between a "qualified" trust and a "non-qualified" trust. If the beneficiary of an IRA is a qualified trust; for purposes of distribution, the life expectancy of the oldest beneficiary of the trust can be used for determining required minimum distributions, instead of the five-year rule for a non-qualified trust.

The IRS has four requirements that must be satisfied in order for a trust to be qualified. They are: 1) The trust must be valid under state law, 2) It must be irrevocable at death, 3) the beneficiaries of the trust must be identifiable, and 4) the trust document or required information must be provided to the IRA custodian by the October 31st of the year following the year of the IRA owner's death.

Many IRA owners are tempted to name their living trusts as primary beneficiaries of their IRAs. Most living trusts drafted before 2002 will not qualify as qualified trusts for purposes of IRA distributions. Thus the trust will be forced to liquidate the IRA under the terms of the five-year rule. This is not a good life- or tax-planning strategy. In most situations the preferred beneficiary designation is to name the spouse as the primary beneficiary and the trust as the contingent beneficiary.

Furthermore, it is essential to consult with an attorney to make sure that the trust is a qualified trust for purposes of IRA distributions. This strategy provides the maximum flexibility for post-mortem planning. The spouse as primary beneficiary maintains the flexibility of the three spousal distribution options. If it makes sense to have some or all of the IRA go into the trust, the spouse can execute a qualified disclaimer which is a legal "no thank you". A qualified disclaimer must be executed within nine months of the date of death, the surviving spouse cannot have exercised dominion or control of the IRA, it must be in writing, and the surviving spouse cannot direct the disclaimed asset. Unfortunately I have seen many cases where the spouse has moved IRA assets from one company to another, or changed investment choices within the IRA shortly after a spouse's death. By doing so, she foregoes the possibility of using a disclaimer because she has exercised control. In the event of death, it is important not to make any hasty decisions until you can talk with a financial planner and/or an attorney.

IRA Owner Dies After Required Beginning Date

If the spouse is the sole beneficiary, she retains the same three options as she would if death had occurred before the required beginning date. If there is a non-spouse qualifying beneficiary, that beneficiary must make distributions either under the five-year rule, or over the beneficiary's life expectancy as determined by the uniform table. In the case of a qualified trust, the life expectancy of the oldest beneficiary of the trust would be used. This option is commonly referred to as the "stretch-out IRA". If a child is the beneficiary, she would be able to take minimum distributions over a long period. Life expectancy for a non-spouse beneficiary is determined based on his or her age as of his or her birthday in the year after the year in which the IRA owner died. The life expectancy is then reduced by one each year thereafter. For example, if the life expectancy is determined to be 40 years, the required minimum distribution for the first year would be the IRA account balance divided by 40. The next year it would be the IRA account balance divided by 39, and so forth and so on.

The advantage of this "stretch-out" is that required minimum distributions would be very small in the first years and most of the money in the IRA would continue to grow tax-deferred. If the beneficiary dies before exceeding calculated life expectancy, the beneficiary's beneficiary would be able to take minimum distributions over the remaining life expectancy. The benefits of a "stretch-out" IRA are certainly powerful in theory. However in practice and reality, most beneficiaries will be tempted to spend the inherited IRA money as fast as they can get it. It is tragic to see the money that a mother and father have worked a lifetime to accumulate and pass along to children, be recklessly spent within several years. In my experience most children perceive an inherited IRA to be a financial windfall rather than a legacy that should be managed prudently for the benefit of not only themselves, but their children as well. If parents are concerned about this spendthrift tendency, they should consult with their attorney to explore setting up an IRA trust. IRA assets within a trust can be subject to a maximum amount that the beneficiaries can withdraw per year which is specified by the parents. As the saying goes, "It doesn't matter what you own, it's what you control!"

On the other hand, many IRA owners would do well to consider using their IRA assets while they are alive. For all their advantages, IRAs have one significant disadvantage. IRAs are subject to both income tax and estate tax at death. Many IRA owners have considered using IRA distributions to fund long term care insurance or have used IRA distributions to purchase life insurance which can magnify the potential benefit of IRA dollars many times over. And unlike the IRA, life insurance death benefits are income tax free and also may be free from estate tax if structured properly. Other options include using the distributions to take an once-in-a-lifetime trip or to make gifts to charities.

Finally, if the beneficiary is a non-qualified non-spouse such as the estate, a non-qualified trust, or a charity; distributions must be made either under the five-year rule, or by using the IRA owner's remaining life expectancy.

As mentioned at the beginning of this section, for most Americans, the money in their IRAs will probably be their largest asset besides the equity in their home. As such, it is critical to make informed decisions in regard to distributions both during life and after death. The IRS has made significant changes to the rules which benefit IRA owners by simplifying the process and allowing IRA owners to magnify the benefit of an IRA, not only to themselves, but also to future generations. However, these benefits are not automatic; they must be assured by thoughtful planning.

Invest For Probability

Over the long run, there are very few exceptionally successful stocks in the stock market. The majority of companies are average. This is not to say that these companies are poorly run. On the contrary, because of global competition and competitive markets, the standard for performance is quite high. The problem arises in that when a company becomes very successful due to a particular product or process, other companies in a similar market will soon develop their own products or processes that will be in direct competition. Because of the very nature of competition, it is very difficult, if not impossible for any company to sustain a large advantage in the marketplace. On the other hand, companies that consistently perform poorly will either recover, be taken over, or go bankrupt.

Benjamin Graham, the father of value investing, wrote in his and David Dodd's seminal book, *Security Analysis*,

The truth of our corporate venture is quite otherwise. Extremely few companies have been able to show a high rate of uninterrupted growth for long periods of time. Remarkably few also of the large companies suffer ultimate extinction. For most, this history is one of vicissitudes, of ups and downs, with changes in their relative standing.

We have a number of sayings which reflect this phenomenon such as "what goes up must come down", "whatever goes around, comes around", or "nothing lasts forever". The scientific term for such phenomena is "regression to the mean". It is an extremely powerful effect and can be observed in nature as well as economics. The lesson of regression to the mean is that performance that is dramatically higher or lower, better or worse than the average is difficult to sustain and that at some point in time that performance will be reversed.

For example, when very tall parents have children it is unusual for their children to be taller than the parents, in fact most of the time the children will be shorter. Conversely, it is rare when very short parents have children that are shorter than they. Again, most of the time, the children will be taller than their parents. This is regression to the mean in action in nature. Very tall or very short humans are a rarity, in statistician's terms they are outliers. If the tall kept having taller children, and the short kept having shorter children, over time we would be comprised of people of great height or very short stature. Our general observation tells us that this is certainly not the case. The vast majority of humans tend toward average height. Nature does not tend toward the production of individuals of unusual height. The graphic illustration of regression to the mean is the bell curve. Whether you are measuring human height, temperature variation in a given location, or rainfall in an area over the years; the results will gather toward the median with fewer and fewer results the farther you proceed from the median.

It was Francis Galton, the Englishman who lived from 1822-1911, who developed the foundation upon which regression to the mean is built. It was through his meticulous observations and eye for detail that he was able to revolutionize the implications of probability. Before Galton, the study of probability was based on simply the randomness of results. His breakthrough was the realization that although results were random, there was a process at work in which "the successors to the outliers are predestined to join the crowd at the center. Change and motion from the outer limits toward the center are constant, inevitable, and foreseeable."[xliv]

For the Enlightened Investor, the implications of regression to the mean are profound. Whether it is the performance of stocks, bonds, or mutual funds; if you track the top performers from a given period, their subsequent performance over time will invariably regress such that their long-term performance will settle at or near the median. It is impossible to forecast winners and losers over a five or ten year period. It has been demonstrated that it would take thirty years of data to confirm at a 95% probability level that an investment manager's short term outperformance was due to skill and not merely benefiting from measurement error.[xlv]

Placing your bet on the stock, asset class, or mutual fund that is currently at the top of performance charts is a prescription for investment disappointment. Consider the average performance of the following mutual funds within different sectors of the market. The data was compiled by Morningstar for two periods of five years each ending March of 1989 and March of 1994. The results are clear evidence of regression to the mean within markets.

Fund Type	Performance 4/1/1984-3/31/1989	Performance 4/1/1989-3/31/1994
International Stocks	20.6%	9.4%
Income	14.3%	11.2%
Growth & Income	14.2%	11.9%
Growth	13.3%	13.9%
Small Company	10.3%	15.9%
Aggressive Growth	8.9%	16.1%
Average	13.6%	13.1%

The history of interest rates is also an excellent example of regression to the mean in action. Consider the history of the 1 yr. constant maturity treasury from 1962-2001.

1 yr. treasury 1962-2001

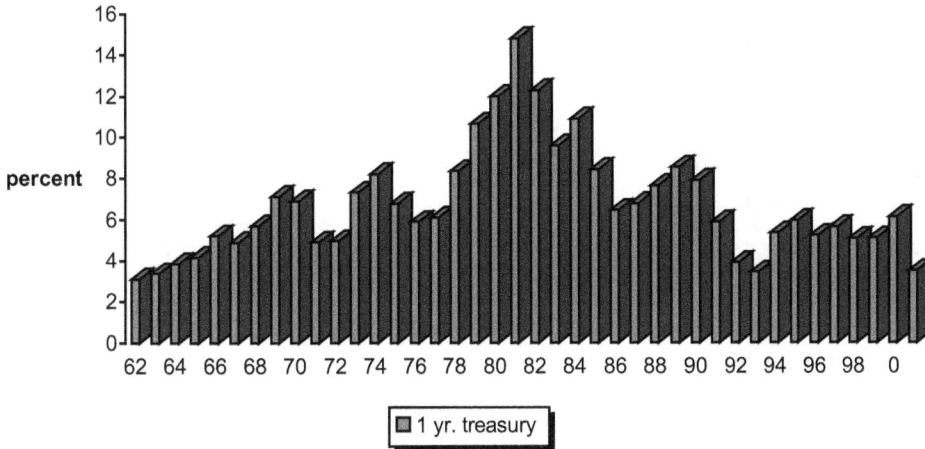

Source: Federal Reserve, 2003

The first thing we notice is the variability of the rates from a high of 14.80% in 1981 to a low of 3.10% in 1962. What then is a reasonable expectation for interest rates on a 1 yr. treasury? If we plot a trend line on the forty years of rate history on the 1 yr. treasury we see that the mean is somewhere around 6.5%. In the early 1980's was it reasonable to expect that double digit rates of return would continue indefinitely? Regression to the mean predicts and the actual history confirms that the answer is no. Conversely, is it wise to anticipate the historic low interest rates of 2001-02 continuing indefinitely? Absolutely not. As a matter of fact, mortgage companies are betting on regression to the mean when they offer the spectacularly low interest-only or adjustable mortgage rates currently available. Since the rates are variable at some point, as interest rates trend more towards the mean, the mortgage payments will increase. Eventually, many consumers will be faced with much higher mortgage payments on their adjustable or interest-only loan, or they will have to refinance at much higher interest rates. Although, at this writing in 2011, it would appear that will be quite some time before interest rates revert to the mean. Again, our short-sightedness betrays us in the long run.

1 yr. treasury with trendline

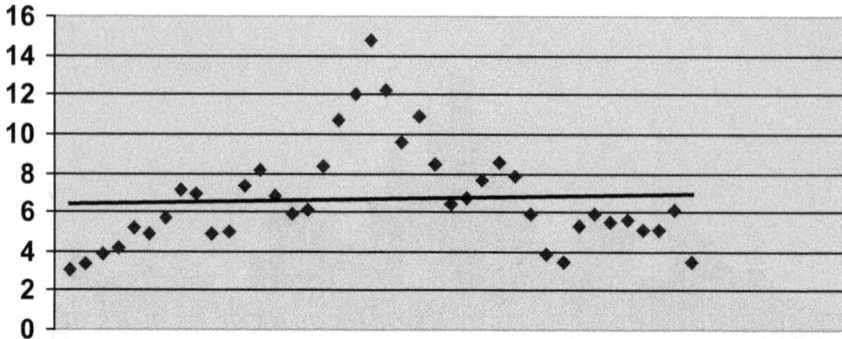

The Enlightened Investor understands that the implication of regression to the mean is to never blindly pursue short-term, above-average performance; nor to avoid short-term, below-average performance. However, human nature is near-sighted; it focuses on the short-term and extrapolates it into an imagined long-term trend. The Enlightened Investor will be aware of the conventional wisdom, and then assume that it is wrong.

If it is my intention to invest in a large-cap stock mutual fund, I should know that the historical mean return of such stocks is approximately ten percent. If my choice is between Fund A which just posted a -25% annual return, and Fund B which finished the year with a +20% annual return, I will resist the temptation to invest in Fund B and instead put my money into Fund A. While this is no guarantee that Fund A will outperform Fund B during the next year, based on regression to the mean, it is the choice with the highest probability of success.

It is important to realize that just as short-term performance cannot predict long-term success; regression to the mean is not an infallible short-term predictor of investment success. Markets are a random walk, particularly in the short run. Markets are not unlike the walk of an inebriated man, there's no way to predict where he'll take his next step! To take the analogy one step further, investors rely on short-term performance like a drunk leaning on a lamppost, more for support than illumination! Markets over-react and under-react, there is no way to predict its next move, nevertheless be this as it may, eventually regression to the mean will assert itself. However, there are reasons why investors have difficulty applying regression to the mean to their investment decisions. The first is that the process of regression to the mean may take a long time, five or ten years or more. Most investors simply do not have the patience to wait. The second reason is that regression to the mean may proceed so quickly within an asset class that investors are frightened by its volatility. And finally, sometimes political and economic events may be so cataclysmic that the mean is completely redefined.

The summer of 2002 provided a vivid illustration of regression to mean in nature. The southwest U.S. experienced the worst drought and wildfires in a hundred years. It seemed as if every day brought news of a new wildfire outbreak in California, Arizona, Colorado, New Mexico, Nevada, and Utah. National Forests were closed due to the extreme fire danger. A heavy price was being paid for the hubris of thinking that nature could be coerced into a steady state. Ever since Europeans gained dominance in the New World, they have used every technological means at their disposal to attempt to tame and control nature. They believed that they could tame wild nature; harness it to do their bidding. Eventually, however, nature will assert its will. In the summer of 2002, nature provided an object lesson in the power of regression to the mean. Because of our suppression of fire through the years, fuels built up in the forests, and it was only a matter of time before nature corrected the situation. Nature had decided that there were just too many trees for the health of the ecosystem.

I was struck by the parallels to the stock market crash of 2000-2002. The summer of 2002 was also the height of a record-breaking drought and wildfire in the stock market. Nobody thought it could happen. We had established the Federal Reserve, the Securities and Exchange Commission, accounting rules and regulations, etc. to tame the fires of market uncertainty. And yet, wildfire cut across the investment landscape, leaving charred portfolios in its wake. We had become too complacent. We lost sight of regression to the mean. We forgot that what has been will not always be.

As investors, we seek certainty. We want to believe that markets are a steady progression of gain. How many false constructs, bankrupt theories, and outright lies have been devised to make us believe thus? Fire is nature's self-renewal program. You may suppress it for a time, but inevitably regression to the mean will assert itself and the fires will come. So also with investing, we look at the beautiful forest of investment opportunities and are mesmerized by their beauty. We believe that the forest will continue to grow and grow. Once again, we deceive ourselves. We project the recent past into the everlasting future.

Eventually the wildfire will come. We must constantly remind ourselves that life and markets are ever-changing, that regression to the mean will eventually assert itself. And just as the fire clears the over-growth and the underbrush to make way for a new forest, low prices that produce future opportunity are not possible without periodic catastrophe and risk.

The Internet bubble and market crash of 2000 is an object lesson in regression to the mean. The extraordinary returns of internet stocks and the stock market in general during the years of the late 1990's should have been a clear warning that such extraordinary returns could not continue indefinitely. Looking back, we see regression to the mean in action. If the long-term average of stocks is around ten percent per year, regression to the mean would tell us that we may be in a period where stock returns will average below the historical mean.

In mid-summer of 2002, we witnessed a dramatic exodus from stocks and stock mutual funds into money markets and bonds. Unfortunately, those investors who re-positioned money into bonds and bond mutual funds set themselves up for more losses once regression to the mean asserted its will in 2004 in the form of rising interest rates and lower bond prices.

The Enlightened Investor will invest with probability. The odds are that markets will rise over time, and that investment patience will be rewarded. However, we know that the possibility always exists that fate may intervene and our best laid plans may go astray. Peter Bernstein, in his remarkable book, *Against the Gods, the Amazing Story of Risk*, relates a humorous anecdote which illustrates the problem of probability versus possibility. I have used this anecdote in seminars to help people understand the central challenge when it comes to achieving financial independence. It always draws the biggest laugh of the evening; however I can see the light bulbs of understanding flash as people realize the wisdom of the story.

It seems there was a professor of mathematics in Moscow during World War II. The Luftwaffe conducted bombing raids over the city every night. As the air raid sirens sounded, the citizens of Moscow made their way down into the bomb shelters below the city streets. Everyone except the professor. When questioned about his refusal to go into the shelters he arrogantly replied, "I am a professor of mathematics, I understand probability. There are four million people in Moscow and every night only a few are killed by the bombs. Thus the probability that I will be killed is very small indeed. Therefore I choose to stay in the relative comfort of my apartment, rather than go into the dark, cold, and smelly bomb shelters!" And so it was until a week later. When the sirens went off, people were surprised to see the old professor heading to the bomb shelters along with everyone else. "Why are you now going to the shelter?" asked his neighbors. To which he replied, "I am a professor of mathematics. I understand probability, but I now also understand possibility. There are four million people in Moscow and one elephant in the zoo. And last night they got the elephant!"

Our next chapter is a discussion of possibility, in other words the contingencies that we may face during our financial lifetime. This is the most neglected, and yet the most critical element, to achieving financial independence. Because, as the professor so eloquently demonstrated, you never know when you will be the elephant!

Insure Against Possibility

Mark Twain was fond of telling the story of his uncle who never owned any insurance, and was always sorry about it afterward! Twain spent his happiest years in Hartford, which in the late 1800's was the insurance capital of the United States. About Hartford he would say,

> *Hartford is comprised of the triple band of brothers, working sweetly hand-in-hand. First, as the Colt Arms Company, making the destruction of our race easy and convenient. Second, as our life insurance companies paying for the victim when he passes away. And finally, our fire insurance companies taking care of him after he's gone!*

As someone who started his career selling insurance, I know that most Americans share Twain's somewhat skeptical and suspicious attitude towards insurance. However, the idea of insurance is one of the greatest inventions of mankind. Properly utilized, insurance can reduce or remove risk from many aspects of human endeavor. Without insurance our economy would not be able to function. However most people would rather focus on what might go well rather than focus on what might go wrong and thus insurance is an afterthought unless it is mandated by law.

The Enlightened Investor understands that as we move through our financial lives, we face several contingencies that can destroy any hope of financial independence. The major contingencies are: death, disability, illness, and financial catastrophe. The value of insurance or risk management strategies is that regardless of what might befall you as you journey through your financial life, you and your loved ones can maintain some degree of financial independence.

In Seamus Heaney's wonderful translation of <u>Beowulf</u>, Hrothgar the elder exhorts Beowulf to be mindful of the fragility of life. Hrothgar declares,

> *O flower of warriors, beware of that trap.*
> *Choose, dear Beowulf, the better part, Eternal rewards.*
> *Do not give way to pride.*
> *For a brief while your strength is in bloom,*

but it fades quickly; and soon there will follow
illness or the sword to lay you low,
or sudden fire or surge of water
or jabbing blade or javelin from the air
or repellent age. Your piercing eye
will dim and darken; and death will arrive
dear warrior, to sweep you away.[xlvi]

We may not face as many risks as did Beowulf in his time, for instance we probably don't have to worry about javelins from the air, but then Beowulf never had to worry about automobile crashes. Consider the top ten causes of death for all Americans in 2009:

1. Heart Disease   598,607

2. Cancer   568,688

3. Chronic Respiratory Disease   137,082

4. Stroke   128,603

5. Accidents   117,176

6. Alzheimer's Disease   78,889

7. Diabetes   68,504

8. Flu and Pneumonia   53,582

9. Kidney Disease   48,714

10. Suicide   36,284

All other causes   600,280

Source: National Vital Statistics Report, Vol. 59, No. 4, March 16, 2011

There is no doubt that in general Americans are living safer and longer lives. The risk of premature death is not as great as it was just fifty years ago. However, in 2009, 2,436,652 Americans died from all causes. What is it that makes us believe that we will not be among that group in any given year? If the open discussion of money is taboo in American society, so also is the subject of death.

When death arrives unexpectedly, it is a financial event as well as being a traumatic, emotional experience. In thirty years as a financial advisor and working with other financial advisors, I have witnessed many situations of unexpected death. After the initial shock, the surviving spouse always has the same questions about his or her financial future:

Will I have enough money?

How long will it last?

Will I be able to stay in my home?

Will I be able to provide my children with an education?

It does not matter what the financial circumstances, the questions are invariably the same. I remember working with Mort, a financial advisor in Nevada. He called me one day to discuss investment alternatives for a large IRA that his client had inherited because of the death of her spouse. The size of the IRA was around $1.5 million and the net worth of the couple was approximately $6 million. While discussing the options for the IRA, Mort said, "You know it's interesting. No matter how much money someone has, when a spouse dies, the survivor always has the same concerns: Will I have enough money? How long will it last? Will I be able to stay in my home? Will the children be able to go to school?"

To the objective observer, Mort's client should not have had any financial concerns. Her wealth put her in the top one percent of American households. However, that is not the point. It is the psychological uncertainty that causes the anxiety. The miracle of life insurance is that no other investment can guarantee a specified amount of money at the exact time that it is needed. No one can predict when their life may come to an end. If the Enlightened Investor is serious about financial independence for her loved ones, insuring against the possibility of premature death is a critical component in the quest for financial independence.

It so happened that I was at a conference with Mort and other top performing financial advisors in Montreax, Switzerland in May of 2000. On a beautiful, sunny spring day, Mort and his wife, I and my wife, as well as a number of other couples took a day trip to Chamonix, France. Our plan was to take the tram up to the Aguille de Midi to admire the view of the Alps and in particular Mont Blanc. The tram ride was spectacularly heart-stopping as it ascended several thousand feet to a narrow rock outcropping. Stepping out onto the viewing platform induced vertigo as we looked over the cliff edge into the abyss several thousand feet below. The view of Mont Blanc was fantastic. We were literally and figuratively on top of the world.

Unfortunately, shortly after our return to the United States we received word that Mort had been diagnosed with terminal lung cancer. Within six months he was gone. The life insurance agent is often ridiculed for their attempts to use emotional and heart-wrenching stories to compel people to buy life insurance. However, these unfortunate events happen all the time. Who's to say that tomorrow it won't be you or I? It has been reported that after 9/11 sales of life insurance increased as the tragedy had a profound impact on how people viewed the uncertainties of life. And yet the numbers of Americans who do not have or do not have enough life insurance is still shocking. A 2004 study by MetLife of New York revealed that:

- 25% of working Americans who purchased a house in the previous 18 months had no life insurance.

- 32% of workers who had a baby in the previous 18 months did not have any life insurance.

- 40% of working Americans aren't sure whether they have enough life insurance.

- 63% of working women are very concerned about the effect a premature death would have on family finances.

- 70% of widows say the death of their spouses had a "major" or "devastating" impact on the family's finances.

It is not my task to advocate certain types of life insurance over others. Suffice it to say that the Enlightened Investor understands that life insurance is a key component of any plan to achieve financial independence.

The question arises: How much life insurance should I own? There are many different ways to approach this question. There is the simplistic approach which states that you should own life insurance equal to ten times your income; or there is the analytical overkill of a comprehensive financial analysis which factors in inflation, investment earnings on individual assets, income growth, etc. I would suggest that the best approach lies somewhere in between these extremes. A colleague of mine, Brad Tansom, developed a life insurance calculator which can be used as an easy way to determine how much life insurance you need, and also how much you are willing to afford.

There are two aspects to determining the amount of life insurance you should own. The first is immediate expenses. These are expenses that typically will be incurred within the first six months after a death. Examples of immediate expenses are funeral costs, costs to relocate, building a cash reserve for emergencies, and paying off short- or long-term debt. Depending on the surviving family's financial situation, they may have adequate resources to deal with these expenses without the aid of a life insurance death benefit. Nor is it necessary to provide funding for all of the expenses. For example, the surviving family may choose not to pay off debts, rather they may continue paying on them from income.

The second aspect of determining the life insurance need is funding for goals in the future. Such goals would include replacing the income of the deceased, providing funds for children's education, funds for the down payment on the purchase of a home, or funding retirement. Life insurance provides dollars at death which can be invested such that there will be funds available to pay for these goals in the future. Therefore we call them Pre-funding Goals.

The "Life Insurance Calculator" provides two columns; the first is the amount of funds that you would want to provide in the event of premature death, and the second column is how much you can afford. Unfortunately for most families, the amount of life insurance that they would like to have is much higher than the amount they can afford or want to afford. This calculator enables the family to determine a range of life insurance need based upon both want and affordability.

The most important of the pre-funding goals is the amount necessary to replace the income of the deceased. For most families, income is the lifeblood of their financial lives. We noted earlier that a survey of Americans indicated that most families would need financial assistance in less than six months if their income was lost due to unemployment. In one sense, premature death is permanent unemployment. And only life insurance can guarantee an amount of money to generate income at the exact moment it is needed. No other financial investment can deliver that guarantee at death.

In determining the amount of life insurance needed in the event of death, the first step is to calculate the amount of income that would need to be replaced. In most circumstances, that number will be less than 100% of the income that was being earned by the deceased. Typically a percentage of 75% of after-tax income is used. The income generated by life insurance will not be subject to payroll taxes, and depending upon where the life insurance is invested, may not be subject to income taxes. Furthermore, if there are four members of the family before death, there are only three remaining after death. Household expenses will not be as great, however they will not be reduced pro-rata by 25%. A majority of expenses such as a mortgage, utilities, etc. continue to be the same.

The second step is to determine how many years of income need to be replaced. If the surviving family has young children, the family will probably need more years of income than an empty-nest couple. I am often asked, "Do we need to provide income until the survivor is eligible for Social Security?" The answer is not clear cut. You will notice on the "Life Insurance Calculator" that there are two columns, "Want" and "Will Afford". The fact of the matter is that most people cannot or will not afford as much life insurance as they may need.

Determining the amount of life insurance is a compromise between, "How much would I ideally like to provide my surviving family?" and "How much do I want to spend on life insurance?" Income replacement is far and away the largest component of the life insurance needed by most families. I have never been an advocate of replacing income until age 62 or 65. If someone wants to do that and can afford to do so, more power to them. However, I usually recommend a period of years that will allow the surviving family to adjust to their new financial and emotional circumstances.

The third step is to make an assumption as to the growth rate of the invested life insurance proceeds. This rate of return can have a tremendous impact of the amount of life insurance needed. Obviously if I can earn 7% on the invested life insurance death proceeds, it will produce more income than if I can earn 3%. Let's assume that we can average an 8% return on the invested death benefit. Having determined a gross rate of return, we must then decide if we want to include a cost of living factor. Inflation increases the cost of living and thus $50,000 twenty years from now will not have the same purchasing power as $50,000 today. In our example we will incorporate a 3% cost of living factor. We then subtract the 3% cost of living factor from the 8% rate of return. The net discount rate to be used for our calculation is therefore 5%. The higher the discount rate, the less life insurance is needed to create the desired income. The lower the discount rate, the more life insurance is needed to create the same amount of income.

The fourth step is to go into the discount factors table. Based on the net discount rate and the number of years of income to be replaced we would determine the discount factor to be applied to our calculation. For example: If the net discount rate was 5% and we wanted to replace 10 years of income, the discount factor would be 7.722. We would then multiply the amount of income to be replaced times the discount factor. For our example, let's assume that we wanted to replace $50,000 of annual income. The calculation would be $50,000 x 7.722 = $386,100. Therefore, $386,100 invested at a gross rate of 8% would produce $50,000 a year with a 3% cost of living increase each year for ten years.

Life Insurance Calculator

Name of Insured: _____

Current Age: _____ **Sex:** _____

Need	**Can Afford**	**Immediate Expenses:**
_____	_____	Funeral
_____	_____	Relocation
_____	_____	Cash Reserve
_____	_____	Short Term Debt
_____	_____	Long Term Debt
_____	_____	Other _____

Need	**Can Afford**	**Pre-Funding Goals**
_____	_____	Income Replacement
_____	_____	Education Fund
_____	_____	Purchase Home
_____	_____	Retirement Fund
_____	_____	Other _____

Total Need: _____ _____

Existing Insurance: _____ _____

Insurance Needed: _____ _____

Income Replacement Calculator

_____ **% Rate Of Return On Death Benefit**

Minus _____ **% Cost of Living Factor**

Equals _____ **% Net Discount Rate**

_____ **Years Of Income To Be Replaced**

_____ **Discount Factor (From Table)**

Times $_____ **Current Annual Income To Be Replaced**

Equals $_____ **Life Insurance Needed To Replace Income**

DISCOUNT FACTORS TO REPLACE CURRENT ANNUAL INCOME*

Years	1%	2%	3%	4%	5%	6%	7%
1	0.990	0.980	0.971	0.962	0.952	0.943	0.935
2	1.970	1.942	1.913	1.886	1.859	1.833	1.808
3	2.941	2.884	2.829	2.775	2.723	2.673	2.624
4	3.902	3.808	3.717	3.630	3.546	3.465	3.387
5	4.853	4.713	4.580	4.452	4.329	4.212	4.100
6	5.795	5.601	5.417	5.242	5.076	4.917	4.767
7	6.728	6.472	6.230	6.002	5.786	5.582	5.389
8	7.652	7.325	7.020	6.733	6.463	6.210	5.971
9	8.566	8.162	7.786	7.435	7.108	6.802	6.515
10	9.471	8.983	8.530	8.111	7.722	7.360	7.024
15	13.865	12.849	11.938	11.118	10.830	9.712	9.108
20	18.046	16.351	14.877	13.590	12.462	11.470	10.594
25	22.023	19.523	17.413	15.622	14.094	12.783	11.654
30	25.808	22.396	19.600	17.292	15.372	13.765	12.409
35	29.409	24.999	21.487	18.665	16.374	14.498	12.948
40	32.835	27.355	23.115	19.793	17.159	15.046	13.332
45	36.095	29.490	24.519	20.720	17.774	15.456	13.606

- Discounting is a method used to determine the principal amount needed today to provide for a future amount. For example, if you need $1,000 in one year from now you would need only $971 of principal growing at rate of 3% today. The mathematical equation for determining the discount factor in this example would be $1,000/ (1.0 + .03) = $971.

We would then take our life insurance needed to replace income calculation of $386,100 and enter it under the Income Replacement section of the first page. We would then add all of the other cash needs and pre-funding goal needs to arrive at a total need for life insurance coverage. The next step would be to subtract any existing life insurance that may be owned such as group term life insurance or any other personally-owned life insurance. The difference would represent the additional amount of coverage needed.

The "Life Insurance Calculator" has been provided as a tool to help the Enlightened Investor begin to think about how much life insurance she may need to provide for her surviving family in the event of her death. However, I must emphasize that it is important to seek the advice of a competent financial advisor when it comes to the decision of what type of life insurance to buy. The value of a financial advisor is that they can work to put together a package of different combinations of life insurance products that can help the investor afford the amount of life insurance that they truly want and need.

Insuring against possibility also applies to more than just life insurance. We have previously discussed the use of stop losses to reduce the risk involved with investing in stock or bonds. It is beyond the scope of this book to discuss all the possible risks we face as we walk the path of our financial lifetime. Suffice it to say that we live in a world of uncertainty, guarantees are becoming scarce, and the unexpected will always happen and may happen to us. However, through the thoughtful use of insurance and risk management techniques, we can live our financial lives fully, knowing that we have protected ourselves from the "slings and arrows of outrageous fortune."

Education Funding

Many families with children are concerned about providing an education for their children. Saving for college education is often identified as one of their primary financial goals. According to the College Board, for the school year of 2011-2012, 44 percent of all full-time college students attend a four-year college that has published charges of less than $9,000 per year for tuition and fees. At two-year colleges the average price for tuition and fees is $2,963. At the other end of the spectrum, approximately 28 percent of all full-time private nonprofit four-year college students are attending institutions charging $36,000 or more in yearly tuition and fees.[xlvii] If that wasn't sobering enough, the College Board reports that college costs are increasing at two to three times the rate of inflation.

The cost of a college education is significant; however the cost of not obtaining a college degree is much greater. The effect of a college education on future income potential is profound. Although there are many other significant factors which make a college education beneficial, it is the future income potential that is most often cited as the most important reason for attending college. The following graph illustrates the difference in median annual household income by education. The graph ascends from no degree, high school degree, some college, college degree, Master's degree, PhD degree, and professional degree such as JD or MD.

Median Annual Household Income by Educational Attainment

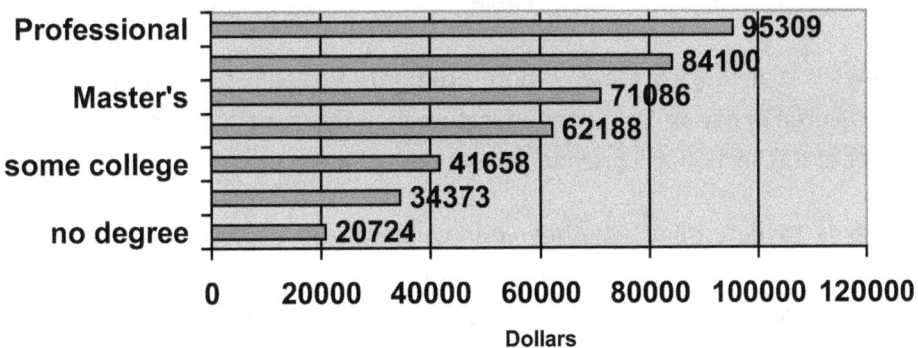

Source: U.S. Census Bureau

It is evident that a college degree and higher education has a profound impact on earnings potential throughout a financial lifetime, thereby explaining why providing for the cost of higher education is a priority for many parents. It is also evident that it is expensive and bound to become more so. These facts cause many parents consternation as they consider the question: "How will I be able to afford to send my children to college?"

Although funding their children's education is a worthy goal, most parents would do much better to concentrate on their own goal of financial independence before focusing on providing the funding for their children's education. If the parents have achieved financial independence or are well on their way to doing so, then by all means provide for children's education. The fact is that the parents have much less time to achieve financial independence than the children do to pay off college loans. For most Americans, if it is a choice between saving for their own financial independence or funding their children's education; they are better advised to concentrate on their own future. I write this as someone who financed his own way through college. Through a combination of work, scholarships, and grants I paid 100% of my tuition, fees, room and board. I will admit, however, that while I was in college I was quite envious of my peers whose parents had the financial wherewithal to pay for their education.

Many of the programs we will examine are better used by grandparents to assist their grandchildren. As opposed to parents who are still striving for financial independence, many grandparents have already achieved it. They are in a financial position to be able to help fund their grandchildren's education. I have often advised grandparents to help grandchildren when the grandchildren are young and need it the most, rather than keeping their wealth until they die.

The good news is that there are many more programs available today to assist families and children in paying for higher education than there were in years past. The remainder of this section will provide an overview of these programs.

The first step is to determine whether your child will be eligible to receive financial aid. Financial aid is a complicated and confusing area. The best place to start your exploration of the world of financial aid is www.finaid.org. This website contains an excellent guide to financial aid as well as a financial aid eligibility calculator to help estimate the amount of financial aid the child may expect to receive.

It is important to note that any investments and savings that you have can affect eligibility to receive federal financial aid. For instance, savings in a parent's name can reduce federal financial aid eligibility by at most 5.6%; however savings in the child's name can reduce financial aid eligibility by 35%. Pre-paid tuition plans reduce eligibility for federal aid on a dollar-for-dollar basis. Depending on the state or private college, they may have their own rules regarding financial aid. It is also critical to realize that 60% of all financial aid given in the 2001-2002 school year consisted of loans which must be paid back. Financial aid at both public and private colleges is typically available to families with household income below $40,000; however aid may be available at private institutions for families with incomes as high as $120,000.

Our discussion of college funding alternatives will first examine the various programs that are available if parents do not have the financial wherewithal to save or pay for their children's education.

Loans

In seeking loans it is advisable to apply for the lower-cost federal loans before looking to private loan funds. Furthermore, the best loan rates are typically available if the student is the borrower. The following loan programs are available:

Federal Perkins Loans: Federal Perkins Loans are available to both undergraduate and graduate students with exceptional financial need. The interest rate is 5.00% and the loans are made through a school's financial aid office. The school is the lender; however the loan is made with government funds.

A student can borrow up to $5,500 for each year of undergraduate study up to a maximum total of $27,500. For graduate students, the limit is up to $8,000 per year up to a maximum of $60,000. However the $60,000 includes the amounts, if any, borrowed as an undergraduate.

Other than interest, there are no other charges assuming payments are made in full and on time. Repayment of the loan begins nine months after graduation, leaving school, or dropping below half-time status.

Direct Stafford Loans: There are two different versions of this program. The first is the Direct Subsidized Loan and the other is the Direct Unsubsidized Loan. Direct Subsidized Loans are for students with financial need. The school reviews the results of the Free Application for Federal Student Aid (FAFSA) and determines the amount that can be borrowed. Interest is not charged while the student is in school at least half-time, during grace periods, and deferment periods.

Students are not required to demonstrate financial need to receive a Direct Unsubsidized Loan. This loan differs from a Direct Subsidized Loan in that interest charges accrue from the time funds are first paid out. Interest can be paid while the student is in school or the interest charges can be accrued and added to the principal of the loan which is to be paid after the student leaves school and the grace period has expired.

Direct PLUS Loans for Parents, Direct PLUS Loans for Graduate and Professional Students, and Direct Consolidation Loans: The terms and conditions of PLUS loans for both parents and graduate or professional students are the same. The primary conditions are: 1) a determination that the applicant for the loan does not have an adverse credit history; and 2) a fixed interest rate of 7.9%.

The Direct Consolidation Loan allows the borrower to combine federal education loan debts into a single loan.

The maximum PLUS Loan amount that can be borrowed is the cost of attendance, which is determined by the school, minus any other financial assistance the student may receive.

Before July 1, 2010, Stafford, PLUS, and Consolidation Loans were also made by private lenders under the Federal Family Education Loan program. However, recent legislation eliminated the private option. All new Stafford, PLUS, and Consolidation Loans beginning July 1, 2010 come directly form the U.S. Department of Education under the Direct Loan Program.

Other Federal Sources of Student Aid: The Department of Veteran Affairs offers several programs administered by its Education Service. Aid is available for veterans, reservists, National Guard personnel, widows, and orphans.

In memory of the late Secretary of Veteran Affairs, Jesse Brown, the Disabled American Veterans has established the Jesse Brown Memorial Youth Scholarship Program.

The United State Army offers educational benefits for individuals enlisting in selected military occupational specialties.

Administered by the Corporation for National and Community Service, AmeriCorps allows individuals of all ages and backgrounds to earn educational awards in exchange for a year of community service.

Parents and students will want to go to the website: www.students.gov which can provide links to scholarship and grant sites, state aid information and much more.

State Programs: States may offer their own programs so it is wise to check with the state where the student resides. Typically these programs offer discounts to the federal loan rates.

Grants

Grants are financial aid given by federal, state, and local governments and usually they are based on financial need. Unfortunately, most families do not qualify. The most familiar of the grant programs is the Pell Grant. The Pell Grant was created in the 1970's with the idea that it would be the cornerstone for the federal college aid program. Unfortunately, inflation has eroded its effectiveness. At present, a Pell Grant covers only about 40% of all expenses at four-year public colleges and only 15% at four-year private colleges. The maximum annual award for the 2011-2012 award year (7/1/2011-6/30/2012) is $5,550. A Federal Pell Grant, unlike a loan, does not have to be repaid by the student.

Federal Work Study Programs (FWS)

The Federal Work Study Program provides funds for part-time employment to help needy students finance the cost of postsecondary education. Approximately 3,400 postsecondary institutions participate in the program. Students must file a Free Application for Federal Student Aid (FAFSA) as part of the application process for FWS assistance. The FAFSA can be completed online at www.fafsa.ed.gov.

Tax Credit Programs

American Opportunity Tax Credit: The advantage of tax credits is that they are a dollar-for-dollar reduction in your income tax. The credit comes right off the bottom line. If your income tax is $20,000, a tax credit of $1,000 reduces the tax to $19,000.

The American Opportunity Tax Credit expanded and renamed the already-existing Hope Scholarship Credit program. This tax credit can be claimed for expenses for the first four years of post-secondary education. The credit includes expenses for course-related books, supplies and equipment that are not necessarily paid to the school. It differs from the old Hope scholarship credit because it allows the credit to be claimed for four years instead of two.

The credit is allowed up to $2,500 of the cost of tuition, fees, and course materials paid during the tax year. Also, 40% of the credit up to a maximum of $1,000 is refundable. This means that the taxpayer can receive this money even if they owe no tax. The credit is calculated based on 100% of the first $2,000 in expenses, plus 25% of the next $2,000.

The credit is available for taxpayers with a modified adjusted gross income of $80,000 or less for a single filer, $160,000 or less for joint filers. The credit is reduced if the taxpayers modified adjusted gross income exceeds those limits. Modified adjusted gross income in excess of $90,000 for single filers and $180,000 for joint filers cannot claim the credit.

Lifetime Learning Credit: The Lifetime Learning Credit is equal to 20% of the first $10,000 of qualified tuition and related expenses. The maximum credit available is $2,000. The credit can be claimed if you, your spouse, or your dependents are enrolled at an eligible educational institution. The Lifetime Learning Credit can be taken every year in which qualifying education expenses are incurred. This also includes graduate school expenses.

Since the American Opportunity Credit is only available for the first four years of postsecondary education, most taxpayers choose to take the American Opportunity Credit first, and then take the Lifetime Learning Credit after the first four years of college. The Lifetime Learning Credit is also subject to income phase-outs. For tax year 2012, the full $4,000 credit is allowed if earnings are less than $65,000 as single filer, or less than $130,000 as a joint filer. The credit is limited to $2,000 if income is between $65,000-$80,000 for single filer and $130,000-$160,000 for joint filers.

Distributions from Traditional IRA's and Roth IRA's

In general, early distributions from traditional IRA's and Roth IRA's are subject to a 10% penalty tax, in addition to regular income tax, on distributions before age 59-1/2. However, qualified higher education expenses are an exception to the premature distribution penalty tax. The definition of qualifying education expenses is rather broad. It includes tuition, books, supplies, room and board. The student must be in school at least half time in order for room and board to qualify. Even though such distributions are exempt from the penalty tax, the regular income tax is still due on the distributions.

Although this exemption exists to help pay for children's education expenses, it is typically not a wise financial decision to access the parent's retirement assets to pay for education expenses. This exemption does represent an opportunity for grandparents. Many grandparents have sufficient sources of income for their retirement and their IRA's are comprised of money that they will probably never need. If this is the case, the grandparents should consider taking distributions from IRAs to assist their grandchildren with education expenses. As I have stated previously, it is a far better thing to help children and grandchildren when they need it the most, rather than waiting until death to distribute assets. It is important to note that the money must be sent to the college directly for the benefit of the particular student rather than giving the money to the student. Such direct payments are not deductible as a charitable contribution; however the payments are not subject to gift, estate, or generation-skipping tax.

Employer-Paid Tuition Programs

For those individuals who wish to pursue higher education while employed, the Employer-Paid Tuition Program is an excellent option. If the employer has established a tuition program, up to $5,250 of employee tuition costs can be paid for, or reimbursed to, the employee with absolutely no tax to the employee.

In terms of financial aid and assistance, there are many avenues available to students, parents, and grandparents. Sorting through the myriad requirements and limitations can be time-consuming. However, the rewards make the effort worthwhile. We will now turn our discussion to the programs available to help save and invest for a college education. The first step is to decide how much you need to save or can afford to save. As mentioned earlier, many families will realize that they are unable to put aside money for their children's college education. The *Circles of Financial Independence* tells us that the first priority is securing financial independence. Once that goal is being adequately funded, then the parents can turn their attention to saving and investing for college education for their children. If and when they decide that they have the ability to save for college, the next step is to decide which savings vehicles will be most effective in helping them reach their goal. The following is a summary of college savings programs available.

529 Plans

These plans are named after the section of the IRS tax code which addresses these issues. A 529 plan is a program that is set up by a state or a participating eligible education institution that allows the taxpayer to prepay college tuition or to contribute to an account established to pay higher education expenses. Almost all the states, as well as many colleges now offer a 529 plan. As a result, there are many choices available. Unfortunately, the tax advantages, investment choices, restrictions, and fees can vary dramatically. It is important to spend the time necessary to make an informed choice. The assistance of a qualified financial advisor can help sort through the many options. Another excellent source of information is www.savingforcollege.com which contains information on many 529 plans.

The most important advantage of 529 plans over other college savings options is the tax advantage they offer. Investment earnings grow tax-free and beginning in 2002, withdrawals are also tax-free as long as they are used to pay for "qualifying higher education expenses". Another advantage of the 529 plan is that you can contribute up to $55,000 in one year. IRS gift tax usually limits tax-free gifts to $13,000 per year; however the tax law provides an exclusion to that rule in regard to 529 plans. It allows aggregation for up to five years of the $13,000 gift-tax exclusion. This allows front-loading of the plan to take advantage of additional investment compounding. Contributions to 529 plans may not exceed the amount necessary to fund the higher education expenses of the beneficiary of the plan account These expenses include tuition, room and board However the expenses may not exceed the maximum amount established by the state or educational institution, in most cases $300,000 per beneficiary.

If the education plan for the child includes attendance at an expensive college and possibly graduate school such that qualified expenses would exceed the maximum established by the state or educational institution, the parent or grandparent has the option of opening an additional 529 plan in another state or educational institution. The final advantage is that anyone can contribute to a 529 plan. Unlike most other college savings and financial aid programs, there are no income limitations. For families with above-average income, the 529 plan is one of the few tax-advantaged college savings programs available.

The state tax treatment of a 529 plan varies widely by state. In many states the contributions are tax deductible if you are a resident of the state that is sponsoring the 529 plan. Furthermore, many states do not tax the investment earnings or the qualified withdrawals from a 529 plan. In most circumstances, you must live in the state and have invested in its 529 plan.

Before we proceed with our discussion of the two types of 529 plans, it is important to note that once a 529 plan has been established and the contributions are made, there is no individual control of the investment of plan assets. This control is in the hands of the state or the private institution that has established the plan. A question that is frequently asked is, "What happens to the money in a 529 plan that is not used to fund higher education expenses?" IRS Section 529 provides for a 10% penalty on any withdrawals from the plan that are not used for higher education expenses. This penalty would be in addition to the income taxation of the plan earnings.

There are a number of exceptions to this penalty. The penalty may be waived if the child gets a scholarship or is disabled. Another typical concern is, "What happens if the plan's originator, usually a parent or grandparent, wants to change the beneficiary of the 529 plan?" For example, an older child decides not to go to college and the parents now want to name a younger child as the beneficiary of the plan. The good news is that 529 plan regulations do allow a change in beneficiary as long as the new beneficiary is a "family member" of the beneficiary of the 529 plan from which the transfer was made. The definition of family member is fairly broad. It includes the account owner's spouse, son, daughter, grandchild, niece, nephew, and first cousins. In addition, the rules allow for a tax-free rollover from one 529 plan to another, provided that the plans are for the benefit of the same beneficiary. These rollovers are limited to one during any 12-month period. Thus, if one becomes dissatisfied with a 529 plan because of excessive fees or poor investment performance, there is an opportunity to move to a different plan.

There are two types of 529 plans: College Savings Plans and Prepaid Tuition Plans.

College Savings Plans

The first type of 529 plan is the College Savings Plan. College Savings Plans cover all "qualified education expenses" at eligible colleges, universities, and other post-secondary institutions. These expenses include tuition, fees, books and supplies, equipment, and room and board. Withdrawals from College Savings Plans can be used at most colleges, universities, and graduate schools throughout the United States. The advantage is that you could live in Arizona, contribute to a plan in Minnesota, and send the child to college in California. It is important to note that plans differ in their provisions and restrictions, thus it is imperative to investigate a plan thoroughly before signing up and investing. Unlike a Prepaid Tuition Plan, a College Savings Plan does not lock in tuition prices. Also the plan doesn't back or guarantee the underlying investments. The investment risk is solely borne by the account owner.

For all of their advantages, College Savings Plans can be relatively expensive in regard to fees, charges, and expenses. It is critical to take into account the expenses of a particular plan when selecting a College Savings Plan. Larger fees and expenses can have a dramatic impact on the value of the account over time. The following are some of the most common fees, charges, and expenses found in College Savings Plans:

Enrollment fee- Many plans charge an enrollment fee ranging from $25-$100.

Annual Maintenance fee- These fees will typically range from $10-$50. A number of plans will reduce or eliminate this fee for state residents if you make automatic contributions, or if you maintain a certain cash balance in the plan.

Sales Charge or Load- Many plans will assess a sales charge if you buy certain investment options within the plan, or if you buy your plan through a financial advisor instead of directly from the state or educational institution. These charges are not unlike those found within many mutual funds.

Deferred Sales Charges- These are charges that you may pay when you withdraw money from a particular investment option or from the plan itself. It generally starts off at approximately 2.5% for the first year and then diminishes over several years to zero. Again, this is similar to back-end loads within a mutual fund.

Administrative/Management Fee- This is also referred to as the expense ratio. This is the annual percentage that is assessed to each account for expenses related to investment management and administrative expenses. These expenses can be relatively expensive compared to mutual funds. It is important to compare several different plans in regard to their expenses.

Summarizing the advantages of a College Savings Plan, they are:

- They can be used to pay for all "qualified higher education expenses".

- They have high contribution limits, some in excess of $200,000.

- No age limits and no residency requirements.

- The ability to begin a plan at any time.

- Tax-deferred growth of plan investments.

- Current tax-free withdrawals for "qualified higher education expenses".

The disadvantages are:

- No lock-in of college costs.

- No investment guarantees as the account owner takes on the investment and market risk.

- Relatively high expenses.

Prepaid Tuition Plans

A Prepaid Tuition Plan is the second type of 529 plan available. It features the ability to lock-in tuition rates today for the education expenses of a child in the future. Unlike a College Savings Plan, most Prepaid Tuition plans require that either you or your child must be a resident of the state offering the plan when you apply. Some Prepaid Tuition Plans limit enrollment to a certain period each year and also have age or grade limits for beneficiaries. Typically most of these plans do not cover the expenses associated with room and board.

In order to contribute to a Prepaid Tuition Plan, you pay for tuition in terms of years or credits in one lump sum or through installment payments. The price of the contract is determined prior to purchase. It is the responsibility of the state or the educational institution to make investments so that the earnings meet or exceed the increase in tuition cost until the child is ready to go to college. Therefore the account owner bears no investment or market risk. Prepaid Tuition Plans are based on the assumption that the child will attend an in-state public college, or a particular private college in the case of a Private School Prepaid Tuition Plan. However, if the child decides not to attend an in-state public college, or the particular private school, the money is not lost. All Prepaid Tuition Plans allow for the use of plan money to pay tuition at most private and out-of-state public colleges. A formula is applied to determine the amount that will be paid, in no case to exceed the actual cost of tuition.

Prepaid Tuition Plans allow the transfer of a plan to a child's brother or sister, although age restrictions may prevent a transfer to an older sibling. If a child decides not to go to college and a sibling doesn't use the plan, or the plan is cancelled, most states will only give back your original principal. There will usually be a reduction or elimination of any interest earned. And in some cases, a cancellation fee will apply. Although a Prepaid Tuition Plan guarantees college tuition costs, it is more restrictive in its provisions than the College Savings Plan.

Coverdell Education Savings Accounts (ESA's)

The Coverdell Education Savings Accounts function much like an IRA. In fact they were formerly referred to as Education IRA's prior to the passage of the tax reduction bill (EGTRRA) in 2001. With an ESA, the taxpayer makes contributions that are nondeductible. However, investments within the ESA grow tax-deferred and if used for qualified education expense, are distributed tax-free. EGTRRA increased the maximum annual contribution limit from $500 to $2,000 per beneficiary. This is important because a parent or grandparent can establish an ESA for every child or grandchild and put away up to $2,000 per year per child. Furthermore, they can make contributions to an ESA and a College Savings Plan for the same child or grandchild in the same year. As often is the case, the ESA is subject to income phase-outs. However the limits are much higher than some of the other programs we have reviewed.

The Coverdell ESA is easy to establish. The donor sets up an account in much the same way as he would for an IRA. It is critical, however, that the account be designated as an ESA. Contributions must be in cash. Also, a donor cannot contribute to an ESA after the beneficiary turns 18 years old. The beneficiary of an ESA must use the funds or designate a new beneficiary before he reaches 30 years old. A change of beneficiary is a tax-free event if the new beneficiary is a member of the prior beneficiary's immediate family or a first cousin.

No matter who makes the contribution to an ESA account, the beneficiary's parent or legal guardian controls the account until the beneficiary reaches the age of majority. Contributions to an ESA are considered a gift for gift tax purposes; however they are not included in the donor's estate for estate tax purposes.

In terms of distribution, the ESA offers an advantage not found in the other programs. Qualifying education expenses can include elementary and secondary education expenses and may be public, private, or religious schools. The ESA offers families the ability to set aside funds for education expenses without undo complication. There is no need to tie the program to a particular state or private institution plan.

Education Savings Bond (Series EE)

Education Savings Bonds are another simple alternative to 529 plans. The Education Savings Bond offers flexibility not found in other college savings plans. The parent does not need to designate up front that the savings bond will be used for educational expenses. There is no requirement that the bond be used to pay for educational expenses. The face values of Series EE bonds range from $50 to $10,000. Issue price is one-half of the face value and the Series EE bond reaches face value no later than 17 years from its issue date. Interest earnings on Series EE bonds are exempt from state and local income taxes, and if the bond proceeds are used to pay for qualified higher education expenses, they are also exempt from federal income tax.

For purposes of Education Savings Bonds, qualifying higher educational expenses only include tuition and fees. In order for the interest to be exempt from federal income tax, the bonds must be issued in 1990 or later in the name of one or both of the parents. The parent must be at least 24 years old as of the first day of the month the bond is issued. As is the case with many other programs, there are income limitations and phase-outs to the interest exclusion. For specific amounts you can refer to IRS Publication 550 at www.irs.gov. A key factor to consider is that the phase-out limits apply to the owner's income in the year of distribution of the bond, not the year it is purchased.

If the bond is cashed and the principal and interest are not used to pay for qualifying higher education expenses or the owner exceeds the income limitations, the interest earned will be subject to federal income tax. However, unlike other college savings programs, there will be no penalty. The disadvantage of Education Savings Bonds is that the investment is limited to Series EE bonds which historically have not been a high-return investment. Families that do not have the luxury of time on their side may find that the return on Series EE bonds is not sufficient to accumulate the amount needed for college. If however, a family begins to purchase Series EE bonds after a child's birth, the Education Savings Bond may be a low-risk method to pay for college.

UTMA/UGMA Accounts

Uniform Transfer to Minors Act (UTMA) or Uniform Gift to Minors Act (UGMA) laws have been adopted in every state to eliminate the usual requirements that a guardian be appointed or a trust be established when a minor is the recipient of a gift. It is the most simple and straightforward of education savings plans; however it is not the most advantageous. The disadvantage of these accounts lies in the fact that a gift made via an UGMA or UTMA vests absolutely in the beneficiary of the account once he or she reaches the age of majority. Furthermore, the custodian of the account is liable to the child for negligence in the handling of the account, and also must, at the child's request, provide a complete accounting as to the transactions in the account.

It is no wonder that there are many stories of parents establishing either an UTMA or UGMA account for their children with the express purpose of funding college, only to watch helplessly as the account reverts entirely to the child at the age of majority and is spent recklessly. Another disadvantage is the "Kiddie tax". It provides that if the child is under age 14, all income above $1,500 per year earned by assets within an UTMA/UGMA is taxed at the parent's maximum income tax rate, whether or not the parent is the custodian of the account. For a child age 14 or older, the income is taxed at the child's rate. Many parents who established and gifted assets into UGMA/UTMA accounts prior to the change in the tax law which established the "Kiddie tax" did so in anticipation that all earnings within the account, no matter what the age of the child, would be taxed at the child's lower tax rate.

Unfortunately, the "Kiddie tax" eliminated this advantage for UGMA/UTMA accounts where the child is under age 14. As a result, many parents who have existing UTMA/UGMA accounts have transferred assets to a life insurance policy. Because of the tax-deferred accumulation within life insurance, the "Kiddie tax" can be avoided. This "UTMA/UGMA Rescue Plan" must be structured properly to avoid adverse gift and estate tax issues, however if properly done, it can reposition UTMA/UGMA assets to provide tax-deferred growth and a self-completing education fund in the event of the death of one or both parents.

Taking Care of Long Term Care

The Baby Boomer generation is frequently referred to as the "Sandwich Generation" due to the fact that Baby Boomers' parents are living much longer than previous generations and that Boomers' children tend to depend on their parents' support much longer than earlier generations. This puts the Baby Boomers in the possible, or perhaps we should say impossible, situation of providing care not only for themselves, but also their children and parents simultaneously. We have discussed the many ways that parents can assist their children with funding the costs of higher education. We will now turn our attention to the issue of providing long-term care for either ourselves or our parents.

In the language of actuaries, the problem of long-term care lies in the fact that mortality is decreasing, however morbidity is increasing. In layman's terms, Americans are living longer lives, yet those later years are characterized by increasing periods of chronic illness and disease. A study by the U.S. Department of Health and Human Services indicates that 60% of Americans age 65 and over will need some form of long-term care at some point during their lives. Of that group, nearly 1 in 3 will spend three months or more in a nursing home, 1 in 4 will spend one year or more in a nursing home, and 1 in 10 will spend five years or more in a nursing home. Currently the average stay in a nursing home is nineteen months.

As we age, the probability of entering a nursing home increases dramatically. Statistics indicate that at any given time, twenty-two percent of Americans age 85 and over are in a nursing home. And because women typically outlive men, they have a fifty percent greater probability than men of entering a nursing home after age 65.

In the year 2002, seven million men and women over the age of 65 required long-term care. This number is anticipated to grow to twelve million in 2020. Most of these people will be cared for at home by family members or friends. In fact, family members and friends are the sole caregivers for seventy percent of the long-term care population. However, if an individual needs the assistance of a home health care aide, costs average $27/hour for such care. If specialized care is required, the costs can be much higher. For those Americans that will need nursing home care, the costs are substantial. According to the <u>MetLife 2011 Market Survey of Nursing Home, Assisted Living, Adult Day Care Services, and Home Care Costs</u>:

- The national average daily rate for a private room in a nursing home rose 4.4% from $229 in 2010 to $239 in 2011.

- The national average monthly base rate in an assisted living community rose 5.6% from $3,293 in 2010 to $3,477 in 2011.

- The national average daily rate for adult day care services rose 4.5% from $67 in 2010 to $70 in 2011.

- The national average hourly rates for home health aides ($21) and homemakers ($19) were unchanged from 2010.

The probability that you or your parents will need long-term care at some point in life is very high indeed. It is also evident that the costs of such care, either at-home or nursing home is expensive. Who pays for such care? Currently 40% of all nursing home bills are paid out-of-pocket by individual families. This number includes payments from long-term care insurance. However, private long-term care insurance currently accounts for less than 7% of the out-of-pocket total of all long-term expenditures. Another 12% is paid by Medicare for short-term skilled nursing home care following hospitalization. Almost half of nursing home costs are currently being paid by Medicaid, either immediately for those Americans meeting federal poverty guidelines, or after nursing home residents spend down their own savings and then become eligible for Medicaid.

Qualifying for Medicaid differs from state to state as does the level of savings and assets that the individual is allowed to keep and still qualify for Medicaid. The first step in addressing the risk of long-term care is to familiarize yourself with your state's rules and regulations regarding Medicaid eligibility.

The next step is to decide how you want to deal with the financial risk of long-term care. You can decide to take your chances hoping that you or your parents will be the fortunate ones who never have to face the issue of long-term care, or that if you do, the need for long-term care will be short-lived. And if you are not so fortunate, you can pay for long-term care out of current income or savings, risking financial impoverishment and loss of choice.

The other alternative is that you can transfer some or all of the risk to an insurance company through the purchase of a long-term care insurance policy. The decision whether to purchase long-term care insurance is not a particularly enjoyable experience. No one likes to think of their own death, yet I find that clients' denial of the possibility that they will someday need long-term care is even stronger than their denial of their own mortality. The purchase or non-purchase of long-term care insurance is a matter of risk management. It is simply a decision to transfer the risk to an insurance company by paying a known premium that offsets the risk of a much greater, though uncertain, financial burden in the future. The alternatives are to self-insure and hope for the best, or at worst rely on the safety net of Medicaid.

Most Americans are choosing to self-insure. According to the American Council of Life Insurers less than ten percent of Americans age 60 and over have purchased long-term care insurance. There are several reasons for the hesitancy of consumers to buy long-term care insurance. The first reason is the denial factor that I referenced earlier. Many people refuse to acknowledge the high probability that they will someday need long-term care, either for themselves or their parents. The second reason is that long-term care insurance is relatively expensive and can be complicated to understand. The third reason is that long-term care insurance is a relatively new business and it has been difficult for insurance companies and their actuaries to determine the correct amount to charge for premiums and still allow the company to make a profit, while at the same time avoiding pricing the product so high that consumers will not buy it. This uncertainty of future cost discourages many consumers from purchasing coverage.

Over the last decade, we have seen a wave of premium increases on long-term care products due to the fact that claim experience is running much higher than the companies anticipated when they first introduced their products. Premium increases of 35-90% are not uncommon. It has been estimated that only five out of every one hundred 60 year olds that purchased long-term care insurance in 1995 will still have the insurance when they need it because the increase in the cost of the premiums has either forced them, or will force them to discontinue their policies.

Long-term care and how to finance its cost is one of the most difficult issues the Enlightened Investor will face during her financial lifetime. There is no simple or easy answer. A compelling case for the purchase of long-term insurance can certainly be made. One needs look no further than the current probability that a 65 year old faces a one out two probability of spending some time needing long-term care. And as the individual grows older, the probability becomes much higher. In light of these odds, does it make sense to risk the financial independence that one has worked forty plus years to achieve? Is it fair to expect family or friends to provide both personal and financial care? Many retirees' greatest fear is becoming a burden to their families. The purchase of adequate long-term care insurance coverage preserves the ability to choose the type of long-term care desired.

A compelling case can also be made for self-insuring until impoverishment, then relying on Medicaid. The strongest evidence for self-insuring is that the average stay in a long-term care facility is currently nineteen months. It is a sad reality that once someone enters a nursing home it isn't long before death follows. Could you or your family afford to pay two years of long-term care expenses? At an average daily rate of $239, this would amount to a total of $174,470. Other than purchasing long term care insurance, there may be alternative ways of paying the costs associated with long-term care if and when it occurs. Two of the best methods of creating additional cash flow are a medically-underwritten annuity and the reverse mortgage.

Reverse Mortgages

For most Americans, the equity in their home represents their largest asset. Until the advent of reverse mortgages, there were two ways to create cash from your home. 1) Sell your home, or 2) borrow against the equity in your home. Both methods have significant disadvantages. If you sell your home, you are then faced with having to find some other place to live. If you borrow against your home, you have to make monthly loan repayments. Reverse mortgages created a third way to cash in on the equity of your home without having to sell or make monthly repayments. Sounds too good to be true, doesn't it?

The idea of a reverse mortgage is quite straightforward. It is a loan against the equity in your home, however the loan principal and accrued interest is paid back when you sell the home, permanently move out of the home, or at death. As opposed to a conventional mortgage where you borrow money to purchase a home and make monthly mortgage payments which decreases your debt and increases your home equity over time; with a reverse mortgage you are drawing down the equity in your home in the form of cash advances which increases debt and decreases home equity. Reverse mortgages typically must be "first" mortgages. This means that there can be no other debt against the home. If there is existing debt on the home it must be paid off before you apply for a reverse mortgage, or you can pay off the debt with part of the money you get from a reverse mortgage.

The money from the reverse mortgage loan can be paid in a lump sum, as a monthly income, or in amounts and at the times you choose. Furthermore, you can never owe more than your home's value at the time the loan is repaid. One common misconception is that when you take out a reverse mortgage the bank now owns your home. This is not true, you continue to own your home and as such you continue to be responsible for property taxes, insurance, maintenance, and repairs.

Reverse mortgages are offered as either a "public sector" or a "private sector" loan. "Public sector" loans are offered by state and local governments and must generally be used for the payment of property taxes or home repairs. "Private sector" loans are offered by mortgage companies, banks, and savings associations. These loans can be used for any purpose. The borrower has sole discretion as to how they use the proceeds of this type of loan. For example, the loan proceeds could be used to pay for long-term care expenses or for premiums on a long-term care insurance policy. "Private sector" reverse mortgages tend to be much more expensive than their "public sector" counterparts. The costs include such things as an appraisal fee, credit report, origination fee, closing costs, insurance, and a servicing fee. The costs can be financed as part of the loan and thus not paid out-of-pocket. Although the costs may be higher than conventional mortgages, one must bear in mind that the reverse mortgage is a loan that does not require income, asset, or credit underwriting approval and does not require monthly repayments.

Although the qualification process is easy, reverse mortgage applicants must receive reverse mortgage counseling from an approved HUD/Fannie Mae counseling agency before the loan process can proceed. This is a necessary protection to make sure that the loan applicant understands the process and consequences of such a loan, as well as exploring possible alternatives.

Counseling agencies can be located by calling 1.888.466.3487 or by searching on-line at www.hud.gov/offices/hsg/sfh/hcc/hccprof14.cfm.

One concern that is often expressed by those considering a reverse mortgage is, "Will my heirs be responsible for repaying the reverse mortgage loan at my death?" The answer is no, they will not be responsible. A reverse mortgage is a non-recourse loan which means that in the event that the sale price of the home is not adequate to cover the amount due on the loan, the bank has to accept the lesser amount as payment in full. Another related concern is that by using a reverse mortgage, the value of the home or the home itself cannot be left to heirs. This is true. In return for cash and income during life, the reverse mortgage loan must be paid at the death of the last surviving borrower, or when the house is sold, or when the borrower permanently leaves the home.

There is a way, however, to have your cake and eat it. By using life insurance on the homeowner's life it can create a replacement fund that can be used to pay off the reverse mortgage loan, thus allowing the home to be transferred to heirs. Reverse mortgages combined with life insurance on the homeowner's life make a great combination in the right circumstances. It allows the homeowner to create cash and income by accessing the equity in their homes while still allowing them to continue to live in the home. Furthermore, the homeowners do not have to make monthly loan repayments. At the death of the homeowner, the life insurance pays an income tax-free death benefit to the heirs to replace the value of the home, or to pay off the reverse mortgage loan and thereby retain the home within the family.

Types of Reverse Mortgages

There are three primary types of reverse mortgages available. They are:

- Single-purpose

- Proprietary

- Federally-insured

Single-purpose reverse mortgages can only be used for a specific purpose. For example, they may be used to pay property taxes or assessments; others may only be used to make home repairs. Single-purpose loans are usually offered by state and local governments and are the least expensive reverse mortgages available.

Proprietary reverse mortgages can be used for any purpose. They are typically available to homeowners age 62 and over without consideration of income. Proprietary loans are offered by banks, mortgage companies, and other private lenders. They are usually the most expensive type of reverse mortgage.

Federally-insured reverse mortgages are also known as Home Equity Conversion Mortgages (HECMs). These loans are available throughout the United States and Puerto Rico to homeowners age 62 and over without regard to income. These loans are offered by banks, mortgage companies, and other private lenders. They are backed by the FHA which means that the government guarantees that HECM borrowers will get all the cash advances that have been promised to them regardless of how long they live in their home, what happens to their home, or what happens to the lenders.

The HECM reverse mortgage provides the borrower with a number of cash-advance options. The options are:

- A single lump-sum.

- A credit line of a specific amount. The borrower decides when to make withdrawals and in what amount.

- A monthly cash advance for a specific period of time, or for as long as the borrower lives in the home.

The amount of cash a borrower can get depends on the borrower's age, current interest rates, and the value of the home. The maximum amount available is subject to limits that vary by county. The limits are based upon a county's median home value and subject to change at least annually. To find the current maximum mortgage limit per county, often referred to as "203-b" limits, go to the website https://entp.hud.gov/idapp/html/hicostlook.cfm. If you find that your home is worth more than the maximum limit for your county, you are still eligible for a HECM loan. However, the maximum amount available will be based on the "203-b" limit rather than your home's actual value.

The following table summarizes and compares the three types of reverse mortgages available:

	Single-Purpose	Proprietary	HECM
Backed by	State, local government	Private companies	**FHA**
Offered by	State, local government	Banks, mortgage co.	**Banks, mortgage co.**
Availability	varies	varies	**Throughout U.S.**
Can be used for	Property tax, home repairs	Any purpose	**Any purpose**
Loan types	Permitted uses only	Most types	**All types**
Loan amounts	Smallest	varies	**largest**
Income eligibility	Limited to low income	No limit	**No limit**
Cost	**low**	**high**	**Moderate**

As mentioned earlier, all reverse mortgages become due upon the earlier of death of the last borrower, sale of the home, or if the borrower moves out of the home for more than one year. Lenders can also require payment if the borrower fails to pay property taxes, fails to maintain and repair the home, or fails to insure the home. These failures are referred to as "conditions of default". Other default conditions may include declaration of bankruptcy, donation or abandonment of the home, fraud or misrepresentation, or condemnation proceedings involving the home.

Reverse mortgages also may include what is known as "acceleration clauses" that can cause the loan to become due. They include such things as renting out part or the entire home to someone else, adding a new owner to the home's title, changing the use of the home from residential to commercial, or taking out new debt against the home.

As with any significant financial transaction, you must take care to understand all the conditions that pertain to a reverse mortgage. If upon closing, you then decide that you do not want the loan, the law provides a window of three business days after the closing date. This must be done in writing using the form provided by the lender at the closing.

Reverse mortgages may have tax consequences and also affect eligibility for assistance under State and Federal programs. An American Bar Association guide states that generally "the IRS does not consider loan advances to be income." The guide also states that if you receive SSI, Medicaid, or other benefits with similar eligibility rules, that the loan advances are counted as "liquid assets" only if they are kept in an account past the end of the calendar month in which they are received. If these monies are kept longer than the calendar month in which they are received, eligibility for these programs could be lost if the total liquid assets exceed the limits the various programs allow.[xlviii] As always, it is critical to seek professional advice from tax, legal, and financial planning counsel.

Medically Underwritten Annuities

One of the most interesting techniques to create additional funds for long-term care expenses is through the use of a medically-underwritten annuity. Traditional annuities are not underwritten. This means that the applicant does not have to submit medical evidence of insurability. The reason is that in pricing a traditional annuity, the insurance company relies on the law of large numbers and probability theory to predict how many people will die in any given time period. They are amazingly accurate with their predictions. When an insurance company pays an annuity it knows that some people will die sooner and some will die later, however they can accurately predict how much they can pay given the age of the annuitant and still make a profit.

In contrast, a medically-underwritten annuity is computed only on the life expectancy of one individual. If the individual is young and in good health, the insurance company would anticipate that it would have to make payments for many more years than it would if the individual were older and in poor health. Therefore, a medically-underwritten annuity paid on an older individual in poor health would pay out more per year than a standard annuity.

This presents an opportunity to create greater cash flow in the case of someone who needs long-term care. By the fact that the individual needs long-term care, their health and life expectancy is probably not good. By using existing financial assets to purchase a medically-underwritten annuity, greater cash flow can be created to help pay for long-term care.

Other Long-Term Care Issues

Another question concerning the issue of whether to purchase long-term care insurance is, "How much money do I need before I don't need long-term care insurance?" The genesis of this question stems from the fact that if an individual does not have much wealth, they probably can't afford long-term care insurance and they will be covered by Medicaid anyway. Conversely, an individual with substantial wealth can afford to pay the premiums but doesn't need to because they have enough wealth to self-insure. Unfortunately there is a lot of misinformation in the financial media concerning this issue. Typically the media advice-givers will claim that if you have less than $500,000 in assets, you can't afford and therefore shouldn't buy long-term care insurance. If you have more than $1.5 million, you don't need and therefore shouldn't buy long-term care insurance because you can afford to pay the costs of any long-term care you may require.

People love easy answers to complicated problems. As you probably have surmised by now, I believe that there are easy answers to every problem and that almost every one of them is wrong! I am fascinated that long-term care insurance is the only insurance subjected to this simplistic analysis. I don't think I have ever heard anyone suggest that at a certain level of wealth, health insurance is not needed. Nor would anyone suggest that at a certain level of wealth, homeowners or automobile liability insurance would not be needed. I remember asking a successful businessman the secret to his success. He replied, "I never kept a risk that I couldn't transfer to an insurance company." The consensus among long term care insurance specialists is that households with net worth's between $100,000 and $2,000,000 should consider the purchase of long-term care insurance.

The Enlightened Investor will not be led astray by simplistic formulas when it comes to the decision to purchase long-term care insurance. As noted earlier, it is perhaps one of the most difficult and complex decisions that will be faced during a financial lifetime. Just like life insurance, it is an issue that is freighted with emotion and colored by family experience.

We can, however, look to several guidelines in deciding whether the purchase of long-term care makes sense. First, you should be able to pay the long-term care premium without sacrificing your lifestyle. Do not buy what you cannot afford. Furthermore, realize that if the premium is barely affordable today, it may become impossible if premiums increase in the future. And it would probably be a safe bet to assume the premiums will continue to increase. Second, if you need to dip into your nest egg to pay for long-term care premiums it is probably a warning signal that the coverage may not be affordable. Finally, if you have the financial means to self-insure, it may make sense to consider long-term care insurance from an estate-planning or risk management perspective.

If after due consideration you decide to purchase long-term care insurance, there are many factors to consider. The following is an overview of what is available and what to look for in purchasing long-term care insurance.

What Does Long-Term Care Insurance Cover?

There are two basic types of long-term care insurance in terms of how claims are paid. The first type is what is known as an indemnity policy. This means that the insurance company will pay a fixed dollar amount for each day that you are receiving care either in a nursing home or at home. An indemnity policy does not take into consideration the actual costs incurred for long-term care. When a claim is approved, a check in the amount of coverage is issued regardless of the actual cost of care. For example, if an individual has an indemnity type long- term care policy that has a $200 daily benefit, the policy will pay $200 per day even though the actual cost of care may be $150 per day.

The other type of long-term care policy is known as a reimbursement policy. This type of long-term care policy only reimburses the individual for the actual expenses incurred up to, but not exceeding the policy benefit limits. In our previous example of a policy that had a $200 daily benefit, however the actual cost of care was $150 per day, a reimbursement policy would pay only the actual cost of care of $150 per day.

Indemnity type policies are advantageous because they pay the actual benefit regardless of the actual cost of care. Administration costs for the insurance company are much lower than a reimbursement type policy because the insurance company does not need to spend the time and money to track the actual incurred cost of care. Once the claim triggers are satisfied, they pay the actual dollar amount specified in the policy. The advantage to the policyholder is that they may receive more money from the insurance company than they actually paid for long-term care. The disadvantage of an indemnity policy is that they are typically more expensive than a reimbursement type policy.

The advantage of a reimbursement type policy is that they are usually less expensive per dollar of benefit than an indemnity policy. The reason for this cost advantage is that the insurance company does not have the risk of potentially overpaying claims. The choice of whether to purchase an indemnity type policy or a reimbursement type policy must be considered on a case-by-case basis. One type is not necessarily better than another. It depends on the cost of premiums and the individual insured's situation.

The newest generation of long-term care insurance policies features "integrated" or "pooled" benefits. This contract provides a total dollar amount that can be used for different types of long-term care such as nursing home, assisted living expenses, or home care. This type of policy will provide a total benefit subject to a per day limitation. For example, it may provide for $300,000 total benefit with a maximum of $200 per day. Several long-term care policies now offer benefit payments in terms of a dollar amount per month as opposed to a daily benefit. This can be an advantageous feature, especially for those claimants receiving home care.

Many policies also offer an inflation adjustment feature which increases the benefit amount by a specified percentage. With long-term care costs increasing faster than the rate of inflation, adding an inflation rider is an important consideration. If you bought your policy at age 60 and don't have a claim until you are age 80, the benefit that was sufficient twenty years ago probably will not be sufficient to cover the current cost of care.   Unfortunately, an American Association of Retired Persons study indicates that sixty percent of long-term care insurance is being purchased without inflation coverage. This is due to the fact that an inflation rider may add from 40% to 80% more to the base premium. Recently we have seen a trend among insurers to discontinue offering inflation riders on long term care insurance.

The daily benefit amount available usually ranges from $50 up to $500 per day for nursing home coverage. It is important to determine whether the policy's benefit differs for home care. In many policies the daily amount for home care is less than the amount for nursing home care.   The average daily benefit being purchased for long-term care insurance averages $130-$140 per day. Typically an individual purchasing long-term care insurance will choose a daily benefit that is

90% of the average cost of daily nursing home care in his or her geographical area. It is important to note that any nursing home care or home care expenses that exceed the daily maximum of the policy will be the responsibility of the individual.

Many policies have an elimination period. This refers to the number of days that the individual must be in residence at a nursing home or the number of home care visits received before the policy benefits will begin. For example, a thirty day elimination period means that the policy will begin to pay a benefit beginning the 31st day. The longer the elimination period selected, the lower the premium. Another advantage of a longer elimination period is that the medical underwriting tends not to be as stringent as it is for a short elimination period. Elimination periods from 0 to 100 days are common, although up to one year is available on some policies. Most long-term care insurance buyers choose an elimination period between 60-90 days.

The cost of long-term care insurance is determined by your age at purchase, the benefits selected, and the elimination period. It is advisable to determine the amount of time that you could cover long-term expenses out-of-pocket before such expenses would threaten your financial security. As noted earlier, the longer the elimination period, the lower the premium. Current statistics indicate that forty-five percent of nursing home stays last three months or less, however more than one-third last one year or longer. It is important to keep in mind that the primary purpose of long-term care insurance is to provide coverage in case of a prolonged nursing home stay or home care period.

If an individual is in reasonably good health and between the ages of 18 and 84, you may be able to purchase long-term care insurance. The age limitation applies only to the age at the time of purchase of the policy, not the age at which you might need the insurance. Almost all long-term care insurance that is sold to individuals is guaranteed renewable. What this means is that the company cannot cancel your policy as long as premiums are paid and you have honestly and fully disclosed the state of your health on the initial policy application. Guaranteed renewable does not, however, mean that premiums cannot be increased. Premiums are subject to increase only if they are increased for an entire group of policyholders. Many policies also contain a provision for waiver of premium. This provision means that you do not have to continue to pay premiums if, and when, you are receiving benefits from the policy. Usually there is a period of ninety days of care required before the premiums are waived.

Many long-term care insurance policies now offer an optional benefit which is known as nonforfeiture benefits. The most common types of nonforfeiture benefits are a return of premium provision or a shortened benefit period. The return of premium benefit typically provides a return of a percentage of the sum of premiums paid after a policy has been terminated due to death of the insured or lapse of the policy. A shortened benefit period provides that if the policy is lapsed, the long-term care coverage continues, but the benefit period or benefit amount is reduced. Without optional nonforfeiture benefit coverage, if the long-term care insurance is terminated, there is no refund of premium to the policyholder. Standard long-term care policies are similar to car insurance, homeowners insurance, and term life insurance. If there are no claims, the premiums cannot be recovered. Long-term care policies with the nonforfeiture option are similar to cash value life insurance. As with other optional coverage, a nonforfeiture benefit can add twenty to one hundred percent to the policy's premium cost. Because of this additional cost, very few long-term care insurance policies are purchased with such return-of-premium provisions.

Long-term care insurance policies are categorized as either qualified or non-qualified. The categories were created by the Health Insurance Portability and Accountability Act of 1996 (HIPAA) which became law in 1997. HIPAA went a long way towards standardizing long-term care insurance provisions. It also mandated that if a long-term care insurance policy were to be eligible for tax-favored status, it would have to meet the requirements of HIPAA. These policies are referred to as "qualified". Policies that do not meet the requirements of HIPAA are referred to as "nonqualified".

Qualified long-term care insurance will pay benefits when a need is established by either: 1) the inability of the insured to perform two out of six functions or activities of daily living. The six activities are bathing, dressing, eating, continence, toileting, or transferring; or 2) when care is needed due to cognitive impairment such as Alzheimer's disease. Qualified policies also require that a qualified physician must certify that the insured will spend 90 days or longer in need of long-term care.

Non-qualified policies also will pay benefits when there is inability to perform the activities of daily living or upon cognitive impairment. Non-qualified policies also have one additional "trigger" to pay benefits which is "medical necessity". Both "qualified" and "non-qualified" policies are available for purchase. Both types of policies are valid and legitimate forms of long-term care insurance. The primary difference lies in when benefits will be paid and also the tax treatment of premiums and benefits.

Most policies issued today are comprehensive in scope and cover skilled, intermediate, and custodial care in state-licensed nursing homes. They also provide for home care services such as skilled or nonskilled nursing care, physical therapy, homemakers, and home health aides provided by state-licensed and/or Medicare-certified home health agencies. Coverage is also often provided for assisted living, adult daycare, alternate care, and respite care for the caregiver.

There are certain things that long-term care insurance will not cover. It is important to determine exactly what exclusions and limitations are contained within the long-term care insurance policy you may be considering. Typically the insurance company will require that a certain period of time pass before the policy will pay for long-term care related to a health issue that the insured had before they applied for the policy. These are referred to as preexisting conditions. Alcoholism, drug abuse, some mental and nervous disorders, and care necessitated by an intentionally self-inflicted injury are usually specifically excluded from coverage.

In considering the purchase of long-term care insurance, I recommend that the consumer follow a three-step process. The three steps in order of importance are:

1) Analyze the insurance company offering the policy. What are their ratings for financial strength from the various rating agencies? How long have they been in the business of long-term care insurance? It is recommended that you only consider companies that have been offering long-term care insurance for five years or more. Has the insurance company ever raised rates on its long-term care policies? And if so, by how much and when?

2) What features and benefits does the particular policy offer?

3) How much does it cost?

The National Association of Insurance Commissioners, an organization of state insurance commissioners, has developed standards that aim to protect consumers in the purchase of long-term care insurance. Their recommendations as to what to look for in a long-term care insurance policy are as follows:

- The policy should provide for at least one year of nursing home or home health care coverage. This should also include intermediate and custodial care. The nursing home or home health care benefits should not be limited primarily to skilled care.

- Alzheimer's disease should be covered if the policyholder develops the condition after policy purchase.

- The policy should offer an inflation protection rider. This option should offer a choice between automatically increasing the initial benefit on an annual basis, a guaranteed right to increase policy benefits periodically without providing evidence of insurability, or providing coverage for a specific percentage of actual or reasonable charges.

- The policy should contain an "outline of coverage" that describes the policy's benefits, limitations, and exclusions. It should also offer a long-term care insurance shopper's guide that can assist in deciding whether long-term care insurance is appropriate.

- The policy should contain a guarantee that it cannot be canceled, non-renewed, or otherwise terminated because of increasing age or deterioration in physical or mental health.

- It should contain the right to return the policy within 30 days after you have purchased the policy and to obtain a full refund.

- It should not have any requirement that states that the insured must first be hospitalized in order to receive nursing home or home care benefits, or first receive skilled nursing home care before receiving intermediate or custodial nursing home care, or first receive nursing home care before receiving benefits for home health care.

In addition, there are several other important elements. In the policy language it is important to compare how the company will reimburse benefits. The best definition is one that states, "The Company will reimburse for actual expense". If the definition contains phrases such as, "The Company will pay the prevailing" or "The Company will pay the usual and customary", it is possible they may use these ambiguous definitions to weasel out of paying the actual expenses incurred for care.

It is also important to ask how the insurance company treats care coordination. Is it at the Company's discretion or the policyholder's? Also, it is critical to be sure you know exactly how the home health care benefits function.

Hybrid Products

As mentioned earlier, many consumers do not purchase traditional long term care insurance because of two reasons:

1. Uncertainty of claim. Most traditional long term care insurance policies do not have cash values or any money-back provisions. Therefore, if you do not have any claims, the money you paid in premiums can never be recouped.

2. Uncertainty of price. Insurance companies can raise the premiums on previously issued policies. They cannot randomly raise premiums on any given policyholder, however they can raise premiums on a given policy issued within the particular state. We have seen dramatic premium increases over the last decade and this uncertainty of future price has discouraged many consumers from purchasing traditional coverage.

As a result, insurance companies have introduced hybrid long term care insurance products that address these concerns. The hybrid products fall into three categories:

- Long term care insurance coverage riders as a part of an annuity contract.

- Single Premium Life Insurance that provides a long term care benefit.

- Traditional life insurance with a long term care rider.

All of these hybrid products feature some variation that provides for the payment of long term care benefits if the client cannot do two or more of the activities of daily living. Furthermore, once the product is purchased, there is a guarantee of premium and either a money-back guarantee or cash value that can be accessed if the client wishes to discontinue coverage.

The rationale for the purchase of this type of product is to take some assets and move them from a "self-insured" position into a "reinsurance" position. In return for the insurance benefit, the client is giving up the "opportunity cost" of the asset repositioned. For example, a hybrid product may credit an interest rate of 3.00%. If I reposition assets that I thought could earn 6.00% elsewhere, I would have an opportunity cost of 3.00%/yr. (6.00% - 3.00% = 3.00%)

Since the risk of paying for long term care is the biggest financial risk most Americans will face, it makes sense to take a serious look at transferring some or all of that risk to an insurance company.

Tax Considerations

Recent Congressional legislation provided that the tax treatments for "qualified" long-term care insurance would be the same as for major medical coverage. If a long-term care insurance policy is considered qualified, meaning that it contains the provisions mandated by the HIPAA act, benefits paid will generally not be subject to income tax. If the policy is not HIPAA compliant, it is considered non-qualified and thus benefits payable may be subject to income tax. It is important to ask whether the long-term care policy you are considering is qualified or not. "Non-qualified" policies do not receive such preferential tax treatment.

Since qualified long-term care insurance now receives the same tax treatment as accident and health insurance, premiums for long-term care insurance and any out-of-pocket expenses for long-term care can be applied toward meeting the 7.5% floor for medical expense deductions. There are limits applied to the total amount of premiums paid for long-term care insurance that can be applied toward the 7.5% threshold. These limitations are based upon the age of the taxpayer.

Employers are now able to deduct as a business expense, the cost of establishing a long-term care insurance plan for employees as well as any contributions the employer makes towards paying premiums. Such employer contributions will be excluded from the taxable income of employees.

In 1950, average life expectancy in the United States was 69. In 2000, the average life expectancy had risen to 76.5, an increase of 7.5 years. We have witnessed extraordinary advancements in medicine and pharmaceuticals. However, living longer is no guarantee of enjoying complete health and mobility. Medicine can keep people alive, but it has not solved the chronic health problems associated with old age. We are therefore confronted with a new reality of a rapidly aging population, many of which will require some form of long-term care. Such care imposes a heavy emotional and financial burden. At present, the federal Medicaid program is the payer of choice for most long-term care patients. Along with the increasing cost of Medicare and Social Security, it will present a financial challenge unprecedented in United States history.

Private long-term care insurance is an alternative that can preserve the luxury of choice in care providers, as well as preserving the financial security of the family. It can provide a modicum of certainty in an age of increasing financial insecurity.

14 GIVING BACK TO THE COMMUNITY

If we command our wealth, we shall be rich and free; if our wealth commands us, we are poor indeed. Edmund Burke

In this world, it is not what we take up, but what we give up, that makes us rich.
Henry Ward Beecher

One of the benefits of financial independence is the ability to give back to our community through the use of charitable giving. When I speak of community, I am using the term in the broadest sense of its meaning. Community can mean the world, a community of people united in a particular faith, a local town or city, a state, or an organization dedicated to a particular goal or cause. Charitable donations are the down payment we make on a future we believe in, the values we cherish, and the benefits such organizations add to all our lives. The individual donor is the most significant source of giving to charities and communities. The Enlightened Investor never thinks her gift too insignificant to make a difference. A charitable gift connects the head and the checkbook by and through the heart. It truly is planning from the heart.

As with so many other aspects of life, the act of giving is simple, but it is certainly not easy. Giving is a difficult and unnatural act. It goes against the grain of our human instinct for survival and control. You are giving away a portion of what you have accumulated during a financial lifetime to someone else's control for a hoped for, yet nonetheless uncertain benefit. If anyone thinks this decision is easy, imagine separating yourself from 25% of your wealth. And yet people make the decision to give all the time.

Why do people give? There are several possible explanations. The first is to support a cause that they believe is just and right. Charitable organizations are fond of appealing to this desire in their fund raising efforts. Unfortunately, many times these appeals are little more than "it's us versus them, and we've got to outspend them." Just as in political campaigns, many organizations go negative in their fundraising appeals. It is not so much what they are for, but rather what they are against, that gets emphasized in these campaigns. They appeal to their donors' worst fears rather than their highest hopes.

Another reason that people are motivated to give is because of guilt. Some people who have had the good fortune to accumulate significant wealth, they harbor feelings of guilt about having so much. The act of giving back to the community can help assuage these feelings of guilt. With the advent of the astounding era of greed and avarice beginning in the 1980's and continuing into the present, guilt isn't quite the factor that it used to be. Now it seems that large donors are looking for recognition. Many donors see giving as a means to enter a higher social circle of influence.

Congress has recognized the value of charitable organizations and thus has encouraged giving by providing substantial tax benefits for charitable gifts. Charitable giving can result in income, capital gains, and estate tax reduction. In essence, the tax laws allow the donor to "do good while doing well!" Although tax benefits may provide the push that tips the balance towards giving, I have worked with very few donors whose sole motivation for giving was because of the tax benefits such gifts would create.

Perhaps the motivation to give back to the community is a combination of all these factors. However I think there is more to it than just this. One of the profound benefits of a successful journey along the path to financial independence is the realization that survival is not the first law of life, it is the second. The Enlightened Investor realizes that the first law of life is that we are all truly one. It is a spiritual breakthrough that informs our financial life. How else to really explain why someone would transcend self-interest to give to others?

The philosopher Arthur Schopenhauer framed the question this way:

How is it possible that suffering that is neither my own nor of my concern should immediately affect me as though it were my own, and with such force that it moves me to action?..... This is something really mysterious, something for which Reason can provide no explanation, and for which no basis can be found in practical experience. It is nevertheless of common occurrence, and everyone has had the experience. It is not unknown even to the most hard-hearted and self-interested. Examples appear every day before our eyes of instant responses of this kind, without reflection, one person helping another, coming to his aid, even setting his own life in clear danger for someone whom he has seen for the first time, having nothing more in mind than that the other is in need and in peril of his life.[xlix]

We need look no further than the heroism and selfless acts of those rescue workers who rushed to the World Trade Center in an attempt to save the victims. In addition, the outpouring of spontaneous compassion in the weeks following the tragedy provided further proof that the first law is that we are all truly one. Professor Joseph Campbell provides an eloquent summary of this truth:

Such a one is then acting, Schopenhauer answers, out of an instinctive recognition of the truth that he and that other in fact are one. He has been moved not from the lesser, secondary knowledge of himself as separate from the others, but from an immediate experience of the greater truth, that we are all one in the ground of being.[l]

The act of a fireman rushing into a burning building to save a child, or someone jumping into a river to save a drowning stranger are certainly dramatic examples of this truth in action. However, we see examples of this all the time in people helping others with no thought of repayment, in financial gifts to the community. Such acts are subtle manifestations of this truth.

Unfortunately for many Americans, they believe that they must keep their eyes close to the ground, struggling for financial survival. It is the curse of capitalism that would have us believe that meaning in life can only be found through the financial equivalent of the survival of the fittest. The Enlightened Investor will resist this temptation; she will know that giving back to the community is the spiritual bouquet of financial independence.

There are many ways to give, however they can be broadly categorized as: 1) Making an outright gift of cash or property, 2) A gift of a remainder interest. This is a gift that will be completed at some future date. 3) A gift of current income or lead interest. This is a gift that is given currently to the charity, however at some point in the future, the property or income will revert back to the donor.   The following is a summary of the methods available. I would encourage consultation with a qualified financial and tax advisor to determine which of these methods would best meet your charitable and financial goals.

Outright Gifts

Outright gifts can be in the form of cash, real estate, stocks or bonds, life insurance, artwork, etc. Typically the asset has appreciated in value from its original purchase price. The advantage of such a gift is that the asset can be sold to create either current income or an addition to the endowment fund of the charity. The benefit to the donor is that it generates an immediate income tax deduction based on the fair market value of the property as of the date of the gift. There is no capital gains tax on such appreciated gifts and the value of the gift is removed from the taxable estate of the donor.

Bequest

A testamentary bequest is made by will at the death of the donor. The form of the bequest can be cash, real estate, personal property, a percentage of the donor's estate, or the remainder of the donor's estate after all other obligations have been satisfied. The advantage to the charity is that the bequest can be used to fund current expenses or added to the endowment of the charity to be held in perpetuity. The advantage to the donor is that they can specify how the bequest must be utilized by the charity. The gift will also qualify for an estate tax deduction.

Charitable Remainder Trust

Charitable Remainder Trusts (CRTs) were established in the Tax Reform Act of 1969. In using a CRT, the donor transfers assets to a trust and retains an income from the trust for a period of years or for a lifetime. Upon the termination of the trust at the death of the income beneficiary(s), the remaining value of the trust passes to the charity(s) of the donor's choice. CRTs have become very popular because they provide significant tax incentives. There are seven important benefits of CRTs:

1) The gifted, appreciated asset is sold tax-free by the trust. The sale is not subject to capital gains tax.

2) The gift creates a current income tax deduction. The deduction can be up to 30% of the adjusted gross income of the donor. If the value of the deduction exceeds the per year limit, it can be carried forward for an additional five years. The

actual deduction is a function of the age(s) of the income beneficiaries of the trust and the percentage payout of the trust.

3) The trust can create a stream of income for life for the donor(s). The income stream is typically 5% to 9% depending on the donor's choice. The lower the payout percentage, the higher the current income tax deduction; the higher the payout percentage the lower the current income tax deduction.

4) The gifted asset is removed from the taxable estate of the donor thus reducing potential estate tax.

5) The undistributed earnings in the trust grow tax-free.

6) Donor recognition for making a significant gift to charity.

7) Professional investment management.

CRTs are irrevocable trusts which mean that once established they cannot be changed. However the donor does retain the ability to change trustees and they can also change the charitable beneficiaries of the trust.

There are two types of CRTs. The first is a Charitable Remainder Annuity Trust (CRAT). With a CRAT, the annual payout rate to the income beneficiary is a *fixed* percentage of the initial market value of trust assets. For example: a 7% payout rate on a CRAT with assets valued at $1,000,000 would pay the income beneficiary(s) $70,000 per year regardless of the fluctuation in value of the trust assets. Once the donor has made the initial gift, they cannot gift additional assets to the CRAT.

The second type of CRT is known as the Charitable Remainder Unitrust (CRUT). With a CRUT, the annual payout to the income beneficiary is a percent of the market value of the trust, thus the income may fluctuate from year to year. The CRUT is by far the most popular type of CRT because it has the potential to increase the income stream over time, however it also may decrease based on the performance of the trust investments. The donor can make additional gifts to the CRUT.

How the Charitable Remainder Trust Works

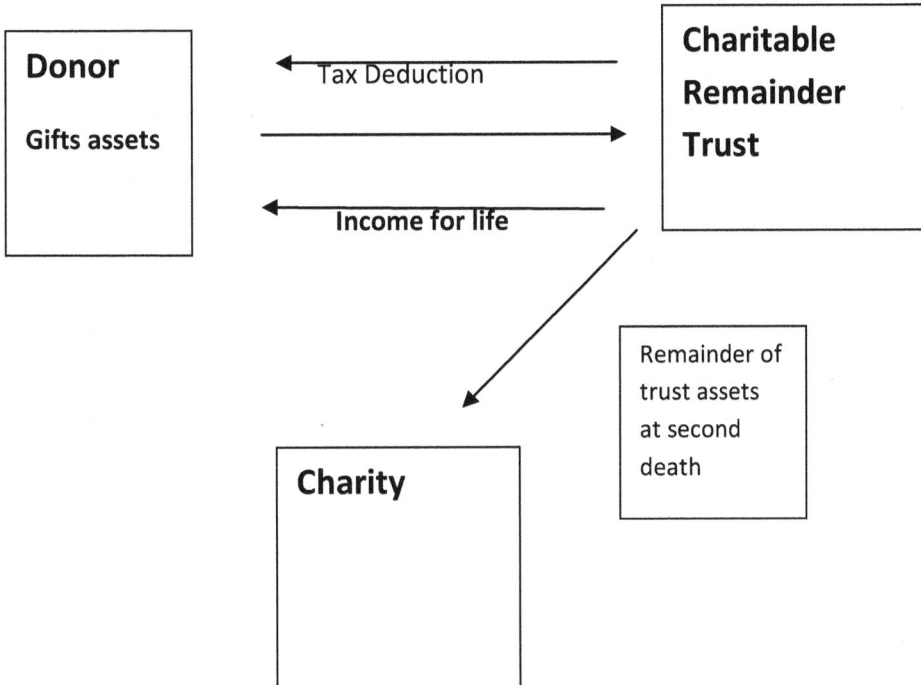

```
┌──────────────┐                              ┌──────────────┐
│  Donor       │ ◄──── Tax Deduction ─────    │  Charitable  │
│              │                              │  Remainder   │
│  Gifts assets│ ──────────────────────►      │  Trust       │
│              │                              │              │
│              │ ◄──── Income for life ───    │              │
└──────────────┘                              └──────────────┘
                                                     │
                                                     ▼
                                    ┌──────────────┐
                        ┌───────────│ Remainder of │
                        │  Charity  │ trust assets │
                        │           │ at second    │
                        │           │ death        │
                        │           └──────────────┘
                        └───────────┘
```

The type of assets that make sense for gift into a CRT include securities, real estate, closely-held businesses, royalty interests, collectibles, patents, or trademarks. The assets should generally be highly appreciated assets. The lower the cost basis of the asset, the greater the benefit of the CRT because all appreciation will escape capital gains tax. Inappropriate assets for gifting include leveraged assets and most partnership interests.

In order to illustrate the potential benefits of a CRT we will compare selling an asset worth $250,000 outright versus setting up a CRT and gifting the asset to the CRT and having the CRT sell the asset within the trust.

	CRT	**Outright Sale**
Sales proceeds	$250,000	$250,000
Cost basis	- $ 75,000	- $ 75.000
Gain on sale	$175,000	$175,000
Tax rate (15%)	no tax	- $ 26,250
Tax due	$ 0	$ 26,250
After-tax proceeds	$250,000	$223,750
payout rate (10%)	$ 25,000	$ 11,187 5% tax-free
Income	$ 25,000	$ 11,187
Tax rate (25%)	- $ 6,250	- $ 0
After-tax income	$ 18,750	$ 11,187

The income paid to the donors by the CRT is subject to income tax. However, the CRT would generate $18,000 per year (assuming the trust assets always earned 10% per year), compared to the outright sale which would generate $11,187 in annual income if invested in a tax-free municipal bond paying 5%.

Furthermore, we have not calculated the income tax deduction that the donor would receive upon making the gift to the CRT. Based on a male and female age 65 and a 10% Charitable Unitrust payout rate, the deduction would be worth $37,585. Assuming that the donors are in a 25% tax rate, the tax savings would amount to $9,396!

Using a CRT can benefit the donor, the charity, and Uncle Sam. You may say, "Wait a minute, Uncle Sam is losing a lot of potential tax revenue." And you would be correct, however the government has granted favorable tax advantages to charitable gifts such as the CRT because they would prefer private funding for various social causes rather than the government having to fund the programs for health research, education, the arts, etc. A dollar provided by charitable organizations for these types of activities is one less dollar Uncle Sam has to spend.

There are potential losers in the CRT strategy. Because the value of the trust will ultimately pass to a charity(s) at the death of the last income beneficiary, there may be a concern about reducing the potential inheritance of children. A simple solution to this problem is the establishment of a second trust that would own life insurance on one or both of the parents. The children would be the beneficiaries of this wealth replacement trust. The parents would make gifts to the wealth replacement trust to provide the money for the premiums on the life insurance policy. With the increased income from the CRT and the income tax savings as a result of making the gift to the CRT, in many cases there is more than enough money to pay for the life insurance.

The children will receive more, not less, because the life insurance within the wealth replacement trust is income- and estate-tax free. Some donors may not choose to use a wealth replacement trust in conjunction with the CRT because both spouses are uninsurable, they have no heirs, the heirs are provided for with other assets, or they do not wish to leave an inheritance to heirs.

Charitable Lead Trust

The Charitable Lead Trust (CLT) is another significant form of charitable giving. The CLT is the reverse of deferred giving such as the Charitable Remainder Trust. In a CLT, the donor transfers property into the trust. The trust pays an income to a designated charitable organization for a period of years. After the specified number of years the remainder interest in the trust returns to the donor or is given to a noncharitable beneficiary such as family members.

A charitable deduction is allowed for income, gift, and estate tax purposes as long as the CLT is set up under one of the following conditions: 1) that the income interest to the charity is in the form of a guaranteed annuity. This is referred to as a Charitable Lead Annuity Trust. 2) The income interest is a fixed percentage of the fair market value of the trust property. This is referred to as a Charitable Lead Unitrust.

For purposes of the income tax deduction only, there is an additional requirement that the donor be treated as the owner of the income interest. In other words, the income of the trust is taxed to the donor. As a result, the CLT is a trade-off of future income tax obligations for the benefit of a current tax reduction. This may be a worthwhile trade in a circumstance where the donor's income is unusually high in a particular year. If the donor does nothing to reduce the taxable income, it will be taxed at very high rates. The CLT would enable the donor to generate a current charitable deduction to reduce his taxable income in that year. The CLT can also be an effective strategy in a year preceding a substantial reduction in income tax rates.

The CLT can offer advantages in terms of estate and gift tax planning. Instead of retaining the remainder interest in the trust themselves, parents may designate children as the owner's of the remainder interest. Such a gift can reduce the tax costs of making lifetime family transfers, since the value of the gift, for gift tax purposes, is reduced by the value of the income interest that is received by the charity. Estate tax costs can be reduced because any subsequent appreciation in value of the property in the CLT is not includible in the donor's estate.

Gifts of Life Insurance

Gifts of life insurance offer several distinct advantages as a method of charitable giving. From the donor's perspective, the gift of life insurance can be made out of current income instead of some portion of the donor's wealth, thereby offering the ability to make a large gift on the installment plan. Family assets and investments do not need to be impaired in order to make a gift. If the gift of life insurance is properly set up, an income tax deduction is available to the donor. Furthermore, the donor can get the recognition of making a substantial future gift in the here and now. Life insurance offers the opportunity for almost everyone to make a substantial gift to charity.

From the perspective of the charity, life insurance gifts are attractive because the amount of the future gift is certain (assuming premiums are paid), and the charity is assured of a source of future income or endowment. It is estimated that a charitable organization needs an endowment that is at least ten times its annual expenditures. Gifts of life insurance can help build a strong endowment for the future of an organization. With gifts of cash value life insurance, the charity has access to the cash value of the policy. At the death of the insured, the charity receives the death benefit free of income and estate tax without any probate or administrative costs or delays.

Compared to testamentary bequests, which are gifts made through the last will and testament of the deceased, life insurance offers distinct advantages. The gift of life insurance is self-completing; at death the benefit is paid. A bequest may be subject to will challenges and probate. Cash value life insurance has a value that the charity may access for current needs; a bequest has no current value that the charity can draw upon. Life insurance may be used as collateral by the charity to secure loans, a bequest cannot.

There are many ways to use life insurance as a means to make gifts. The following is a list of some of the most popular methods.

- Purchase a new policy. The donor is the insured; the charity is the owner and beneficiary. The donor gifts the premiums to the charity which in turns pays them to the life insurance company. This assures the donor of being able to deduct the premiums as a charitable gift.

- Sell an existing life insurance policy to the charity at cost.

- Trade a life insurance policy for a gift annuity from the charity.

- Use life insurance to replace the value of other property that you gift to charity.

- Assign dividends or cash value to the charity.

- Replace a charitable bequest with a gift of life insurance.

- Give an existing policy and continue to gift future premiums to the charity.

- Purchase life insurance within a wealth replacement trust in conjunction with a Charitable Remainder Trust.

Charitable Gift Annuities

Charitable gift annuities are another form of giving that is quite popular among donors. A charitable gift annuity arrangement involves a transfer of cash or other property by the donor to the qualified charitable organization. In exchange for this transfer, the charitable organization makes a commitment to pay the donor a specified amount each year for the remainder of the donor's life. The transfer is not a quid pro quo, since the value of the cash or property transferred to the charity exceeds the value of the annuity that is guaranteed by the charity.

The amount required to purchase an annuity from a charitable organization is greater than the amount required to purchase a comparable annuity from an insurance company. It is this excess cost that generates the charitable deduction for the donor. Thus the transaction is both a purchase of an annuity and a charitable contribution.

Whether the charitable gift annuity is acquired for cash or for appreciated property, the donor will be taxed in accord with the general rules for taxation of annuity income. The rules allow the annuitant to recover a portion of each annuity payment as a return of principal. This is known as the "exclusion ratio". It is determined by dividing the donor's investment in the annuity by the expected return on the contract. Should the annuitant die before fully recovering their principal, the unrecovered principal is allowed as a tax deduction on the final income tax return.

Pooled Income Funds

Charitable gifts can also be made through the use of a pooled income fund. In this arrangement, the donor transfers property to the fund and retains a life income interest in the property for one or more individuals. The remainder interest is contributed to the charitable organization. Like other charitable gifts, the pooled income fund also qualifies for income, gift, and estate tax deductions.

The requirements of a pooled income fund are as follows:

- The donor must transfer an irrevocable remainder interest in the property for the use of charitable organizations that qualify for the 50% income tax charitable deduction, and must retain an income interest in the property for the life or lives of one or more beneficiaries.

- The property must be commingled with the property transferred by other donors, hence the name pooled income. A charity can maintain more than one pooled income fund so long as the maintenance of such funds does not permit the creation of a fund that can be manipulated by its donors.

- The pooled income fund can neither receive as a contribution, nor invest in tax-exempt securities.

- The fund can include only those amounts received from transfers that meet the requirements for pooled income funds.

- The fund must be maintained by the organization to which the remainder interest is contributed, and it cannot have a donor or a beneficiary of the income interest as a trustee.

- The income received each year by the income beneficiary must be determined by the rate of return earned by the fund for that year.

It has been said that if you want to know how much someone is worth, look not to the value of all he owns; look instead to the value of all he has given. One of the great rewards of a financial life well-lived is the ability to bestow gifts upon the community. There is great and important work that is being done every day by charitable organizations, and more to do in the future. They, and the good people that work within such organizations, enrich our lives in many ways. The Enlightened Investor will pursue the adventure of her financial life, making a path where there was none before, living the life that is waiting for her. Knowing that her own life was sustained by the support of others both known and unknown, she will return to the community to make gifts that will sustain others. The community is not unlike a net of jewels, each jewel reflecting the light of the others, on and on, back and forth, to create a tapestry of brilliant light.

15 THE VALUE OF FINANCIAL ADVICE

There are terrible people who, instead of solving a problem, bungle it and make it more difficult for all those who come after. Whoever can't hit the nail on the head should, please, not hit it at all. Nietzsche

Over the course of this book, we have taken an honest look at the state of American financial life, we have described a new vision of financial independence, we have exposed the prevalent investment fallacies that the investment industry uses to confuse investors, we have explored the perennial investment wisdom of the ages, and we have examined the great challenges and opportunities of a financial lifetime.

At this point, one might be tempted to exclaim, "Eureka, this is simple. I can do this myself!" If only this were true. The ideas and concepts we have discussed are indeed simple. That is the mantra of the Enlightened Investor, simplify, simplify, simplify. However simple does not imply that the path is easy.   Granted, there may be some among us who have the discipline and time to successfully walk the path to financial independence without assistance, but they are few and far between. There is an old saying in the legal profession that, "He who serves as his own lawyer has a fool for a client". A fool may be too strong of a pejorative for the investor who tries to go it alone, but one thing I am sure of, they are definitely fooling themselves.

Over the last decade we have witnessed the explosion of that segment of the investment industry that promotes and profits from encouraging investors to "do it themselves". At the height of the bull market in the late 1990's, the media was awash with direct brokerages, investment managers, mutual funds, analysts, newsletter and magazine writers all proclaiming that the road to riches is easily traveled by yourself, if only you bought their map. I recall the comment of one of the more successful prophets of "do-it-yourself" investing. In 1998, the brothers

Investment management is an art, not science, it is engineering. . . We are in the business of managing and engineering financial investment risk. The challenge is to not take more risk than we need to generate the return that is needed.

In traveling the path to financial independence, the Enlightened Investor will employ three layers of protection to defend herself from the slings and arrows of outrageous investment fortune. The first layer of protection is self-control and wisdom. We must seek to educate ourselves, not only of financial fallacies, but also our own all-too-human foibles. We must resist the temptations of fear and desire, which always lie in wait to lead us astray.

Although we may be motivated to exercise self-control, motivation has a bad habit of coming and going. When motivation and self-control are on vacation, we must look to our second layer of protection, disciplined strategies. In an earlier chapter we discussed perennial investment wisdom. These are the strategies that provide a means to invest with discipline. The strategies of diversification, dollar-cost-averaging, constant ratio rebalancing, stop loss, and tax diversification deliver the highest probability for superior long-term investment results. Their strength lies in their disciplined approach. The rules apply regardless of whether the investment markets are up, down, or sideways. The Enlightened Investor knows that investment success is not so much due to unusual and uncanny insight; rather it is the employment of a systematic approach to investing. The failure of most investors arises from the all-to-human tendency, as my grandfather used to say, "To shut the barn door after all the horses have gone." These disciplined investment strategies allow us to ignore the short-term noise and concentrate on the long-term signal.

However, even these best laid plans are susceptible to the whims of human nature. I have seen too many investors abandon disciplined strategies such as dollar-cost-averaging, constant ratio rebalancing, and diversification in the face of the current investment fad du jour. I am reminded of Charles Shulz's <u>Peanuts</u> cartoon character Linus when he pronounces, "It doesn't matter what you believe as long as you are sincere!" Although this may be true in the world of cartoons, politics, and religion; it is not true in the quest for financial independence. Sincere belief will not suffice. No matter how firm our belief, in matters of finance we need a second opinion. Therefore, we must rely upon our third layer of protection, the financial advisor.

The value of an objective and wise financial advisor is inestimable. Finding someone who measures up to these standards is much easier said than done.

Unfortunately many financial advisors attract their clients by holding out the promise of market-beating investment returns. The Enlightened Investor knows that when a financial advisor solicits business based upon promises of investment returns, it is a clear signal to run.

The Certified Financial Planner Board of Standards, Inc. conducted a consumer study which was completed in 2002. Not surprisingly it found that the majority, eighty-two percent, of investors make financial decisions without a financial advisor. However, the use of financial advisors increases with age and net worth. When investors were asked what was important in the selection of a financial advisor, ninety-seven percent stated that the advisor must be trustworthy. Ninety-six percent said that it must be someone who listens to them; ninety-five percent wanted an advisor who was more interested in helping them than merely selling them financial products. When seeking a financial advisor, one-third of the respondents look for solid credentials, one-third look for experience and expertise, and one-third rely on a referral from family and friends. No surprises here, these are good, common sense guides to choosing a financial advisor. However, the survey revealed that two-thirds of the respondents said it is difficult to tell if a financial advisor is truly qualified and trustworthy. Ah, there's the rub! It is my task in this chapter to 1) make the case for the use of a financial advisor, and 2) provide a guide to choosing an advisor that is qualified, experienced, and trustworthy.

The value of a financial advisor lies solely in their ability to function as an *investor* manager rather than an *investment* manager. Professor Meir Statman compares the ideal financial advisor to an optometrist. He states that investors are either myopic or hyperopic, that is either short- or long-sighted. Myopic investors can focus very well on short investment horizons, but lose clarity when taking the long view. Hyperopic investors can focus on the long-term horizon, but not the short. Both types of investors need the help of corrective lenses.

The myopic, or short-sighted investor, is keenly aware of the hottest investment sector or trend. They are always chasing the newest thing. However, they are always a day late and a dollar short. They are a rudderless boat tossed upon the ocean. The value of an investor-oriented financial advisor is that she can provide the myopic investor with corrective lenses to focus on the long-term goal, to see the forest as well as the trees.

As for the hyperopic investor, they suffer from the illusion that in the long run everything will come to a happy end. They buy and hold forever, unaware that what is, will not always be. The unimaginable can, and does happen. We only need look at the devastating bear markets of 2000-2002 and 2008-2009. The majority of individual investors demonstrated great resolve and forbearance during the first year of the market crash. They had learned the lesson of buy-and-hold. Unfortunately they did not possess the experience and wisdom to understand that sometimes markets don't recover right away. Sometimes markets can destroy portfolios in the blink of an eye. Without sound risk management strategies in place, the individual investor can sometimes experience losses of 50%-80% or more. The value of an investor-oriented financial advisor is that she can provide objective advice in the midst of market chaos, correcting our investment sight, either long or short.

Money is the last American taboo. As a society we talk openly about subjects that fifty years ago were never discussed in public. Almost everything is open to examination and personal confession. We are eager to discuss anything relating to the other circles of emotional, physical, social, and spiritual concerns. Most people will seek assistance if they encounter problems in these areas of life. The exception is our relationship to money. We identify too closely with our money. We believe net worth correlates with self worth. Thus we are embarrassed and humiliated to reveal that we have not managed our income and wealth successfully. We are hesitant to seek assistance.

Investors resist paying for financial counseling; however they are happy to pay outrageous fees and commissions to anyone promising exorbitant investment returns. The Enlightened Investor realizes that she needs assistance to offset her weakness in financial self-control and discipline. She needs assistance in making money the servant of the larger dimensions of life, rather than the master of them. She needs assistance to help develop a vision of how she truly wants to live, rather than an endless and mindless pursuit of income and wealth. This then is the true value of a gifted and caring financial advisor: to help clients distinguish between goals that reflect the greed to be rich – such as having more money and toys than my neighbor; from those that reflect the fear of becoming poor – such as a secure retirement income.

The Enlightened Investor will seek a financial advisor that embodies three elements of expertise. Although most financial advisors are well-meaning individuals, many are unable or unwilling to embody these three areas of expertise.

The first area of expertise is life experience and wisdom. Just as the financial advisor's first responsibility is to get to know who you are and what your dreams and goals are, so too, it is your first duty to determine the experience of a potential financial advisor. Experience can be defined in terms of financial education, years in the business, and most importantly, how their life experience has shaped their approach to financial advice. If a financial advisor speaks only of investment performance and returns, run, don't walk to the exit. The following are some suggestions for questions that you can ask as you interview prospective financial advisors.

Where are you from?

Tell me about your education.

Tell me about your financial experience and credentials.

What principles do you follow in regard to managing your money and investments?

Tell me about the best financial advice you ever gave someone.

Tell me about the worst financial advice you ever gave someone.

How do you define financial independence?

How do you work with clients?

Are there any investments that you would refuse to recommend on principle?

I think you get the idea. I have always been amazed at how quickly investors will hand over their money and their financial futures to financial advisors. Most people will spend more time and effort planning a weekend getaway than they will spend interviewing and questioning a prospective financial advisor. It is easy for a financial advisor to make glowing promises of investment success, or make a dazzling presentation in a seminar. The Enlightened Investor must explore beyond the veil of promise and hype, she must seek to understand the substance of a potential advisor. I have seen too many investors, lured by the promise of quick riches, get taken to the cleaners by inexperienced or unethical advisors.

Many investors make the decision to work with a financial advisor based on a "gut feeling". Trust based on intuition is all well and good, but it should be developed with more information than simply an impressive sales presentation. Just as you want a financial advisor to understand you as a person and your history and your dreams, so it is also your task to gain a complete understanding of a potential financial advisor. The purpose of this process is to determine whether the potential financial advisor is more interested in pursuing and promoting their financial agenda than in understanding and promoting yours.

The second area of expertise that a financial advisor must possess is a working knowledge of financial concepts and strategies. The first role of a financial advisor can be likened to that of an architect designing a house. The financial advisor is there to help you design the financial house that you would like to live in. Do you want a large house, or will a smaller house fulfill your needs? What do you want your house to look like? How many rooms? How many people will live in the house, and for how long? And if your desire is to live in a Cape Cod, and the advisor insists on designing a Spanish Colonial, you know it is time to find another financial architect.

The second role of the financial advisor is that of the general contractor who will actually build the house. Just as a general contractor must have working knowledge of building materials and construction techniques, so too the financial planner must have the experience and skill to determine which financial strategies and concepts are best suited to building the financial house in which you want to live. The Enlightened Investor will ask a prospective financial advisor for examples of how she has helped build other clients' financial houses and what strategies and concepts were used.

The final role of the financial advisor is that of maintenance and repair. Just as any house needs continuing maintenance and repair, so too does your financial house. Unfortunately, this is the role that most financial advisors are unwilling or unable to fulfill. Markets change, tax laws change, life circumstances change, life goals change, all things change. The financial advisor must have a system for excellent customer service in order to provide maintenance and repair to his clients' financial houses.

Most investors do not have the time, training, or temperament to effectively negotiate the journey to financial independence by themselves. Over the last twenty years, the information revolution has flooded us with a deluge of data and opinion. Even though we now have the internet, television, radio, and cell phones, the transmission speed of information has not increased since the invention of the telegraph. However, the number of sources and the volume of information transmitted have exceeded our ability to intelligently digest it. And this is especially true in the investment business. With the advent and explosion of the financial media: talk radio, magazines, cable television, newsletters, internet websites, newspapers; there is financial and investment information available twenty-four hours a day, seven days a week, three hundred sixty-five days a year. We have too much noise and not enough time to find the true signal. There are too few filters available to eliminate the noise.

Most investors just don't have the time to filter and analyze the torrent of information. At the turn of the twenty-first century, Americans are overworked and stressed-out. The average American workweek has expanded. Study after study concludes that Americans are sleep-deprived. Between the demands of work, family, and pursuing the American dream, most Americans simply do not have the time necessary to process the raw financial and investment information flooding their lives into financial and investment wisdom.

Even if they have the time, or choose to make the time, it is my belief that they would be better served, and pursue more fulfilling lives if they would make a decision to ignore all the noise. We have allowed our lives to become too much about the pursuit of information at the expense of the development of wisdom.

Consider the universe of investment options: treasury bills and bonds, money market, municipal and corporate bonds, options, open- and closed-end mutual funds, exchange-traded funds, derivatives, mortgage-backed securities, unit investment trusts, hedge funds, separately managed accounts, equity-indexed annuities, real estate investment trusts, precious metals, small- mid- large- and micro-cap stocks, variable life insurance, fixed and variable annuities, certificates of deposit, universal life insurance, the list goes on and on.

And these are only financial and investment products! Add to the mix, investment, tax, and financial planning strategies such as asset allocation, 1035 and 1031 exchanges, 72(t) and 72(q) distributions, family limited partnerships, dollar-cost-averaging, rebalancing, laddered maturities, charitable trusts, irrevocable life insurance trusts, living trusts, split dollar insurance, unified credit, gift tax, defective trusts, etc. There are very few financial advisors, say nothing of average investors, that have the training and experience to make an informed decision as to which financial or tax strategy makes sense in a given financial situation. And it is the proper, or improper, use of such strategies that can have a profound effect for good or ill upon the pursuit of financial independence.

Of the three attributes, temperament is the one that ultimately trips up the "do-it-yourselfer" on the path to financial independence. If I have not done so already, let me state clearly, very few investors have the emotional and psychological self-control to effectively manage their investments through the uncertainty of a financial lifetime. It takes a strong, yet humble constitution to face the fact that we are often self-deceived.

The dark side of capitalism is financial uncertainty. You may lose your job, your business may fail. The companies you invest in may go bankrupt. Corporate executives may lie, cheat, and steal. You may be sued and held liable for damages. You or someone in your family may become disabled by accident or illness. You may die prematurely. The uncertainties of a financial life in a capitalistic system are many. We fool ourselves if we believe that such uncertainties do not lead to anxiety or fear. As Shakespeare's Hamlet declares, "Our wills and fates do so contrary run that our devices still are overthrown."

The bright side of Capitalism is its dynamism, its opportunity. It holds the promise, through hard work, good fortune, street smarts, or a combination of all, of income and wealth. Theoretically there is no limit on the financial success that is possible. However, hand-in-hand with such opportunity is the temptation of over-reaching desire and greed.

It is the temptations of fear and desire, in all their manifestations, that cause us to take more financial risk than is necessary, or avoid as much risk as possible. In 1948, Friedman and Savage pointed out in an article entitled, "The Utility Analysis of Choices Involving Risk" that risk-taking and risk-avoidance play roles in our investment behavior. As they put it, "People who buy insurance policies often buy lottery tickets as well.[ii] Unfortunately, our risk-taking behavior is not rational.

During our financial lifetime we find ourselves in one of two domains. We are either in the "domain of losses" or the "domain of gains". When our financial situation is less than our aspirations we dwell in the "domain of losses". We are tempted by a combination of fear and desire to take financial risks that we would not be willing to take otherwise. We play Russian roulette with our investments. In Russian roulette, there are five bad outcomes and one good. As Nassim Taleb points out, if you keep playing eventually the bad outcomes will catch up with you. Cases in point, the Internet bubble and the housing collapse. Professor Meir Statman wrote,

Consider the United States, where swift technological and societal changes once made some middle-class people feel as poor as Albanians relative to dot-com millionaires. Such people allocate increasing proportions of their portfolios to the upside potential goal and choose lottery-like securities.[lii]

Conversely, if our financial situation is equal to or exceeds our aspirations, we dwell in the "domain of gains". The temptation of the fear of losing what we have compels us to become risk averse, to take less risk than we should; or the temptation of desire compels us to take extraordinary risk because we believe that fate is on our side, we are omnipotent, and we can beat the odds. The Enlightened Investor understands that she is ultimately undone by fear and desire. She will endeavor to resist such temptations. She will concentrate on the still point of the financial wheel of fortune, her own life goals. She will understand that in the temporal moment, no matter how much noise nor how fast the wheel of fortune is spinning, nothing is happening. The key is to focus on the still point.

Perhaps the most significant revelation for the Enlightened Investor is the realization that no matter how intelligent, self-controlled, and well-informed she may be; in the contest between intelligence and emotion, emotion will prevail. This is not necessarily a bad thing, it is our human condition. However, in matters of financial security it can be extremely hazardous to financial independence. Most of us need the assistance of a financial guide to help us eliminate our emotional static. Someone who, when the wheel of fortune is spinning madly, can stand beside us and remind us of the still point, remind us of the perennial investment wisdom, and who can guide us calmly along the path to financial independence

16 THE MULTI-GENERATIONAL IRA
(THE BEST PLANNING IDEA EVER)

When I analyze a client's financial situation, I separate their assets into three general categories:

1. Current. These are assets that the client needs to create current income in order to meet the expenses of living.

2. Contingent. These are assets that are not currently needed to create income. However, at some point down the road, these assets may be needed to create income.

3. Custodial. These are assets which the client still owns and controls, however they will never be needed to create income. As a result, the client has begun thinking, or perhaps already decided, to allocate these assets to charity or family.

When the Individual Retirement Account (IRA) was created, I am sure the congressmen who drafted the legislation never imagined the success of the concept. There are billions and billions of dollars that are held within IRAs. For most retirees, the amount held within IRAs is the second largest financial asset they have, second only to the equity in their home. And with the Housing Bubble collapse, it may be the largest.

It remains to be seen how the Baby Boomer generation and succeeding generations use their IRAs, however many of the "Greatest Generation" of Americans have put themselves in the fortunate situation of having significant assets within their IRAs, and not needing the income from the IRAs to support their lifestyle.

My experience in working with many retirees is that between their defined benefit pension and Social Security, they have more than adequate income to meet their wants and needs. However, the IRS will not let you accumulate money in your IRA forever. In the year in which an individual reaches age 70 ½ , they are required to begin taking Required Minimum Distributions (RMD). This was discussed in depth in the section on IRA Distributions.

The typical distribution plan for an IRA is as follows:

- The IRA owner will take RMDs until their death.

- The beneficiary of the IRA is the spouse. The spouse will convert the IRA into his/her name and take RMDs based on the spouse's age.

- At the surviving spouse's death, the children will be the beneficiaries of the remainder of the IRA.

This is all well and good; however there are distinct disadvantages to this wealth transfer strategy. First of all, my educated guess is that most children will be tempted to take their share of the IRA as a lump sum. Therefore they will have to pay income tax on the value of the IRA received. This can amount to many thousands of dollars in tax and seriously erode the net value of the transferred IRA. Second, I suspect that most children will end up spending the net IRA assets during their lifetime and thus there will be nothing left for the benefit of grandchildren.

What if there was a way to provide the children with the benefit of the IRA, without having to pay income tax on the transfer? What if there was a way to provide grandchildren with a lifetime pension? And what if there were a way to preserve the control and benefit of the IRA during the lifetimes of the IRA owner and spouse?

There is such a way and we call it The Multi-Generational IRA. Perhaps the best way to describe the concept is through the use of a hypothetical example. We will assume that Mr. Jones is currently age 70 and his wife, Mrs. Jones is currently age 65. Mr. Jones owns an IRA with a current value of $500,000. We will assume that the IRA grows at a 7.00% annual rate. Finally, we will assume that Mr. Jones will live another 10 years and that Mrs. Jones will live another 20 years. Therefore Mr. Jones will be 80 at his death and Mrs. Jones will be 85.

Mr. Jones will be turning age 70 ½ this year and he will begin to take Required Minimum Distributions from his IRA. That would result in an RMD of $18,000 this year. At a 7.00% annual growth rate, the RMD at his age 80 would be $33,000. At his death, Mrs. Jones would inherit the IRA and most likely convert it to her name. At her age 85, the RMD would have grown to $48,000. At her death at age 85, the value of the IRA would be $711,519.

At her death, she would have named their daughter as the beneficiary of the IRA. The daughter would have the option of taking lifetime distributions over her life expectancy and thus spreading the taxation of the IRA asset over many years, however she will be tempted to take the entire $711,519 in one fell swoop. If she were in a combined federal and state tax rate of 35%, she would end up with a net $462,487. And being the good Baby Boomer that she is, she will end up spending the entire amount during the course of her remaining life, leaving nothing to her children, Mr. and Mrs. Jones grandchildren.

We will suggest another approach. Mr. Jones will change the contingent beneficiary of his IRA from his daughter, to specially designed IRA trusts for the benefit of his grandchildren. Mrs. Jones will continue to be the primary beneficiary. At Mr. Jones death, Mrs. Jones will likely put the IRA into her name and she would then name the IRA trusts for the benefit of the grandchildren as the primary beneficiary of the IRA. The IRA trusts will stipulate that the grandchildren will receive distributions based on lifetime stretch out provisions.

At a 7.00% assumed annual growth rate, we project the value of the IRA to be $711,519 at the last death of either Mr. or Mrs. Jones. Mr. and Mrs. Jones will apply for a survivorship life insurance policy in the amount of $711,519 and name their daughter, or a Life Insurance Trust for the benefit of the daughter, as beneficiary. The premium for the policy is approximately $11,000/yr. Since the Jones' do not need the RMD's for current expenses, there is more than enough after-tax cash flow from the RMD's to pay for premiums.

By putting this plan into effect, the Jones' can create as additional $8,000,000 of benefit for their child and their grandchildren. Consider the following:

- At the second death, the child will receive the death benefit of the life insurance in the amount of $711,519, income tax free and potentially free of estate taxes. Compare this to the net amount of $462,487 she would have received as beneficiary of the IRA.

- If the Jones' have three grandchildren, ages 16, 12, and 8, the grandchildren's trusts will receive $237,173 each as beneficiary of the IRA.

- With stretch out payments, Grandchild A at age 36 will receive lifetime income in the amount of $2,177,083, Grandchild B at age 32 will receive lifetime income in the amount of $2,642,181, and Grandchild C at age 28 will receive lifetime income in the amount of $3,233,270. A total of $8,052,533.

- Through their foresight and planning, Mr. and Mrs. Jones would provide their grandchildren with an additional, and perhaps necessary, stream of income. For example: at age 65, Grandchild A would receive $45,163.

Consider the following comparison of their current IRA plan to a Multi-Generational IRA plan:

	Current	Multi-Generational IRA
Net Amount to Daughter	$ 462,487	$ 711,519
Income to Grandchildren	$ 0	$8,052,533
Total	$ 462,487	$8,764,052
Less Insurance Premiums	$ 0	$ (230,881)
Total	$ 462,487	$8,533,171

Mr. and Mrs. Jones were fortunate to have lived during a period of American Economic dominance. As a result, Mr. Jones worked for 35 years with one company and once retired, collected a handsome pension. Between the pension, Social Security, and the Jones' prudent spending, they have more than adequate income to meet their needs and wants.

Compare that to the likely financial realties that their daughter and their grandchildren will face. None of them will have the benefit of a defined benefit pension plan. However, if Mr. and Mrs. Jones implement a Multi-Generational IRA plan, they can provide their daughter with a significant income tax free lump sum of money, and provide their grandchildren with a significant lifetime income stream that can go a long way towards replacing the value of a defined benefit pension plan.

This and a number of other compelling wealth planning strategies are available to The Enlightened Investor who takes the time to seek them out and to seek out the financial professionals that can help them implement such strategies.

17 CONCLUSION

I see no special heroism in accumulating money, particularly if the person is foolish enough to not even try to derive any tangible benefit from such wealth. Nassim Talebs

The gods only laugh when men pray for wealth. Japanese proverb

There is more to life than making money and accumulating wealth. I'm sure that most of us, when we listen to our "better angels" would agree with this sentiment. And yet we live, and are dominated by a world in which the acquisitive spirit runs rampant. It is the spirit of materialism. It manifests itself by our insatiable appetite for more and more. It is fed by fear and desire. We want more to stave off the fear of being destitute or the fear of the loss of self-esteem. We want more to satisfy the desire for status, power, and immortality. We imagine that our wants are actually needs. We end up sacrificing that which we hold most dear, our time, our family and friends, our lives, our very souls, to the acquisitive spirit. According to Aristotle, those who seek wealth for its own sake are "intent upon living only, and not upon living well."

The great ideological battle of the twentieth century was between two aspects of the acquisitive spirit of materialism: capitalism and communism. The means of capitalism and communism were distinctly different, yet they shared the same end: material wealth. By 1990 the contest had been decided, capitalism had demonstrated its superior capacity for economic development and material wealth. However, the assumption behind materialism, that more goods and services results in greater happiness, the good life, and the American Dream, was never questioned.

America today is predicated on the mythology of money and wealth. We have been led willingly by the advertisers and marketers into a perverse cycle of growth and consumption. Their mantras are, "You never have enough", "Enough isn't good enough", and "If you don't get it, your neighbor will." We worship at the altar of money. We idolize those who possess it. Whether by hook or by crook, it doesn't matter how you get your money as long as you get more of it. As Madonna quipped, "Having money is just the best thing in the world." Joseph Campbell, the professor and writer of "The Power of Myth" fame, commented on the state of American values in his lectures. He said,

The American workplace is based upon the myth of money. Money is the bottom line today. No value can supersede the value of money. If you want to explain anything that you're doing, turning out third-rate material or anything else, it's cost. You can't turn out what you'd like to turn out because it would cost too much. The hero is one who will do it even sacrificing the money. The value that you stand for is your life. And if money is the final term, that's your mythology.[liii]

Make no mistake; there is nothing wrong with prosperity and material well-being. As Woody Allen put it, "It is better to be rich rather than poor if only for economic reasons." However, when our materialism and acquisitive spirit subsumes and consumes our time, our values, and our deepest sense of ourselves; it is time to say, "Enough!" The economist John Maynard Keynes put it thus:

Why should anyone outside of a lunatic asylum wish to hold money as a store of wealth? The possession of actual money lulls our disquietude, and the premium we require to make us part with money is the measure of our disquietude.

I can imagine an America that understands that the value of an economy is to create a better quality of life for all its citizens, not just the top one percent. That growth for growth's sake is, as the writer Edward Abbey put it, "The raison d'etre of a cancer cell." I can imagine an America where tax and economic policy values labor as much as it does capital. In 1861, President Abraham Lincoln wrote,

Labor is prior to, and independent of, capital. Capital is only the fruit of labor, and could never have existed if labor had not first existed. Labor is the superior of capital, and deserves much the higher consideration.

If only our current political leaders had as much wisdom, perhaps we could imagine an America where narrowing the income gap between the highest earners and lowest earners was a priority.

I can imagine an America where, instead of giving outrageous tax deductions, tax incentives are provided for conservation and restoration. I can imagine an

America where, in addition to political democracy, we enjoyed a democratization of capital. A democratization of capital whereby, instead of charging the highest interest rates for credit to those least able to afford it, a reasonable limit would be enacted. In concert with this, credit availability would be tightened such that banks would not be able to indiscriminately solicit credit cards which tempt too many Americans into the overuse of credit.

I can imagine an America where tax and economic policy is enacted for the benefit of the people and not the corporations, an America where corporations do not coerce employees into longer and longer work weeks. Instead, I can imagine an America where every employee is entitled to five weeks of vacation, where every American can devote time to the values of family, faith, friends, and community.

With the advent of the Occupy Wall Street movement, we may yet have a national conversation or debate about what constitutes the good life. However, we have a political, media, and economic system that quashes any meaningful discussion. The special interests are too entrenched; Congress is too indebted to them, and the media too afraid of losing their advertising dollars. Therefore, the Enlightened Investor must, at some point, decide how much is enough? What constitutes a life well-lived? The answer will be as unique as the individual.

In this book, I have attempted to construct the framework for a journey along the path to financial independence. It is not an easy path, it never has been. As far back as the golden age of Athens, Aristotle wrote,

Men are divided between those who are as thrifty as if they would live forever, and those who are as extravagant as if they were going to die tomorrow.

I have written this book, not as a guru who has reached the destination, rather as one attempting to travel the middle path between thrift and extravagance. I grew up in a family that represented both sides of the dilemma. My mother came from a frugal, German-American farming background. They never made a great deal of money, but the key was they spent much less than they earned. Of course those were the days when farmers had chickens, pigs, cows, and large gardens. Most of the necessities of life were grown or processed on the farm. My maternal grandfather never took any risk with his money. It went into the bank. I'm sure he said to himself, "Farming is risky enough as it is, if I'm fortunate enough to make a profit, it surely will not be put at risk." My mother grew up just as frugal. To this day, she can stretch a dollar farther than anyone I've ever known.

My father, on the other hand, spent everything he had and sometimes even more. His philosophy: "Eat, drink, and be merry, for tomorrow we die." He grew up in a small farming town in southwestern Minnesota not very far from my maternal grandparent's farm. After several jobs as a young man, he finally found a home with the U.S. Postal Service. In his mind, this was a perfect scenario; he could spend his entire income secure in the knowledge that once he had worked thirty years, he would receive a generous pension and benefits. Confident in the safety net, he lived life with his friends golfing, bowling, fishing, hunting, watching football, etc.

How my parents survived twenty-seven years of marriage, I'll never know. Money was always an issue. Dad kept spending and Mom did her best to make ends meet. These were the days before the women's' movement and thus Dad's lifestyle took precedence. Mom did the best she could with what was left. And she did very well; we were always well-dressed and well taken care of. After twenty-seven years they divorced.

She was in her mid-forties when the divorce happened. She had very little work experience and no immediate job prospects. To her credit, she moved to the city, rented an apartment and got a job as a salesperson at a department store. After a brief time at the department store, she took a job at a bank and ultimately found a position with an insurance company. Fast forward twenty years and she has her own house, of which the mortgage is paid-off and she is financially secure.

She is representative of that group who have saved and lived frugally in order to accumulate a nest egg for their financial security. Because of the financial discipline they employed during their financial lives, once they achieve financial independence they have difficulty in overcoming their decades-old habits of frugality. They are always concerned about the future, the possibility of running out of money and becoming destitute. This is not an unfounded fear as life expectancies are rapidly expanding and financial uncertainty abounds. In response to these uncertainties, they have struck a psychological deal to sacrifice some pleasure in the here-and-now for the security of the future.

On the other hand, my father retired as soon as he was eligible for his pension. Because of his pension and the supplemental health insurance provided by his retirement plan, he had some degree of financial security. However, he could never stop spending beyond his means. Due to a lifetime of smoking cigarettes, his retirement was one of declining health and activity. In the summer of 2011 he died. In retrospect, perhaps he made the right decision to have enjoyed life while he could. People such as my father are tempted by desire. Their psychological bargain is to satisfy their wants in the here-and-now, knowing that they may be compromising the future.

My parents are representative of the duality of financial personality. On the one hand, live for today for tomorrow we die. On the other, sacrifice today to secure tomorrow. It is a dilemma with no easy answer. Do we live, earn, and spend for today hoping for a fortuitous financial future? Or do we fear for the worst, store up our treasure in the event that fate turns against us in the future? It would appear that people are pretty much one way or the other; there are very few people who have found a middle path. It has been so since the dawn of civilization. Consider the words of Horace when he asked, "What is the difference whether you squander all you have, or never use your wealth?" And yet it is my belief that the key to true financial independence lies in traveling a middle path, the middle path of living fully in the present while preparing for the future.

The idea of the middle path has a long history in religion and mythology. There is the tradition of the Holy Grail. There are many stories of the grail; the most profound of which is where the grail is brought down to earth by the neutral angels during the war in heaven between God and Lucifer. In this tradition, fulfillment is not found by identification with the pairs of opposites, rather it is found by taking the middle path. In Western mythology this idea finds its highest expression in the story of Parzival and the Holy Grail. Parzival travels far and wide in search of the grail. He eventually comes to the enlightenment that we must all travel our own path in seeking the grail, and that the path is to be found in the middle way.

What are the lessons for a financial life? Follow your own path, steering clear of the temptations of fear and desire. Be moderate in pursuing your desires and avoiding your fears.

Consider the words of the Roman poet Horace in his Odes II, 10, as translated by David Ferry,

> You'll do better, Licinius, not to spend your life
> Venturing too far out on the dangerous waters,
> Or else, for fear of storms, staying too close in
> To the dangerous rocky shoreline. That man does best
> Who chooses the middle way, so he doesn't end up
> Living under a roof that's going to ruin

Or in some gorgeous mansion everyone envies.
The tallest pine shakes most in a windstorm;
The loftiest tower falls down with the loudest crash;
The lightening bolt heads straight for the mountain top.
Always expect reversals; be hopeful in trouble,
Be worried when things go well. That's how it is
For the man whose heart is ready for anything.
It's true that Jupiter brings on the hard winters;
It's also true that Jupiter takes them away.
If things are bad right now, they won't always be.
Apollo isn't always drawing his bow;
There are times when he takes up his lyre and plays,
And awakens the music sleeping upon the strings.
Be resolute when things are going against you,
But shorten sail when the fair wind blows too strong.

After the tragedy of 9/11, there was much discussion of a reassessment of life by Americans; taking stock and getting back to basics. For the first time in their lives, many Americans realized the precariousness of existence, that the hand of fate could change the world in an instant. Add to this the excruciating loss of wealth due to the market crash of the first three years of the new millennium, the Great Recession, political and economic instability in the world, and the crisis in the Roman Catholic church; is it any wonder Americans are anxious about all aspects of their lives.

This book was written in response to this anxiety, particularly as it manifests itself in our financial lives. The path to financial independence is simple, yet not easy. It requires that we block out the noise and listen to the signal of our true selves. Life is too precious to waste on obsessing about money. Granted, we live in a world where money is necessary, but it need not be all-obsessing. I have attempted to lay the groundwork for a different approach to our financial lives and the quest to achieve financial independence. It is an approach that recognizes that life is uncertain, that there are no guarantees. That in spite of the uncertainty, we must have the courage to participate fully in the world. That, in the words of the Japanese proverb, we must "walk in the dark, in your best clothes." Erich Fromm wrote, "The quest for certainty blocks the search for meaning. Uncertainty is the very condition to impel Man to unfold his powers."

We have exposed the fallacies of the noisemakers of the financial world and explored the perennial investment wisdom of the ages. In the Bible, the apostle

Mark writes, "What doth it profit a man if he gains the whole world and lose his soul?" The Enlightened Investor understands that the path to financial independence is a psychological breaking-free of the chains of fear and desire in order to set free our true selves. As the old Shaker hymn refrains "Tis a gift to be simple, tis a gift to be free.

Joseph Campbell, the writer and mythologist, summed things up eloquently when he said,

> The warrior's approach is to say "yes" to life: "yea" to it all. Participate joyfully in the sorrows of the world. We cannot cure the world of sorrows, but we can choose to live in joy. When we talk about settling the world's problems, we're barking up the wrong tree. The world is perfect. It's a mess. It has always been a mess. We are not going to change it. Our job is to straighten out our own lives.

I have written this book to hopefully cast some light on the adventure of living a financial life that complements our true life. The path to financial independence is not easy, nor is the journey ever complete. We must constantly strive to resist the temptations of desire for material wealth for its own sake and the paralyzing fear of loss.

O Sancta Simplicitas!

[i] Taleb, 2001

[ii] Shapiro, Greenstein, Primus, 2001

[iii] Ibid

[iv] Shapiro, Greenstein, Primus, 2001

[v] Wolff, 2001

[vi] Stanley and Danko, 1998

[vii] Wolff, 2000

[viii] Gross, 1999

[ix] Wolff, 2000

[x] Wolff, 2000

[xi] Pollan, 1997

[xii] U.S. Census Bureau, 2010

[xiii] Roper Center, 1996

[xiv] Campbell, Converse, Rodgers, 1976

[xv] Langer,1975, Seligman, 1975, Wright, Zautra, Braver, 1985

[xvi] Gladwell, 2002

[xvii] G.K. Chesterson

[xviii] Federal Reserve, 2010

[xix] Carp&Carp, 1982

[xx] Markowitz, 1952

[xxi] Campbell, 1988

[xxii] Callan Periodic Table of Investment returns. Chart is comprised of the S&P 500 index, S&P MidCap 400, S&P/BARRA 500 Growth, S&P/BARRA 500 Value, Russell 2000, Russell 2000 Value, Russell 2000 Growth, MSCI EAFE, and Lehman Brothers Aggregate bond indices.

[xxiii] Dalbar, 2010. Average equity investor returns were calculated by applying the retention rates of investors of mutual funds to the returns of the S&P 500.

[xxiv] Taleb, 2001

[xxv] Wall Street Journal, 6/20/02

[xxvi] Mayer, 2002

[xxvii] Surowiecki, 2002

[xxviii] Ibid

[xxix] Carp&Carp, 1982

[xxx] George, 1993

[xxxi] George, 1992

[xxxii] Brinson, Hood, Beebower, 1986

[xxxiii] Brinson, Singer, Beebower, 1991

[xxxiv] Miller, 1997

[xxxv] Wiesenberger, 2002. Market indices used were the Lehman Brothers Aggregate Bond, MSCI/EAFE, Russell 1000 Growth, Russell 1000, Russell 1000 Value, and Russell 2500.

[xxxvi] Statman, 1999

[xxxvii] Taleb, 2001

[xxxviii] Bernstein, 1996

[xxxix] Jones, 1998

[xl] Kalat, 1990

[xli] Taleb, 2001

[xlii] Siegel, 2003

[xliii] Hockschild, 1973

[xliv] Bernstein, 1996

[xlv] Boldt and Arbit, 1994

[xlvi] Heaney, 2000

[xlvii] The College Board, 2010

[xlviii] American Bar Association, 1997

[xlix] Schopenhauer, 1840

[l] Campbell, 1972

[li] Friedman, Savage, 1948

[lii] Statman, 2002

[liii] Campbell, 1990

www.ingramcontent.com/pod-product-compliance
Lightning Source LLC
Chambersburg PA
CBHW061617210326
41520CB00041B/7474